The Male Chauvinist Pig

The Male Chauvinist Pig

A History

Julie Willett

The University of North Carolina Press CHAPEL HILL

This book was published with the assistance of the Anniversary Fund of the University of North Carolina Press.

Set in Merope Basic by Westchester Publishing Services
Manufactured in the United States of America

The University of North Carolina Press has been a member of the Green Press Initiative since 2003.

Library of Congress Cataloging-in-Publication Data
Names: Willett, Julie A., author.
Title: The male chauvinist pig : a history / Julie Willett.
Description: Chapel Hill : University of North Carolina Press, [2021] |
    Includes bibliographical references and index.
Identifiers: LCCN 2020051253 | ISBN 9781469661063 (cloth ; alk. paper) |
    ISBN 9781469661070 (pbk ; alk. paper) | ISBN 9781469661087 (ebook)
Subjects: LCSH: Sexism in political culture—United States. |
    Anti-feminism—United States. | Conservatism—United States—
    History—20th century. | Conservatism—United States—History—
    21st century. | American wit and humor—Political aspects—History.
Classification: LCC HQ1237.5.U6 W55 2021 | DDC 305.30973—dc23
LC record available at https://lccn.loc.gov/2020051253

Cover illustration: 1970s montage of a businessman with a pig's head sitting at a desk © ClassicStock / Alamy Stock Photo.

*If you think this book is dedicated
to you, you're probably right.*

Contents

Illustrations

Introduction
Taking Humor Seriously

Over the years, the White House Correspondents' Dinner has turned into a celebrity roast in which presidents, politicians, and media moguls take their turn being targeted by satirists. At the 2011 gala, President Barack Obama did his own bit of stand up and skillfully delivered "one-liners at VIPs in the crowd." Among his targets was Donald Trump, who had recently found himself a much-talked-about reality show host and the leader of the Birthers—a movement calling into question the president's citizenship. Like a misbehaving schoolboy desperate for attention, "the Donald" appeared to relish the limelight. Waving to the crowd, Trump beamed with an unmistakable look of satisfaction and later remarked, "I was having a good time. I was actually honored." Obama's shtick, however, served only as a warm-up act for the featured comedian who would hurl a much more powerful political punch. "Donald Trump has been saying that he will run for president as a Republican which is surprising," quipped Seth Meyers, "since I just assumed that he was running as a joke." This time, Trump didn't smile let alone laugh but sat stone-faced surrounded by an uproarious audience. He even complained the comedian was "out of order" and "too nasty." In hindsight, Trump's fateful decision to run for president of the United States in 2016, some speculated, was a simmering reaction to that night when he was cast as the butt of the joke.[1]

Alongside all of the other forces that it drew on, we cannot understand the political phenomenon Trump personifies without understanding that it also functioned on a register that was, at heart, comic. On the path to the presidency, Trump maneuvered through debates and interviews like a comedian zinging his oblivious prey. He relied on ridicule and mockery to stir up huge crowds to a sneering frenzy. And his jabs and one-liners produced a sense of authenticity and connection with his supporters that cannot be ignored. Trump's political adversaries on the right and left played it straight on the 2016 campaign trail, failing to offer any measurable comedic comeback and, too often, becoming the unwitting stooge. Up until that fateful November night, most Democrats, pollsters, and media outlets assumed Hillary Clinton would break through the glass ceiling and become the first female US president as Trump—the laughingstock—was left in the dustbin of history. After all, how could a rich playboy who relied on racist tropes and misogynist jokes beat an overqualified second-wave feminist? A Trump victory seemed impossible, but when we look through a comic lens, we can also recognize it as a punch line waiting to happen.

For all that was historic about the 2016 presidential race, the way it boiled down to a competition between a second-wave feminist and an old-school misogynist may strike a familiar chord to those who remember the 1970s. As the women's liberation movement gathered strength, a new opponent rose to oppose it—the male chauvinist pig. Beginning as an epithet designed to put men in their place, the label soon became a badge of honor— a brand that the resurgent Right embraced.

Much like Trump on the campaign trail, the male chauvinist pig used humor to mock and ridicule his feminist adversaries. Against the backdrop of feminism's battle of the sexes,[2] these paragons of patriarchy maintained an asymmetry of power in the personal and public domains that allowed them to laugh at their feminist rivals in ways that made it difficult for the latter to laugh back. Over time, the male chauvinist's bad-boy image contributed to the trope of the humorless feminist who was at once a punch line and a perceived threat to the *natural* order of things.

Far from static, the political views of the male chauvinist pig ebbed and flowed over time, but his whiteness and entitlement remained foundational to his steadfast appeal. Because the male chauvinist pig or male chauvinist was generally regarded as white, the privileges of race made his indiscretions appear to be more of a nuisance than a threat.[3] Of course, the male chauvinist pig was not exclusively a phenomenon of the Right; men across the political spectrum found common cause in sexist jokes. By the latter half of the 1970s, the moniker was beginning to fade from popular discourse,[4] yet the chauvinist's brand of humor would continue to profoundly shape conservative political strategies. As he roamed across the political spectrum, the chauvinist found his place most unapologetically on the right, where his humor would broaden the appeal of the uptight holier-than-thou Christian conservative,[5] all while perpetuating the image of the feminist who couldn't take a joke.[6] However, it was not just feminists whose humor was erased. In the 1980s and 1990s, liberals and progressives would also lose a measure of their countercultural cool as political correctness became the Right's new political stooge.[7]

To understand the popularity of the male chauvinist pig, we must explore humor's relationship to power. Humor is a vital force that can create in-groups and out-groups, perpetuate falsehoods, and fuel anger, as well as defuse a situation. Comedy can tease, speak truth to power, and even hold out the promise of a reimagined and more inclusive future.[8] Of course, humor has also developed a bit of a bad reputation. Not only have women and other marginalized performers had to negotiate unsavory rituals of self-humiliation, from putting on blackface to playing the dumb blonde, they too often have been the traditional targets of derogatory jokes. Think, for example, of "Take my wife, please," one-liners that shaped stand-up in the mid-twentieth century, or the prevalence of rape jokes that continue to mock victims.[9] When Trump's "grab them by the pussy" remark went viral just before the 2016 election, it was seen as crossing the line for some. Others, like Trump, dismissed it as "locker-room talk"—why apologize for something that was just a joke?[10] While many Americans saw Trump as more of a schoolyard bully than a presidential candidate who used jokes as a defense of bad behavior, others regarded his sense of humor as evidence that he was authentically in step with the *common man*.[11] Either way, Trump's humor is more than just a matter of political style—it's a key source of power.

Scholars have taken a serious look at the rise of modern conservatism, but they have paid far less attention to humor. Natasha Zaretsky, Lisa McGirr, Jefferson Cowie, and Robert Self, for example, have brilliantly revealed how cultural tropes such as hardhats, welfare queens, suburban warriors, NASCAR dads, and the politicized family fueled conservative politics. Tainted by Vietnam and a postindustrial economic slide, Americans have often expressed their politics through anger, and scholars are left trying to understand contemporary political discourse and the aims of the common man as anything but a laughing matter.[12] Indeed, conservatives have often been seen as humorless.[13]

This book dives deep into the belly of the beast and, with the help of an intersectional lens, explores how and why the male chauvinist pig, armed with a biting sense of humor, became such a popular icon. Theories of intersectionality remind us that there is never one single power dynamic. As Patricia Hill Collins and Sirma Bilge put it best, "Peoples' lives and the organization of power in a given society are better understood as being shaped not by a single axis of social division, be it race or gender or class, but by many axes that work together and influence each other."[14] Hence not only do we find that what is funny to some is offensive to others, but we also see why feminists could appear privileged and that mocking them may well be fair game. Keeping intersectionality in mind renders humor's golden rule—that one should punch up and not down—murky and unsettled. A quick glance across social media reveals strong disagreements even among like minds who debate the appropriateness of jokes and comedic stunts in such serious times.

Humor is not straightforward—little wonder that scholars have sidestepped this vital force. After all, humor creates a volatile field in which the meanings of and attitudes about jokes are disputed. And coupled with laughter's messy affects and felt vibes, the meaning of humor is unstable and hard to pin down or define. To ignore humor, however, is to ignore a conduit of power.

Without losing sight of the longue durée of misogynist mockery and ridicule, this book reveals how both male chauvinists and feminists could each be cast as bullies and victims, truth tellers and fools. In so doing we see how the male chauvinist pig could serve as a cruel political weapon for some, as well as an avenue for a kind of inclusion for others. Jokes are a power play, yet among friends they can create fellow feelings and a sense of community, especially when everyone takes their turn exposing their underbelly and engaging in playful moments of self-deprecation.[15] Even roasting a pig can be social play, an invitation, or a measure of recognition for someone who has been ignored or outright excluded. The 1970s battle of the sexes witnessed its fair share of playful banter that, at times like a romantic comedy, turned on teases and taunts as it held out the hope for a happily-ever-after ending. A comic lens reveals the male chauvinist pig as the oppressive patriarch who could be an asshole even as he was also a beloved family member, lover, and friend. Rather than dismissing the male chauvinist pig as a flat, one-dimensional stereotype, I trace a more mixed political consciousness that engendered iconic appeal and whose brand of humor, although problematic and outright caustic at times, was seen as less of a danger than those with no humor at all.

Setting the Stage

If, as comedians often say, getting a laugh is all about timing, then the stage was set in the 1960s and 1970s for the rise of the male chauvinist pig. Having a sense of humor not only made you appear to be politically more flexible, it also made you a rebel. A trilogy of bad-boy stand-ups redefined the comedy and political discourse of the era. Lenny Bruce (1925–66), who was infamously arrested for breaking obscenity laws in the early 1960s and who defied Cold War conformity, inspired a new generation of comedians to reveal the incongruities of religion, sexual propriety, racism, and politics.[16] Inseparable from the protests against the Vietnam War stood George Carlin (1937–2008), who became as infamous as his predecessor. Particularly memorable was a 1972 monologue about the "seven words you can never say on TV": "shit, piss, fuck, cunt, cocksucker, motherfucker, [and] tits," which he listed with the "glee of a classroom cut up and the scrupulousness of a social linguist."[17] Last but not least, joining the pantheon of satirical rebels was Richard Pryor (1940–2005), whose profanity and racial epithets were delivered to white America as a blistering attack on its own homegrown apartheid.[18] Not only were Bruce, Carlin, and Pryor crowned the kings of comedy, they were touted as champions of free speech and the epitome of countercultural cool.[19]

As stand-up began to reflect the politics in the streets, mainstream network television experimented with edgy political satire like *The Smothers Brothers Comedy Hour* (1967–69), *Rowan and Martin's Laugh In* (1968–73), and *Saturday Night Live*, which debuted in 1975 and remains a comedic tour de force in political discourse and even outcomes.[20] These shows not only mocked the powers that be, they sometimes offered a path to redemption. Intellectual historian Daniel Wickberg argues that by the latter half of the twentieth century, having a sense of humor was so important to American identity that it reinvigorated notions of American exceptionalism as it defined political character as distinct from fascists, ideologues, and other sworn U.S. enemies. These villains were believed to lack humor, along with any other measure of political flexibility. This is why, he argues, in 1968 Richard Nixon, touted as the least funny modern president, made a cameo appearance on television's *Laugh-In*,[21] setting in motion a trend of political figures who not only have been willing to engage in a bit of self-mockery but have gone so far as to announce their candidacy on comedy shows.[22]

By the 1960s, then, lacking a sense of humor was a curse and a political liability, and for feminists negotiating the volatile world of humor, it was one of their greatest challenges. In part because comedy, like politics, was a masculine domain, it exacerbated a long-standing stereotype that women in general were not funny. Comedy clubs remained hostile to women well into the 1970s. A drunk clientele, coupled with mostly male talent agents and managers, ensured an atmosphere that found it "peculiar to see a woman on stage doing jokes."[23] And even a quick glance at Carlin's seven dirty words suggests that the terrain of cultural cool was not letting go anytime soon of its "tits and ass" humor. To be sure, there were female comedians who could roll with the punches and who were successful at finding a professional niche, such as Gracie Allen, Lucille Ball, Moms Mabley, Lily Tomlin, and Joan Rivers, to name a few.[24] But telling jokes was a man's gig, and the 1970s was still decades away from the kind of democratization that would bring into view a golden age of feminist comedy.[25] So pervasive was the concept that women lacked comedic skills that as late as 2007 *Vanity Fair* published British writer Christopher Hitchens's evolutionary musings on just "why women aren't funny," in which he argued that men have needed to be funny to get a mate, while women could simply rely on their looks.[26]

If women have struggled to be viewed as funny, feminists attempting to be taken seriously were seen as even more problematic. Media scholars such as Susan Douglas contend that popular culture transformed feminism into a dirty word through its depiction of the typical feminist as a woman with "the complete inability to smile—let alone laugh."[27] Bonnie Dow argues that the "distorting mirror of media attention" assumed its typical reader was a white male who found feminism to be a "bewildering assault on his privileged status,"[28] and who also made feminism the target and appear incompatible with having a sense of humor. Yet ignoring humor in social movements is also understandable. After all, feminism has flourished thanks in part to a history of the female as moral arbiter, something that has allowed women, especially white and middle class, to enter the U.S. political arena formally since the nineteenth century. Whether it was moral reform efforts to end slavery or close down saloons, women's participation in politics was associated with spiritual uplift and piety.[29]

On the one hand, mixing politics with humor seems a man's game. On the other, the all-too-serious feminist was a powerful trope in the 1970s and has been hard to shake. An unwillingness to simply smile was a crucial strategy for feminists who understandably refused to laugh off grave issues. After all, who does not want to be taken seriously, especially if you have always been the butt of the joke? This history of mocking women's rights, along with the moral obligations that forged much of women's entry into formal politics, has made the desire to be taken seriously inseparable from many feminist goals and discourse.

However, just as problematic as being turned into the "tits or ass" of a joke is being cast as unable to take a joke, let alone make one. As Nancy Hewitt reminds us, scholars must recast histories of feminist waves and tune into different frequencies,[30] something that can begin to reveal the rich histories of feminist humor. Second-wave feminism is filled with humor's revenge, or what writer Kate Clinton terms "fumerist," an explosive mix of humor and feminism; as she put it, "It's the idea of being funny and wanting to burn the house down all at once."[31] Numerous studies of the women's liberation movement discuss fumerist acts such as the infamous 1968 Miss America protest, where feminists crowned a live sheep, or when WITCH (Women's International Terrorist Conspiracy from Hell) put a hex on Wall Street that was followed by a mysterious drop in the stock market. Nevertheless, feminist humor is not typically seen as the driving narrative.[32] Dorothy Sue Cobble, Linda Gordon, and Astrid Henry's *Feminism Unfinished: A Short, Surprising History of American Women's Movements*, for example, brilliantly traces the nuances of a century of activism and offers a litany of comedic protests; nevertheless, humor is not a vital force in their narrative.[33] Instead of seeing humor as simply a fleeting moment, scholars such as Regina Barreca, Jessyka Finley, Viveca Green, Bambi Haggins, Maggie Hennefeld, Kirsten Leng, Rebecca Krefting, Linda Mizejewski, Kathleen Rowe and Sara Warner are starting to reclaim the erased history of fumerist acts.[34] In so doing, they reveal humor's ability to claim a feminist stance in a charged space and volatile political atmosphere. Thus, we see how an unwillingness to lighten up and simply roll with the punches does not negate uproarious counteractions of protest that come from feminists and other marginalized social groups.[35]

This book does not ignore fumerism—but to fully understand feminism's troubles with humor since the 1970s, we must dissect the male chauvinist pig and his long-lasting appeal. In so doing, we can see how and why some derisive monikers (the *feminazi*, "crooked Hillary," and "Pocahontas") became inseparable from their targets, while other epithets—such as *male chauvinist pig* itself—proved easier to appropriate. Chapter 1 looks at how the male chauvinist went from an epithet to a popular brand. Bobby Riggs, a middle-aged tennis player, and television's most lovable patriarch, Archie Bunker (*All in the Family*, 1971–79), were both infamous for their irreverent antifeminist stance. Bunker's reliance on monikers, including dubbing a son-in-law "Meathead" and his seemingly clueless wife "Dingbat," made him appear out of touch and cast mocking the male chauvinist as a family affair. Just as fun to hate as Archie Bunker was his real-life counterpart—a once top-of-his-game player who lost to Billie Jean King in 1973 but remained a cultural icon.[36] Like Bunker, Riggs and other male chauvinist pigs of the era turned the battle of the sexes into a comedic routine in which the targets of their ridicule often got the upper hand. The male chauvinist appeared to be a dying breed, and in the process generated laughs and a measure of affection. After all, no one expected Archie Bunker to reincarnate himself decades later and take control of the White House like it was his favorite easy chair. The media's distortion of feminism, coupled with male bravado, breathed life into the male chauvinist pig. As feminist humor was erased, the male chauvinist pig's heterosexual prowess could sell everything from men's shoes to neckties.

The history of the chauvinist and his brand of humor cannot be separated from the history of the pig and the implications of whiteness. The terms *male chauvinist* and *male chauvinist pig* were often interchangeable; however, chapter 2 centers the genealogy of the pig. There were commie pigs and capitalist pigs, but above all else, by the 1960s and 1970s, the pigs were the police and a symbol of white oppression. Therefore, male chauvinist pigs were associated with white privilege. This is not to say that Blacks and Latinos were never called male chauvinist pigs, but it was rare enough to brand the male chauvinist pig as white. In popular discourse the male chauvinist's assumed racial status had multiple implications. Because male chauvinist pigs were cast as white, so too were their protagonists. Hence, women's liberation was often perceived to be white, further limiting its appeal and potentially undermining the movement's inclusivity. At the same time, whiteness made the male chauvinist pig appear as less of a threat. Coming of age with the *macho man*, the male chauvinist pig was given a pass that further marginalized certain social groups. In much the same way that Barack Obama would never have been elected if he behaved like Trump, the white male chauvinist pig benefited from the condemnation of other cultures' and races' assumed machismo. In popular discourse, the male chauvinist pig was a nuisance and, like the playboy, a bit naughty,[37] but the macho man could give you a black eye.

Chapter 3 finds that the male chauvinist pig was easy to spot but hard to define. It offers an exploration of the various incarnations of male chauvinist piggery and provides insight into the confusion surrounding many people's encounters with feminists and the women's movement via the media and in daily life. The media continued to trivialize feminism and the women's liberation movement, using headlines and content to turn serious struggles into an ongoing joke. Meanwhile interviews, surveys, and personal testimonies often revealed through humor that the male chauvinist could possess a mixed political consciousness that was far from settled. In much the way scholars have come to understand feminisms as complicated through the lens of intersectionality, chauvinism was not a singular concept but a set of fluid, sometimes contradictory ideas, attitudes, and moods. Even self-declared male chauvinists had reactions sometimes surprisingly similar to their feminist adversaries'. Thus, the hardest part of the pig to swallow may be the claim that the male chauvinist was a multidimensional, thinking subject who is not so easily dismissed. Tracing discussions and definitions of the male chauvinist from the street level of San Francisco to national debates and dialogues reveals above all else a collective ambiguity about his identity and definition that was complicated by his tongue-in-cheek humor.[38] In fact, there was little agreement on who or what defined a male chauvinist pig, making him more complex than a simple stereotype.

Chapter 4 traces the male chauvinist pig as he found his niche in modern conservatism. More specifically, this chapter explores how the Right began to latch onto the male chauvinist pig label not just for his opposition to feminism and race privilege but to create his own brand of countercultural aesthetics. Even the *redneck* got a makeover as the southernization of American political humor took root. Much like the male chauvinist pig who never got to step foot in the Playboy mansion, let alone get the girl next door, conservatives who lacked the Kennedy mystique or Bob Dylan cool dabbled in misogynist ridicule to play themselves up as heterosexual teases. In so doing, the male chauvinist pig, who took pride in an antifeminist stance, could bolster his (and his party's) political virility in much the way a male chauvinist pig label or tag line marketed sporty shoes and neckties. With heteronormative masculinity under siege in the 1970s from gay liberation, feminism, and deindustrialization, womanizing remained a disturbing form of catharsis. As the playboy lifestyle became even more out of reach, disenchanted men came to embrace antifeminism and adopt the attributes of the male chauvinist pig as a badge of honor. The socioeconomic context remains central for the rightward shift of the male chauvinist pig toward modern conservatism, but it was his misogynist humor that made him so appealing, for he was now naughty enough to disrupt the lingering image of the out-of-touch and uptight square.

Chapter 5 examines the rise in the late 1980s and 1990s of conservative talk radio host Rush Limbaugh, who further transformed modern conservatives from squares into stand-ups. The male chauvinist pig faded as an epithet, but not his brand of humor. As conservatives came to represent the common man, along with his wounded sense of nationalistic pride, Limbaugh, the college dropout, stood in sharp contrast to limousine liberals and narcissistic feminists who put their careers before family. And with a single moniker—the *feminazi*—he further discredited feminism, turning his adversaries into a threat and a joke. It was not only feminists whose humor was being erased, however, but also liberals and progressives. With the publication of philosopher Allan Bloom's 1987 *The Closing of the American*

Mind came an attack on political correctness that would shape politics for decades to come. For conservatives who considered themselves victims of feminism and the Left, a willingness to eschew political correctness was a breath of fresh air.[39] Limbaugh would thus serve as the missing link between the 1970s battle of the sexes and Donald Trump's victory over Hillary Clinton—the second-wave feminist who tried to play it straight.

The epilogue rejoins the discussion of feminist humor and looks at how this golden age of comedy has paved the way for the queens of comedy to take center stage. It begins, however, with Limbaugh receiving the Presidential Medal of Freedom in 2020, which serves as a reminder of his special relationship with the former president of the United States. Like Limbaugh, Trump blatantly ignored humor's golden rule, but in so doing he set himself up as the straight man and a stooge for late-night comedy shows like *Saturday Night Live*. Indeed, a full-frontal attack upset business as usual and bears witness to a rising tide of female comedians whose cross-gender impersonations challenged a president and all of his men. They serve as a reminder of the limitations placed on second-wave feminists like Clinton but also provide hope that the pig's reign as the king of comedy will someday come to an end.

CHAPTER ONE

Oink!

How the Erasure of Feminist Humor
Created a Trademark and a Tease

In her memoir, writer Kate Bornstein recalls her father proudly proclaiming himself a male chauvinist pig. So committed was he to the identity that, she writes, "he oinked—at home and out in front of other people—at parties, at work, in restaurants and bars, on the beach. That's what he'd do. Even my brother remembers that." Not only did he imitate a pig, he had "cuff links with snarling pigs, from some college whose mascot was a snarling pig." And he wore "ties and shirts with piggy patterns—not at the same time," Bornstein adds. "My mother never would have allowed that." Still, he loved pig-themed knickknacks and would transform the once innocent objects into chauvinist pig adornments: "He also kept an adorable stuffed pig on the back shelf of his car, a Buick Riviera, that he adorned with a personalized license plate that read: MCP-I." Whenever she lamented, "Dad, you really are a sexist pig," he always responded, "You're goddamn right I am."[1]

The heyday of the male chauvinist pig came in the first half of the 1970s, less than a decade after the epithet was first popularized in feminist writings.[2] While the television character Archie Bunker and a middle-aged tennis player named Bobby Riggs were the most famous male chauvinist pigs of the seventies, men much like Borstein's father found ways to flaunt their antifeminism with everything from homemade to store-bought iconography. Although the male chauvinist pig was originally an expression of ridicule and rage, men all too easily reappropriated the epithet to bolster their ego and carve out a defensible niche in popular culture. By contrast, in the masculine cultures of both comedy and politics, women were more often than not the butt of the joke. And when feminists snapped back and challenged the deluge of insults and innuendos that cast them as ditsy or dirty sex objects, they were frequently told to lighten up and ridiculed for not having a sense of humor.

Jokes have often been dismissed as mere entertainment, though the reality is that humor is a conduit of power. Filled with subliminal images and humiliating jibes, the sting of sexist and racist humor is often invisible to those in privileged positions caught up in their own laughter at the Other. It was not just that the more feminists demanded to be taken seriously in the 1970s, the less funny they appeared to be. Rather, a moralizing stance can turn anyone into the straight man who is all too easily mocked.

At the moment when the political and comic stage were becoming inextricably bound as a direct challenge to authoritarianism, not having a sense of humor was also seen as a mark of extremism. Thus it was in the 1970s when the fun-loving pig exacerbated an image of the humorless feminist. Feminists' image as too serious to be taken seriously, coupled with the erasure of feminist pranks, gave the male chauvinist pig an advantage in a battle of the sexes where women struggled to be something other than the butt of a joke.

Archie Bunker

In 1971 Archie Bunker (Carroll O'Connor) was the kind of a male chauvinist pig feminists and liberals loved to hate. *All in the Family*'s Archie was a blue-collar antihero who spouted reactionary conjectures about the decline of his neighborhood and country, but his taunts were made to feel more like teases because he was presumably a dying breed. As historian Eric Porter notes, the sitcom "continually poked fun at the bumbling patriarch" and made a mockery out of his longing for the good ol' days when "girls were girls and men were men."[3] For a liberal television audience, Archie was the laughingstock and his wife, Edith (Jean Stapleton), whom Archie routinely called "Dingbat," more often than not stole the punch line. Archie's greatest nemesis was his hippie son-in-law, Michael Stevic (Rob Reiner), whom Archie belittled as "Meathead." Along with calling Michael "one dumb Polack," Archie referred to "African-Americans [as] 'black beauties,' Puerto Ricans 'spics,' and Jews 'members of the tribe.'" But he was ultimately the butt of the joke. "Perhaps the key to O'Connor's Bunker is that he always seems to get things just a little bit wrong. In an Italian restaurant, he'll order the 'veal scalapeepee.' His wife Edith will have to see the 'groinocologist' about her 'mental pause.' And his oversexed son-in-law and daughter will engage in 'floorplay.'"[4] While Michael, above all else, stood for everything that Archie despised, he was also a constant reminder that his precious daughter Gloria (Sally Struthers)—and therefore all women—was an irrational decision maker.[5]

Taking on the most serious political issues of the day, *All in the Family* sought to educate and entertain. In a 1972 episode, for example, Gloria exposes the pervasiveness of gender stereotypes with a riddle that centers on

Carroll O'Connor played Archie Bunker on the hit sitcom *All in the Family* (1971–79). Seen here in a familiar pose mocking his wife, Edith (Jean Stapleton), Bunker came to represent the quintessential male chauvinist pig of the era. Used by permission of CBS/Photofest, © CBS.

a tragic car crash in which a father is killed, and his surviving son is taken to a nearby hospital. Upon seeing the child, the doctor abruptly announces, "I can't operate on my own son." Unable to conceive of a female surgeon, Archie, Edith, and Michael scramble to figure out just who the doctor could possibly be, offering wild guesses that range from mistaken identity to reincarnation. It is only in the last minutes of the show that Edith, the "Dingbat," solves the puzzle, realizing, of course, that "the surgeon was the boy's mother," an answer Archie still cannot fathom.[6]

The entire episode was designed to expose subtle and not-so-subtle ways of chauvinist thinking. After Michael gets a reprimand from his wife, he begins to clumsily mend his own shirt and causes Archie to snap, "No self-respecting American husband would do his own sewing." Gloria not only calls out her father's "male chauvinist attitude," she offers him an impromptu history lesson about the origin of the phrase, which she attributes to a "stupid nationalist who believed everything French was best and that women were no good." Archie, unable to resist, interrupts by demanding, "What does a dead frog soldier have to do with me?" and in so doing brings into sharp comedic relief the long history of overzealous nationalism that fueled contemporary sexism.[7]

Chauvinism's origins do indeed tell us much about the sexist pig. *Chauvinist* is an expression rooted in French history, and more specifically a lingering nineteenth-century etymology of the French word *chauvin*. According to historian Gérard de Puymège, chauvinism implies "'exaggerated, aggressive patriotism, fanatic nationalism' and derives from the name of a French soldier . . . Nicolas Chauvin." In the 1840s *chauvin* became a characteristic that increasingly implied ridicule—especially after the fall of Napoleon when a preponderance of overly exuberant veterans clung to the old empire and were met with derision.[8]

Chauvinism's European lineage, vision of nation-state building, and imperial conquest were inextricably bound to hierarchal notions of race that assumed white and Western superiority, which held true in the United States as well.[9] Chauvinism functioned much like jingoism but by the mid-twentieth century was even more broadly defined as an "ideological doctrine" of "excessive loyalty to or belief in the superiority of one's own kind or cause against others."[10] Throughout most of the 1960s, the *New York Times* deployed the word *chauvinism* to describe a love for one's region and its contributions that presumed a sense of haughtiness. Whether it was the topic of food, art, or politics, chauvinists from various cities, states, and nations stood their ground and defended their culture with a boastful white arrogance.[11]

Although chauvinism was not welded together with sexism and *pig* until the 1960s, the term has a longer history on the American left as well.[12] In the early twentieth century, the Communist Party understood *chauvinism* as another term for the kind of nationalism detrimental to worker solidarity. And in an effort to confront racism, the Communist Party also called out *white chauvinism* or *race chauvinism* in the 1930s.[13] During the campaign to mitigate racism, *male chauvinism* also became part of Communist Party discourse as women sought to expose ubiquitous inequalities in the broader culture. Although the expression faded along with the Communist Party's influence, *male chauvinism* was an expression picked up by the children of the party in the late 1960s. By 1969 chauvinism as a reference to sexism would eclipse its previous association with nationalism in the *New York Times*.[14]

At the same time, there was a generation of feminists who felt they did not have a name for the hypocrisy of the liberals and progressives who dismissed their contributions and complaints. Historian Gail Collins found reports in which women complained that the men who behaved inappropriately were often hippies, "on some very heavy ego trips," or members of organizations such as Students for a Democratic Society that awarded leadership roles only to men. The New Left was a breeding ground for "men who behaved boorishly—like what would soon be known as 'male chauvinist pigs'" And although they were a "sliver" of the population, "they had a profound impact on the culture of the women's liberation movement."[15] Starting in 1968 a plethora of publications "spread the feminist message," and along with this message David Farber found that terms such as "'patriarchy,' 'male chauvinist pig,' and 'sexism' entered the American vocabulary."[16] Humor, however, is messier in practice than it looks on the page, and the "male chauvinist pig" soon enough became the bearer of a set of meanings far beyond what its inventors intended.

The Court Jester

Just like the fictional Archie Bunker, a middle-aged tennis star named Bobby Riggs branded the male chauvinist with a sense of humor. In 1973, Riggs found the limelight by mouthing off that he could beat any woman on the tennis court. And that same year, he challenged women's tennis champ Billie Jean King to what would become the era's most iconic battle of the sexes. Forty-eight million television viewers tuned in to watch an unforgettable spectacle broadcast live from the Houston Astrodome that coupled hardball politics with the nonsense of a screwball comedy.[17] The match profoundly shaped the history of women's liberation but also the legacy of the male chauvinist pig.

By all accounts, Riggs was less the top-of-his-game tennis player at fifty-five years of age and more the showman, who with the finesse of a class clown was simply looking for his next hustle. According to sports historian Susan Ware, "Bobby Riggs supplied about 90 percent of the copy, having realized that outrageous statements against Women's Lib got him more attention than sticking to tennis."[18] A plethora of media interviews before and after the match reaffirm that Riggs was far more interested in money-making schemes and impish humor than challenging the tenets of feminism.[19] Less ace tennis player than a class clown, when Riggs walked into a room, it was more like he was "barging through a saloon door," notes sportswriter Selena Roberts. "He'd step foot in a place, let all eyes fall on him, and create a stir no one could ignore." And he could certainly hold his own with professional comedians. During an appearance on *The Tonight Show*, he outshined guest host Don Rickles, "who lagged behind, unable to outwit the stage hog in the chair next to him."[20]

Riggs gambled and grinned his way into the hearts and minds of the American public looking for a less-than-serious antihero. *Time* magazine called him "the Happy Hustler" because of his love of ridiculous bets. "Ride down the road with him and he may bet you $100 that you would not jump out of the car and turn a quick somersault." If you are hanging out with him in his hotel room, "he will invent a betting game that involves tossing tennis balls over a curtain rod." Many of his boyish antics centered on something athletic with a campy twist. "Ask him to play golf with a tennis racket and he will not only oblige but win. Show up at one of his tennis matches and he may line you up for a side bet."[21]

Perhaps unsurprisingly, Riggs stood apart from the "tennis establishment." He was a loudmouth who cared little about "breaking the amateur rule against taking illicit payments." Ignoring staid etiquette, Riggs once even played a tennis match "while holding a poodle on a leash ('It's harder if the dog isn't housebroken') while tied to his doubles partner, while running around four chairs, while wearing an overcoat, while carrying a pail of water."[22] Riggs poked fun at others as well as himself. In an interview with *60 Minutes* host Mike Wallace, he talked about using Clairol products to mask his gray hair and how he took an outrageous 450 vitamin pills a day "to keep up with the girls."[23] In many ways he was less of a pig and more of a ham.

For Riggs, the shtick mattered more than any political stance. Wells Twombly, sports staff writer for the *San Francisco Chronicle*, vowed that Riggs "wouldn't know Germaine Greer (the feminist author of *The Female Eunuch*)[24] even if she knocked on his hotel door at 2 a.m. with a sad story and desperate need for warmth." Riggs knew little about the women's liberation movement. Indeed, his political commitment to antifeminists seemed less than sincere, especially given that his desire and attempt to win the match against King also remain uncertain—there is even some speculation that Riggs purposely threw the game.[25] Regardless, a rigid antifeminist stance was less important to Riggs than money, infamy, and having a good time. With a wink and nod, he declared himself "the hero of the men's counter revolution." Insisting that women should be pregnant and barefoot, he drolly added, "We aren't going to take this lying on our backs." As the self-proclaimed founder of the fictional organization "WORMS, that's World Order of the Restoration of Male Supremacy," he pulled out every cliché, boasting, "When I get through with Billie Jean, every man in America will be able to hold his head up."[26]

Before the match, Twombly dismissed the event as "sheer nonsense" and wondered "why in hell they are holding this thing." Making clear his own stance on feminism, Twombly lamented that "these are unreasonable times" that pit an "aging roue and a grouchy female" against each other for spectacle. King was no grouch, but there were plenty of men like Twombly, who were all but amused with the challenges and critiques of masculine privilege. As Twombly crudely put it, "It seems that women, formerly called broads, are suddenly unwilling to run the economy, the government and the arts from behind the curtain, as they have been doing since Cro-Magnon man." While it would be easy to dismiss Twombly as out of touch, he did acknowledge something that Riggs also understood: "Being a male chauvinist swine is now big business, if not to say heavy industry."[27]

Riggs served up pregame smack talk that King answered with her own bit of vaudeville. The popularity of the match turned on the fact that King was just as relatable as Riggs. She possessed a "blue collar background, a candid and down-to-earth approach with reporters,"[28] which made her own grand yet campy entrance into the stadium atop an Egyptian litter even more amusing. Not only was King carried by "college hunks from the Rice University track team" dressed in "scanty togas,"[29] her audacious litter was complete "with orange and red feathers as big as palmettos pluming from a gold lamé throne—a tinfoil knock off of Cleopatra's favorite mode of transportation." Adding even more laughs, King came bearing a ceremonial gift for her opponent—a "squealing baby pig" that she had mischievously named Robert Larimore Riggs. Being sure that her affinity for the piglet was known, she warned, "You can take him to a farm, but do not have the little baby eaten. I don't want him hurt."[30] Still, impressive as King's comic routine may have been, it is her athleticism on the court that is remembered.

While Riggs could play the court jester, King carried the weight of a larger feminist struggle on her shoulders that combined a number of hard-fought victories and losses. Several months earlier, in May 1973, Riggs had soundly defeated Margaret Court, who was then the top-ranked female player, in what became known in the popular media as the "Mother's Day Massacre."[31] Before his match with Court, Riggs "came bouncing down the stairs carrying an armful of beautiful red roses," mocking his "dear sweet opponent, Margaret Smith Court," and any feminist aim by acknowledging her not as a worthy opponent but as "mother-of-the-year."[32] After Riggs's victory, King confessed that she had little choice but to accept Riggs's challenge, knowing how important a win would be for women desperate to be seen as equal. Poised to avenge Court's humiliating defeat, King set out to achieve her personal and political goals of being taken seriously as a female athlete.[33] Following her victory, King was crowned not just a winner but an icon in a pantheon of stoic feminist figures.

Yet collective memory has seemed to erase King's own pre- and postgame shenanigans.[34] Perhaps because of the serious significance of King's victory

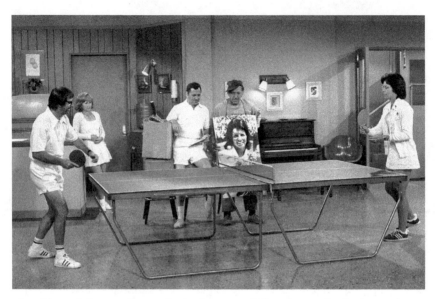

The Odd Couple (1970–75) starred Felix (Tony Randall) and Oscar (Jack Klugman), and in a 1973 episode entitled "The Pig Who Came to Dinner," tennis rivals Bobby Riggs and Billie Jean King continue the battle of the sexes in a game of ping-pong. Photo by Chester Maydole, used by permission of ABC/Photofest, © ABC.

or because feminist humor is all too easily forgotten (recall that Twombly called her a grouch), it may seem surprising that before the match, King joined Riggs in a low-budget commercial for the Sunbeam Mist-Stick Curler Styler. The two athletes played themselves—Riggs, the cheeky tennis ace, and King, the jet-setting "Five Times World Tennis Champion," who "doesn't have time to fuss with [her] hair" but, thanks to her Mist-Stick Curler, can now keep up with anything that comes her way—on and off the court. Looking into her confident reflection in the mirror, King touts, "Sunbeam controls the mist," but "*you* control the heat." As she emerges from an airplane's lavatory freshly coifed, she unexpectedly bumps into her nemesis, who is grinning ear-to-ear and sporting an absurdly large button on his lapel that professes, "I love Bobby Riggs," an encounter that sets up the cheesy punch line. Smiling begrudgingly at her rival, she looks into the camera and quips, "This is enough to curl your hair."[35] After the match, Riggs and King would also appear together in sitcoms. In an episode of *The Odd Couple* (1970–75) poignantly entitled "The Pig Who Came to Dinner," Riggs, a swindler, meets his match only when King makes an unexpected appearance to play out a final bet in a "winner-take-all" game of table tennis.[36]

Even so, Riggs's sense of humor most profoundly shaped the collective memory of the match in ways King's did not. Only at the moment of his impending defeat did sports announcer Howard Cosell remark that the "comedy has gone out of Bobby Riggs."[37] That proved short lived—his loss only enhanced his appeal as the self-deprecating male chauvinist pig. Like Archie Bunker, Riggs was now even less of a threat and more of a tease.

Riggs had no problem playing the fool. He would become the perfect punch line for female comedians ranging from Phyllis Diller to actress Bea Arthur, who played the tough-minded matriarch in the feminist hit series *Maude* (1972–78)—a show inspired by her character in *All in the Family*.[38] And he happily played the object of ridicule in television commercials such as the one for Hasbro's table tennis in which the camera focuses exclusively on Riggs, who is sweating like a pig yet ultimately loses a hard-fought match to his tough mystery opponent. The joke is revealed when the mystery opponent turns out to be not King but an elderly woman who lacks any measure of physical prowess.[39]

It is intriguing to think, as King's doubles partner Rosie Casals would later remark, that "Bobby Riggs did more for women's tennis than anybody."[40] Riggs left his mark on the history of women's liberation with his over-the-top slapstick buffoonery and a loss that made him appear to be even more fun than fury. As Selena Roberts puts it best, Riggs was "feminism's perfect fall guy."[41] His humor felt more like a playful roast than cruel ridicule. When Riggs asserted, "I don't mind being called a male chauvinist pig . . . as long as I'm the No. 1 male chauvinist pig," his humor mitigated the sting associated with calling out a male chauvinist pig.[42] Just as Ware observes, "in 1973 Billie Jean King was the right feminist in the right sport at the right moment in American history,"[43] so too was Bobby Riggs the quintessential male chauvinist of the era.

Although King's celebrated victory would shape the trajectory of women and sports and the larger liberation movement of which she was a part, Riggs's mouthy banter and schoolboy antics would help to further transform the male chauvinist pig into a figure of fun who masterfully turned feminists into grouches. King would be referred to as an "angry woman" while Riggs was the "aging rooster." As the chauvinists snagged the laughs, feminists would *appear* to play the game a bit too straight.[44] As media scholar Patricia Bradley poignantly explains, "He took up the rhetoric of the radicals and denatured it by willingly calling himself a 'chauvinist pig'; indeed, he readily took up the mantle to represent all men who seemingly had been denigrated as a result of the second wave. But no matter how exaggerated his statements, his style was without rancor, and he took a kind of delight in the angry responses he elicited." Riggs's sense of humor allowed him to powerfully return any insults that were served his way. But most important of all, "for his supporters, his humor and good nature suggested that there could be no greater patronization than failing to take the other side seriously."[45]

Not taking feminism seriously was the male chauvinist pig's most dominating trait. *Ms.* magazine founder and feminist icon Gloria Steinem admitted that calling out men as male chauvinists simply boosted the wrong ego. "In fact," looking back from 1995, she insisted, "*male chauvinist* itself is a problem. Since *chauvinist* referred to a super patriot, all we were saying was this was a man obsessed with loyalty to his country."[46] Although men called out as chauvinist pigs did not seem to miss the feminist intent, they easily turned the insult into a source of pride, if not a badge of honor. Steinem remembers how "some male supremacists took advantage of the earlier error by wearing ties and pins proclaiming, 'I am a male chauvinist pig.'" Yet "few of those men would so cheerfully proclaim, 'I am anti-Semite' or 'I am a racist.'" Thus, Steinem recalled, "many feminist writers began to use *male supremacist* as a more accurate description of the problem at hand." For Steinem, however, all of "this was an indication, of course, of the lack of seriousness with which sexism is treated."[47]

Taking the Pig to Market

If humor had laundered the sexism of the male chauvinist pig, commodification rendered him even more benign. When Steinem complained about "the lack of seriousness" surrounding the chauvinist, she also understood that the chauvinist pig had been reappropriated as a marketing tool. In 1971, for example, Hush Puppies, a shoe company, found the male chauvinist a trendy advertising technique. "Attention, Male Chauvinist Pigs," a magazine ad read: "Relax, When 'libs' call us names like that it really means we're rugged, masculine, virile," and presumably like the sporty shoes they sold.[48] Tapping into Hugh Hefner's vision of the good life, chef Cory Kiverst published *The Male Chauvinist's Cookbook*, which featured recipes and a tongue-in-cheek humor designed to lure women into bed and encourage men to become a master in the kitchen. In his preface he insisted that "if you can cook a woman under the table, think of where you can take her from there." With titles such as "Appetizers to Appetize Her" and "Pot Lucks and Other Quickies," each chapter served up a naughty image of the chauvinist pig that encouraged men to stock the pantry and set the mood.[49]

And much like a subscription to *Playboy*, the male chauvinist pig as signifier asserted a cisgender stance against the backdrop of feminism and gay liberation. As historian Carrie Pitzulo argues in her study of the playboy, "Much of the fantasy lifestyle was just that, an unattainable vision of luxury in which many American men could never indulge."[50] In fact, Hefner "compares *Playboy* to the Sears Roebuck catalog of the early twentieth century, a 'wish book' that offered a seemingly infinite number of enticing consumer items to Americans,"[51] but a version that was never as scaled down as what Sears had to offer to middle America. Whether it was homespun or purchased at a fancy department store, male chauvinist pig iconography allowed ordinary men who never donned a club jacket to snag a bit of naughtiness with a jocular flair.

In 1974, upscale Bloomingdale's featured "the M.C.P. tie for the 'discriminating' man." For $7.50 you "could find the perfect gift for your favorite unliberated male—boss, boyfriend, co-worker or all-in-the-family man." Neckwear buyer for Bloomingdale's Karen Pittman described the ties as tasteful and fitting for the businessman who needed something "quite conservative and smart looking." In fact, "at first glance [it] looks like a club tie." Only on closer examination do the "small oval patterns and discreet initials sprinkled over a dark background" reveal themselves to be pigs with "small MCP [male chauvinist pig] initials." Pittman explained that "they first came out around Father's day and sold out," which implies the degree to which male chauvinist pig iconography was a sign of endearment. The humorous but classy Father's Day gift could act as a gentle reprimand as well as a nod to the head of the household's lingering virility, all with an amusing twist.[52]

Similarly, between 1977 and 1979, Avon, a company famous for livingroom sales and kitschy beauty products aimed at suburban housewives, marketed male chauvinist pig novelty soaps as a gag gift. Cast as "a somewhat antiquated, allegedly endangered genus (generally associated with the species, Homo sapiens) found in many parts of the modern world," the chauvinist, Avon proclaimed, was somewhat benign if not altogether harmless. The implication was that some of the pig's more annoying characteristics could simply be masked or washed away with a "Deep Woods" scent. The packaging was playfully marked with instructions like "Handle with Care"—"Fragile Ego" at stake. Avon warned with a wink and a grin that the "Lively Stock" had a "particular fondness for any topic relating to [the] intrinsic superiority of [the] male species," who "especially enjoys the company of other M.C.P.'s." Despite the "fearsome, gruff mannerisms of these

A Father's Day gift? In the 1970s men's ties were one of many consumer items that featured male chauvinist pig iconography. Author's collection.

Between 1977 and 1979, Avon, known for its kitschy toiletries and living-room sales, manufactured and sold chauvinist pig soaps in a decorative box that described the male chauvinist pig as "a somewhat antiquated, allegedly endangered genus." Author's collection.

creatures," Avon customers were reassured that "M.C.P.s have also been described as good-natured," as well as "kind and gentle by their loyal female companions."[53]

In sharp contrast to the cookbook, neckties, and Avon products, cartoonist R. M. Hurley and Betty Swords's 1974 "Male Chauvinist Pig Calendar" featured a pig for every month, with unmistakable feminist intent. Their typical male chauvinist pig is a white professional man wearing a tie who, much like "Mr. January," carried a copy of the *Wall Street Journal*, patronizingly pats his wife on the top of her head and quips, "When I want your opinion I'll tell you what it is." In March, a mother surrounded by her eight young children tells a friend that "the only pill Henry lets me take is aspirin." There was also "the Swinger," who touted a modish turtleneck, sideburns, and a wide-collar shirt. Depicted with a drink in his hand, he jokes, "Of course, I'm broad-minded—I never think of anything else." Some months featured particularly disturbing reminders of how the male chauvinist pig was imbedded in systemic forms of oppression. In an illustration poignantly entitled "The Cop-Outs," the cartoonists drew the image of a young girl clinging to her ripped clothing and surrounded by four lecherous police

SEX IS EVERYTHING!

The erotic memoirs of a

MALE CHAUVINIST PIG

IN COLOR

with
GEORGINA SPELVIN
star of
(The DEVIL IN MISS JONES)

As pornography moved into the mainstream, *The Erotic Memoirs of a Male Chauvinist Pig*—a 1973 XXX-rated film—attempted to cast misogyny and other acts of sexual violence as dark humor. Used by permission of Getty Images.

officers, with a stark caption that reads, "Now, honey, tell us again about this alleged rape."[54] More than just dismissive of female testimony, the male chauvinist pig had no shame to speak of.

With no shame, even the vilest male chauvinist pigs were cloaked in humor. A 1973 XXX-rated film entitled *The Erotic Memoirs of a Male Chauvinist Pig* provides another case in point. Ray Horsch, the film's director, who has come to describe himself as a "villain" and "sociopath," among other things,[55] insisted decades later that the original intent was satirical. "Just about every imaginable sexual deviation is lampooned."[56] And the *Playboy*-esque film poster, which featured a relatively modest drawing of a topless woman in the clutches of a cartoonish man wearing a suit who had a gargantuan double-chinned pig face, made the film appear relatively tame in an era in which porn was becoming mainstream. The film, however, was considered crude and misogynistic. So much so that Al Goldstein, "the scabrous publisher whose *Screw* magazine pushed hard-core pornography into the cultural mainstream," called it "disgusting."[57]

Whether it was through sporty shoes or porn, the commodification of the male chauvinist pig in all of its manifestations revealed a multiplicity of meanings that could range from outrage to adoration. Consumption is a murky process in which cultural transmission and meaning are often up for debate. The purchase of male chauvinist pig iconography could be a measure of affection or sweet revenge. Brandishing a pig logo may or may not be a resolute nod of acquiescence.[58] Nevertheless, the commodification of the male chauvinist pig made him more often than not appear as just a joke who benefited from his position of privilege and ignored serious offenses.

Taking Women Seriously

In the 1970s, as feminists urged men, "Don't be a clown take women seriously," they consciously confronted the fact that issues of gender were easily dismissed as a joke.[59] A second wave that attempted to be taken seriously reflected the degree to which feminism had exposed the personal as political and brought into sharp relief everything from who did the dishes to the redefinition of pleasurable sex. However, against the backdrop of a war in Vietnam and other liberation movements engaged in protest, men on the left who in theory might be sympathetic to issues of inequality often found gendered issues trivial, if not absurd. Given that so many women lived with and loved the men in their lives — even male chauvinist pigs — their concerns appeared even less real. A member of the old and new Left, Barbara Epstein, recalls that in Students for a Democratic Society, "'male chauvinism' was a phrase that one did not utter unless one was ready to be laughed at."[60]

In 1972 *Ms.*, the first mainstream feminist magazine, investigated presidential political candidates' gender politics under the subheading of "Taking Women Seriously."[61] And in so doing, the magazine expressed that not being dismissed as a joke was half the battle. Not taking women's issues seriously is what the male chauvinist pig did best and what philosopher Kate Abramson refers to as gaslighting. The expression is taken from the title of the 1940s Hollywood film *Gaslight*. But it is different from "merely dismissing someone," insists Abramson, "for dismissal simply fails to take another seriously as an interlocutor, whereas gaslighting is aimed at getting

In a 1971 interview with Gloria Steinem, talk show host Phil Donahue became enamored with Steinem and the movement. As a feminist ally, Donahue stood apart from a hostile white and male media. Used by permission of NBC/Photofest, © NBC.

another not to take herself seriously as an interlocutor." Although not necessarily gender specific, it is more often in response to a "woman's protestation against sexist (or otherwise discriminatory) conduct." In much the way feminists have been told to lighten up or that it's just a joke, Abramson points out, protestations are typically greeted with "that's crazy," "it's not a big deal," or "you're overreacting."[62]

As popular talk show host Phil Donahue recalls, the media had little sympathy for women's liberation. In a 1971 interview with Gloria Steinem, Donahue became an ally of the movement and stood apart from what he described as "a hostile white male press." Decades later he described how the press referred to feminists and movement leaders as "these girls" who just wanted "to burn their bras." In his words, "an awful lot of abuse was heaped on" Steinem and others. The media perpetuated bitter falsehoods that feminists "don't like sex, they don't like men, they don't like love." In fact, the general attitude toward feminists was, "Who are they anyway?" indicating the media's assumption that women needed to stay in their place.[63]

In 1972, on *Meet the Press*, Steinem was cast as a laughingstock for an audience made to wonder whether feminists were actually to blame for the sexism that they claimed to endure. The host of *Meet the Press*, Larry Spivak, first reminded Steinem that she and other feminists had insisted that "women are not taken seriously, we are undervalued, ridiculed and not taken seriously by a society that views white men as the norm." Next, he declared, "men are virtually controlled by women from birth onward." Turning to Steinem, Spivak then delivered his punch line. "Why haven't you done a better job. . . . Well, hasn't she had an opportunity to brainwash the male during those early years. Why hasn't she done it!"[64] To be sure, blaming feminists for raising generations of chauvinist pigs was a repetitive theme.

In 1974, just in time for Mother's Day, the *San Francisco Chronicle* similarly urged, "Don't blame men for being 'male chauvinist pigs.' Women wanted them that way," and thanks to a University of Southern California psychiatrist, they had someone with just enough credentials to back them up. At an American Psychiatric Association meeting, Sherwyn M. Woods informed his colleagues, "It should be emphasized that male chauvinism is not simply a problem of men. . . . There are many women who seek chauvinistic males to meet their neurotic needs."[65] From the *Archives of General Psychiatry*, Woods's published version claimed, "Men are chauvinist because their mothers brought them up that way." The research garnered a fair amount of attention despite the findings being based on interviews with only eleven men, something most newspapers overlooked. According to his findings, "The men said they tended not to identify with the chauvinism of their fathers." In fact, Woods found that the men he interviewed complained that "frequently the mothers implied that the fathers were not chauvinist enough." Chauvinistic tendencies were a problem for Woods. "The chauvinistic conditioning by mothers is destructive not only in the man's relationship with women but it also distorts his relationships with other men," he insisted. With the help of the media's spin, the ironic twist that "women actually may be at the base of chauvinism" is what made the headlines.[66]

The male chauvinist pig's cartoonish posturing and use of ridicule disrupted debates about women's pay, work, and reproductive rights with banter that often turned into an insult—but one that could be dismissed as simply a joke and not so serious as, say, the war in Vietnam, civil rights, or stagflation. At the same time, such banter also set up the feminist as the straight man. Being the butt of the joke was not new; the ridicule used against women demanding the right to vote a century ago is strikingly familiar. While earlier generations of feminists were portrayed as "ultra masculine," men were depicted as being laughably feminized, donning aprons, caring for the home, and tending to young children.[67] In popular culture, women were more often than not the targets not the producers of comedy, something that made feminist demands to be taken seriously mistakenly seen as a complete rejection of humor, or what contemporary feminists might embrace as the "killjoy."[68]

To fully understand the rise of the male chauvinist pig as both an epithet and popular masculine icon, the discourse and tone of second-wave feminism[69] must be understood in terms of the murky relationship women have had with political humor. As media studies scholar and cultural critique Susan Douglas contends, popular culture transformed feminism into a dirty word through its depiction of the typical feminist as a woman with "the complete inability to smile—let alone laugh."[70] By the late 1960s and 1970s, comedy began to share much more visibly with the political stage, and having a good sense of humor mattered to the making of a successful campaign or political candidate. Not willing to simply laugh off serious issues was an intentional feminist aim, and not having or possessing humor became a damaging trope. Just as the women's liberation movement reached its second-wave peak and feminists were demanding to be taken seriously, humor became a central strategy of a masculine political game, played out in an often unsympathetic media that further cast the feminist as the straight man and ironically too serious to be taken seriously.

In the 1970s, playing it straight also reflected a history of feminism that rested on the image of the moral arbiter.[71] Feminist humor had a long history, from the double entendres of early twentieth-century blues singers to the 1968 Miss America pageant protest and the "hex" put on Wall Street by the Women's International Terrorist Conspiracy from Hell (WITCH).[72] Founder of the Feminist Party, member of the National Organization for Women, and "Black radical feminist Florynce 'Flo' Kennedy was famous for using acerbic humor to call attention to racism, misogyny, and sexism." In fact, while on a speaking tour with Steinem, she snapped back at a man who wanted to know whether she was a lesbian by asking him, "Are you my alternative?"[73] Not only was that one-liner repeated on the comic stage by professional stand-ups, but so too was Steinem's hilarious 1978 proposition that "if men could menstruate," "they would brag about how long and how much."[74]

Feminist humor was too often ignored. Congresswoman Shirley Chisholm in 1968 became the first Black female elected to the House of Representatives and "had a tough time being taken seriously," especially when she ran for president in 1972.[75] Yet "humor was but one mechanism Chisholm used to showcase her rationality, allowing her cool temper to shine through when the weight of white male hegemony on Capitol Hill threatened to crush her into silent, neutralized oblivion." "'I could curse them out,' Chisholm remarked, 'but I didn't believe in that. Because I believe in being humorous and embarrassing them.'"[76] Every time she entered the House chamber, an Arkansas congressman "began a ritual of coughing, lifted a handkerchief to his face, and spit in it, almost in her face." In response, Chisholm "went out and purchased a handkerchief. The next time the Arkansas congressman began his ritual fit of coughing and spitting, Chisholm coughed in unison, pulling out her handkerchief as she approached him. He spit in his handkerchief. Chisholm spit in hers, close to the congressman's face, imitating and mocking his attack. 'Beat you to it today,' she quipped. Members of the news media caught the encounter from the balcony, and as she recalled, 'they almost fell over the banister' laughing."[77] As Jessyka Finley argues, "Chisholm's performance kidnapped authority in that moment, but there was not transcendence. Even though it was funny and empowering, her renegade gesture was concealed from the public, prohibiting her rhetorical disruption of a paradigm."[78]

There were far more visible feminist pranks. The mastermind behind many second-wave feminist protests, including that of the iconic 1968 Miss American pageant when a live sheep was crowned in a defiant response to the overwhelming images of female objectification, was Black activist and law school graduate Flo Kennedy.[79] Kennedy had no problem telling it like it is. In 1973, speaking in support of a Graduate Students and Teaching Fellows Union strike, Kennedy taunted an Ivy League crowd, "If you had to give the world an enema, you would put it in Harvard yard. This has got to be the asshole of the world." This was just months before she planned the Great Harvard Pee-In. As the story goes, this was a protest designed to bring into sharp relief the lack of bathrooms for the first generation of female applicants taking Harvard's entrance exam. The folklore surrounding the protest suggests that women took jars of urine-colored liquid and poured them down the steps of a Harvard lecture hall to point out the unfair testing conditions for women, who would lose a full fifteen minutes of test time as they were forced to race to another lecture hall to find a women's restroom.[80]

Too often a whitewashing of feminist acts has erased the movement's humor. In part this erasure also reflects the bourgeois aesthetics that paved the way for women who first entered the realm of formal politics. In the nineteenth century, for example, women who moved into various political movements relied on an ascribed pretense of social purity to justify their shift from a female private sphere to a male public one. Strains of feminism, so rooted in long-standing assumptions of innate female morality, were a source of inspiration for more than a century of women's social activism. Challenging everything from the property rights of married women and suffrage to issues of equal rights and equal pay transformed the global landscape. This thread of moral superiority has been crucial to women's continued entry into the political and social movements of the twentieth century. Yet the moral compass on which feminism most visibly operates has often felt not just bourgeois but exclusionary and sanctimonious. In the early twentieth century, Alice Paul and the postsuffrage National Woman's Party's agenda, for example, ignored labor conditions and the disenfranchisement of Black Americans.[81]

Similarly, 1960s feminism was a response to the "left's penchant for privileging class and race over gender," insists historian Alice Echols, and this is why "radical feminists" have a tendency to "subordinate class and race over gender and to speak hyperbolically about a universal sisterhood."[82] All of which was reaffirmed in the media with the battle of the sexes that featured the male chauvinist pig as being just as white and privileged as his feminist adversary. Yet many protests and feminist demands that focus on issues of gender more than race and class, for example, created bitter divisions that have haunted both ideology and praxis that was no laughing matter. It is often hard to see, as Natasha Zaretsky observes, that "feminists were divided along axes of race, class, sexuality, and region, and they were scarcely in agreement in defining organizational goals, tactics, and strategies. But in part because the movement was so diverse, feminism's effects on American culture and society were profound." From establishing battered women's shelters, day cares, and health clinics, to securing in 1972 Title IX, which "mandated equal gender access for sports funding" in public schools, to winning the legal right to an abortion (*Roe v. Wade*, 1973), feminists took on the most serious of issues.[83] And women's entry into formal politics has made the desire to be taken seriously inseparable from both feminist goals and discourse. Nevertheless, feminisms that ignore privilege have been condemned as uptight and out of touch, making feminist fury far less fun.

In the early 1970s, feminists attacked what they saw as a double standard in the masculine world of comedy. In 1973, Stephanie Harrington, writing for the *New York Times*, opined that when it came to the issues of the day, left-leaning political satirists took everything earnestly *except* feminism. In her words, "Women have been made to look ridiculous for too long: And men have had reasons for wanting women to look ridiculous." "Show biz is show biz and almost anything's good for a shtick, but some things are still sacred." She pointed out, for example, that "no television comic has yet done a boffo impersonation of Cesar Chavez slipping on a grape peel. Or gotten off a joke about how the Oglala Sioux would have been too happy to give back Wounded Knee . . . if only they hadn't drunk so much fire water and forgotten where they put it." "No," she continued, "you can bet your sweet radical chic party list nobody's tried routines like that yet. The plight of the farmworkers and Indians is not to be taken lightly." "But women's liberation," that was an exception. "Now there's something everyone can do a number on."[84]

The same year Harrington published her essay, *Ms.* magazine featured an article by feminist psychologist Naomi Weisstein, who asked women, "How can you trust humor when it's a weapon used against you?" "Think of all the cartoons and comic strips you've read." "Now think of all those that didn't include a silly club lady, a domineering mother-in-law, a wife who can't drive a car or balance a checkbook . . . or a big-breasted wide-eyed nurse/stewardess/secretary/victim." In part, Weisstein's mistrust of humor reflected her doubt that women had ever created an oppositional culture that turned on humor. Lenny Bruce, the king of comedy, she recalled, "had a bit about why Jews and blacks were such natural comedians." While racial tropes problematize her analysis, Weisstein's larger point suggests a history that "focused on the survival function of entertaining; you charm your oppressor and then you don't have to work so hard."[85]

However, Weisstein was at a loss when it came to defining a female world of jokes and pranks with political aims. She too had erased the feminist history of mischief. "I know of no comparable traditions of women's humor," she opined. Nor have women to her knowledge "had a tradition of fighting and rebellious humor." Of course, "by women's humor, I don't mean women being funny. I mean humor which recognizes a common oppression, notices its source and the roles it requires, identifies the agents of that oppression."[86] A humorless women's culture was not just a reflection of Weisstein's perspective; the comic stage was undoubtedly set up for male performance where women were at best interlopers in the early 1970s. Nevertheless, there was a culture of feminist humor that has too often been ignored.[87]

Weisstein's 1973 declaration that feminists "are not laughing any more" was a means to challenge specifically humiliating stereotypes. She believed that a woman's all-too-pleasing *nature* was often something that masked pain and frustration. Well aware that feminists were being critiqued for lacking humor, Weisstein asked her readership to think about the hypocrisy entrenched in popular culture. "Why have they been telling us women lately that we have no sense of humor—when we are always laughing?" After all, just "turn on the tube: there we are, laughing away, running in slow motion through warm sand and the Pacific roaring in back of us, goldenrod and grass undulating in sync with our mane of long straight hair, the camera slightly out of focus and the lights diffused and blinking."[88]

Weisstein complained that when it came to popular images of women on television, "all we do is laugh." Sexist television commercials were constantly aired and seemed especially inescapable: "We're sudsing our hair on the color TV and laughing, we're catching taxis in our new panty hose and laughing, we're playing with pink telephones and laughing. Laugh! We're a laffriot." These same expectations followed women through their daily routine. "When we're not laughing, we're smiling at the boss, smiling at the kid (no headache is going to stop me from smiling at my kid), smiling at the old man, smiling at the dog, the baby, the gas man," and even, she despaired, at "the cop who just gave us a ticket, the automobile mechanic who just insulted us, the men on the street who just whistled at us, the guy with his fly open who's following us, (maybe if we are nice he'll go away), smiling through parties, smiling through conversations, smiling when we talk, smiling when we listen."[89] To be sure, women were more often than not the target of ridicule, but who gets the laughs is often about timing.

Politics and the Comic Stage

The second-wave desire to be taken seriously came problematically at the very moment politics became inextricably bound to the comic stage—more specifically, when having a sense of humor helped make political leaders, activists, and movements more appealing. Ironically, refusing to laugh, let alone smile, was both a stereotype and a strategy that could liberate yet also hold feminism captive. The rise of the male chauvinist pig also played on the image of the humorless feminist. This common failure to recognize the importance of humor for feminism might be expected given that all too often feminists themselves have been treated with contempt while humor has more readily been associated with a more exclusively male terrain.[90]

The intersection of comedy and formal politics has had a lengthy and intriguing history. The somewhat distinct trajectories they followed in the nineteenth century became increasingly blurred in the twentieth century. Daniel Wickberg argues that political character, which once seemed to stand in opposition to humor, increasingly demanded at least some degree of self-deprecation. Even the least funny of politicians attempted comic routines or cameos as an outward sign of political flexibility and a democratic ethos.[91]

In the 1960s and 1970s, political figures increasingly did not want to be seen as humorless. A stately embrace of political humor was a trend that reflected a gradual evolution in American political thought. Although humor and other "hidden transcripts" had been a tool of the weak and not typically a signature of state power,[92] those with power had long distanced themselves from playing the joker or class clown. In other words, political character was serious business. According to Wickberg, in the nineteenth century humor had appeared as a threat to political statesmanship. Even through the Progressive Era, "politics was an arena of moral earnestness that could brook no levity."[93] In the nineteenth century, there were political humorists such as Mark Twain, who became known for his anti-imperialism, and they stood in sharp relief to stately politics and bourgeois aesthetics.[94]

The twentieth century, however, saw a gradual evolution of an Anglo-American tradition that found humor and a democratic ethos inextricably bound. By the 1950s, humor was a valuable asset because it guarded against an undue attachment to rigid moral principles, now defined, Wickberg contends, as "ideology." Humor thus became "a sign of political flexibility, moderation, willingness to see both sides of the question, capacity for compromise. It is a feature of a liberal-pluralistic model of politics," he argues. In stark contrast stood "Hitler, Stalin, Mussolini," whom Wickberg describes as "the highest examples of men who lacked the fundamental and necessary attribute of the sense of humor." In the postwar era, "many Americans saw in Germany, Italy, Japan, and the Soviet Union not simply nations headed by dictators who lacked humor, but societies that because they were not democracies, could not possess humor."[95]

Left-leaning causes have often been dismissed as humorless and thus set the tone for mistrust, but issues of gender may have been an exception. Wickberg notes, "The American left in the twentieth century has been pilloried as lacking in humor and thus is regarded by many as politically dangerous."[96] As communications scholar Kembrew McLeod finds, the "Old Left's stoic denial of pleasure was inherited to a certain extent by the sixties New Left, which was sometimes at odds with the Yippies, Merry Pranksters, and other Groucho Marxists."[97] "The credo of the twentieth-century American bourgeois could well be: 'Have a sense of Humor—don't take yourself so seriously,'" Wickberg concludes. In fact, "no politician wishes to be accused of lacking a sense of humor. The demagogue and the fanatic, the autocrat and the dogmatist, it is widely believed, are without a sense of humor." Wickberg poignantly adds, "Even Richard Nixon, the president least likely to be identified as possessing a sense of humor, made it a point to appear on television's *Laugh-In*."[98] It took six takes but the producers finally got candidate Nixon to sound funny. He was nervous and kept insisting that he was "new at the comedy business."[99]

Dan Rowan and Dick Martin's *Laugh-In* (1967–73), along with *The Smothers Brothers Comedy Hour* (1967–69), relied on satire to offer sharp critiques of the war in Vietnam and racism, as well as challenges to other serious issues that became the material for raucous sketches that offered a political punch. Being too serious was going to win few allies. Tommy Smothers recalled that he had an "epiphany" when he "saw Jane Fonda on the *Tonight Show* around this time, and she was talking about burning babies in Vietnam and workers' rights . . . and all the things I *agree* with." In his words, "There was . . . no joy, she had no sense of humor! . . . And I just realized: to have a message, you can't be deadly serious or they're not gonna hear you; you're just an advocate for a point of view."[100] The 1970s, as historian Bruce Schulman reminds us, was characterized by the "irreverent comedy of *Saturday Night Live*,"[101] satire that was as crucial to the era as deindustrialization or the misery index. These variety shows often featured pathbreaking female comedians like Lily Tomlin, who played a sassy telephone operator on *Laugh-In*, and Gilda Radner, who had one of the few recurring female characters as Roseanne Roseannadanna on *Saturday Night Live*. Yet more often than not the top female comedians in the 1970s were still the butt of the joke. *Saturday Night Live*'s Weekend Update Point/Counterpoint featured the hilarious Dan Aykroyd and Jane Curtin. And in much the same way Jackie Gleason got laughs on *The Honeymooners*—a 1950s sitcom—with his familiar "To the moon, Alice," Aykroyd ended every skit with the punch line, "Jane, you ignorant slut."[102] As well, the intimacies between women and men have often meant that gendered strife has a history of being turned into flirty comic relief. Whether it was ancient Greece's *Lysistrata*, Shakespeare's *Taming of the Shrew*, or a 1930s Hollywood screwball comedy, disputes between men and women have been performed as flirty fun.[103]

IN ELLENSBURG, WASHINGTON, the local newspaper featured Larry Braniff, who got "a little piggy [necklace that he now wears] around his neck that touted, 'Billie Jean is No. 1.'" Braniff worked in a department store and had a reputation for taunting two of his feminist coworkers, Linda Schodt and Nancy Daniel, who gave him the piggy necklace, which came complete with homemade valentine that read, "To one chauvinist from two proud libbers." Braniff, who was sporting a tight black T-shirt and thick mustache for his photograph, humbly admitted "he was 'mouthing off a little more than I should have,' about male superiority." As Braniff posed with a gift that seemed a flirtatious combination of humor and masculine posturing, he bragged that "men are big enough to wear it and take the humility, and they [the women] wouldn't have worn it if we [Riggs] would have won."[104] Braniff's off-the-cuff remark that feminists would never have worn such a necklace, even as a joke, reflected a larger assumption—that feminists lacked a sense of humor.

In the 1970s the male chauvinist pig's popularity thrived on being a bad boy who laughed at all forms of authority and political correctness that included the uptight feminist. Over the years, mocking feminists' lack of humor has dominated popular culture. Consider a John Callahan cartoon from the 1980s about the man who could not find the humor section in a bookstore and was chastised by a grumpy woman behind the counter who declared, "This is a Feminist Book Store! There is not a Humor Section!!!"[105] More recently, the notoriously toxic stand-up comic Louis C. K. informed Jon Stewart and his *Daily Show* audience, "Comedians and feminists . . . are natural enemies. Because stereotypically speaking, feminists can't take a joke" and "comedians can't take criticism."[106] Feminists continue to struggle to avoid being pigeonholed as the ones who need to lighten up. Of course, feminism has flourished thanks in part to a history of the female moral arbiter, something that has allowed women to enter the U.S. political arena formally since the nineteenth century. Whether it was moral reform efforts to end slavery or close down saloons, women in politics were associated with spiritual uplift and piety. However, this history of gendered politics also meant that women's political activism became identified with a holier-than-thou attitude, creating a legacy that pervaded the twentieth century and made feminists an easy target for the male chauvinist pig.

In bold relief to other masculine political iconography such as labor's flexed bicep or a Black Power fist, the male chauvinist pig was often an intentionally ironic emblem of masculinity and political suasion. Rather than simply whine, the most famous male chauvinist pigs deployed strategies that tended to be a bit more tongue in cheek. But unlike the embrace of gay pride, the pig kept within the boundaries of white hegemonic masculinity. While this does not mean that queer men could not be male chauvinist pigs, asserting a patriarchal dominance was part of the flirtatious battle of the sexes the male chauvinist was looking for as he wandered into the intimate political terrain of the second wave. The male chauvinist pig had become an icon but, as we shall see, what it meant to be a pig also turned on the privileges of race.

CHAPTER TWO

Feminism's Racial Fault Lines

The Pig and the Macho Man

In the 1970s, coeditor of the *Texas Observer* and well-known political satirist Molly Ivins made a career of mocking conservative politics and male bravado. Blending savvy wit and feminist humor, Ivins attempted to unravel the troubling gender politics of her own home state. In the process, she uncovered the racial assumptions underlying the male chauvinist pig as well as another misogynist villain—the macho man.

In a column that set out to explain her state's resolute sexism, she borrowed a line from a John Wayne cowboy flick, declaring, "Texas is hell on women and horses." "Lone Star State Culture," she observed, reflected the "marriage of several strains of male chauvinism." On the one hand, Texans suffered from the presumably white "Southern belle concept of our Confederate heritage, the pervasive good ol' boyism; the jock idolatry (football is not a game here: it is a matter of life and death) and, most important, the legacy of the frontier, as it was when John Wayne lived on it." On the other hand, she first blamed "the *machismo* of our Latin tradition"[1] and in so doing reaffirmed an all-too-familiar racial trope placed on Latinx cultures that implied unrestrained passion and inherent violence and that for many was even worse than the male chauvinist.

The chauvinist, as Ivins suggested, was taking shape against the backdrop of other masculine tropes that highlight white privilege, its association with state and institutional oppression, and the virulent racism that tends toward violence, especially when directed at minorities. After all, the good old boy to whom Ivins referred was often indistinguishable from the pig—that is to say, the racist cop whose misdeeds also figured prominently in 1950s and 1960s battles for civil rights as well as more contemporary protests.[2] Yet the pejorative use of the term *pig* has a linguistic heritage stretching back centuries, conjuring up images of uncleanliness, stubbornness, and gluttony. Piggish traits applied across genders—women deemed morally questionable or unattractive were piglike, just as men with unrefined table manners, sloppy behavior, or unrestrained diets were called pigs. Being a pig, however, became a point of contention rather than a laughing matter.

Indeed, the authoritarian pig seemed to be everywhere. "All animals are equal, but some animals are more equal than others," insists George Orwell in his 1945 antiauthoritarian novella *Animal Farm* as the pigs turn out to be the barnyard beasts who violate the bonds of trust once held with other creatures. Ultimately, they walk on two legs and become indistinguishable from their human oppressors.[3] Amid the volatile milieu of the late 1960s and early 1970s and as the pig became perhaps the most powerful political epithet used to speak truth to the powers that be, feminism took a more radical turn and made the personal political, calling out the male chauvinist as a pig who was guilty of his own often familial authoritarianism. But the pig was not the only ridiculing epithet around; there was also the macho man, who served to reaffirm the pig's whiteness. In a world where some men were more equal than others, these distinctive manifestations of sexism further exposed feminism's racial fault lines.

How the Pig Became a Man: A Short Genealogy

Before the pig became a man, even the domesticated beast symbolized a threat to that which was safe and sacred. Judaism and Islam, for example, have considered pigs and pork taboo for thousands of years. Sifting through spiritual proclamations and placing them in the context of climate, economy, and resources, cultural anthropologist Marvin Harris has attempted to understand why pigs and pork became tainted when, say, camels or cows did not. In Harris's telling, pragmatic animal behavior in part set in motion much larger cultural ramifications. Pigs lack protective hair and the ability to sweat, which means they need to wallow in the mud to regulate temperature. This simple biological necessity means that pigs do not adapt well to hot climates or confined spaces. The Middle East does not offer pigs a natural habitat, making them seem out of place. Continuing along this line of thought, anthropologist Mary Douglas has found that things out of place are dirty, for the essence of dirt, she contends, is a "matter out of place."[4] Just like Old World taboos, but updated with a political twist, the pig was not just out of place, but also out of line.

While the linguistic origins of *chauvinism* first emerged in the years after the French Revolution as a mocking response to excessive loyalty to Napoleon and lingering overzealous nationalist pride, the pig became a popular political epithet in the same era. During the Revolution, antimonarchical publications cast Marie Antoinette and Louis XVI, along with other members of the royal family, as pigs when in 1791 they attempted to flee Paris in disguise. Historian Timothy Tackett observes how the king, who had a reputation for overeating (something once thought of as an endearing trait), was now reconfigured and pictured as a disgusting beast. "For weeks thereafter the 'pig-king' appeared everywhere in newspapers and brochures, in posters and engravings. Often there were whole families of pigs: a pig-queen and various other pig-members of the royal family in company with the porcine Louis. . . . Someone even attached a sign to the wall of the Tuileries palace shortly after the flight: 'A large pig has escaped from the premises,' it read. 'Anyone finding him is urged to return him to his pen. A minor reward will be offered.'"[5] The pig, already associated with the uncouth, became identified with corrupt state power and backwards politics and manners.

In the United States, *pig* is a centuries-old insult that over time became infused with America's virulent racism. In the post-Reconstruction South, Black codes that were also known in some states at the Pig Laws were designed as mechanisms of labor control used to turn former slaves into prisoners. Corrupt laws were thus embedded with rule by pigs and the history of racial oppression.[6] Whether it was the southern, small-town sheriff or an unsympathetic urban police force, the state's excessive misuse of power led to the use of the term *pig* to describe the police. As a slang term used to refer to a police officer, *pig* had been familiar since the early nineteenth century; however, it was in the 1960s that the term found its most poignant political aim, as a way of stigmatizing an unsympathetic white police force.[7] Everyday acts of white backlash as well as iconic battles to maintain the racial status quo often found nefarious collaboration among the Ku Klux Klan, local police, the FBI, and other notorious pigs. Whether it was by Alabama segregationist governor George Wallace or the FBI's Counterintelligence Program, which put thousands of civil rights and antiwar protesters under surveillance, the South was unmistakably under pig rule.[8] At the height of the Black liberation movement, the term *pig* was unmistakably associated with those who most embodied and misused state privilege, power, and whiteness.

For Black Americans long categorized as animalistic, calling a white man, moreover a police officer or politician, a pig who wallowed in his own filthy corruption seemed more than justified. According to historian Steve Estes, Black Panther theory and praxis centered on discussions of race and masculinity that questioned long-held assumptions of what defined a man. The pig became a pig because of the legacy of white denial of who was a man. In prison, Black Panther Party cofounder Huey Newton, for example, "critiqued the use of the term 'the Man' to refer to white men in positions of power because, he argued, this epithet implicitly denied nonwhite manhood. This was why the Panthers referred to police officers as pigs, to show that they were 'less than a man.'"[9] The use of such epithets quickly filtered into mainstream media along with images of this revolutionary movement. In 1969 *Life* magazine, for example, featured the dramatic trial of the Panthers' other student cofounder, Bobby Seale, who was "ordered bound and gagged" after "peppering Judge Julius J. Hoffman with obscenities and labels that ranged from 'fascist' to 'pig.'" However, there are countless other examples of the police being called out as pigs in a cultural terrain that included everything from Black newspapers, magazines, and interviews to films and music.[10]

Any genealogical study of the figure of the pig in feminist truth-telling must first point out that the chauvinist pig owes much to the pig the Student Nonviolent Coordinating Committee and the Black Panthers confronted in the 1960s and 1970s that turned on violence, oppression, and the dirtiest of dirty tricks.[11] By the end of the 1960s, the chauvinist would become a pig because he was not just an overzealous braggart but also a dirty political figure who had the potential for unsavory attitudes and actions. Even though antifeminist rogues were popularly identified as chauvinists in the early 1960s, as a political target the pig actually predated chauvinism as an insult and a taboo. Although the pig is first and foremost associated with the brutal police oppression of Black civil rights, as an epithet it converted many figures of authority and political adversaries into more villainous figures. The same symbol that channeled Black anger became a means of adding insult to injury for a multitude of political purposes.

Regardless of political leanings, calling someone a pig turned on rage. From capitalist pigs to commie pigs, the "pig" was a surefire way to heat up Cold War discourse and protests. Against the backdrop of an escalating war in Vietnam and antiwar protests surrounding the 1968 Democratic National Convention in Chicago, two leading white political activists, Abbie Hoffman and Jerry Rubin, nominated the actual barnyard animal for president. A pig named Pigasus the Immortal became the Yippies' (Youth International Party members') nomination for president of the United States and an ultimate sign of disrespect for an executive office that was now deemed corrupt. In a bit of street theater, Rubin held his squealing candidate in front of a defiant crowd of supporters and proclaimed with bitter irony, "We want to give you a chance to talk to our candidate and to restate our demand that Pigasus be given Secret Service protection and be brought to the White House for his foreign policy briefing." Rumors and memories suggest that after the protesters were thrown in jail, the police ate the pig

The police manhandling Pigasus the Immortal, the Yippies' 1968 presidential nominee. Photo by Fred W. McDarrah, used by permission of Getty Images.

for dinner.[12] Nevertheless, the violent encounter of the New Left, and in particular Students for a Democratic Society, with Chicago's "Mayor Daley and his fascist pig police" at the Democratic National Convention reaffirmed the power of calling a pig a pig in ways that mirrored the actions and attitudes of Black liberationists.[13]

Calling someone a pig still packs a painful political punch. It emerges to this day in contemporary protests such as the 2010–12 Occupy Movement and the Black Lives Matter protests that have called out everything from the 2014 police shooting of Michael Brown—an unarmed Black teenager in Ferguson, Missouri—to the police murder of George Floyd in 2020, which sparked global outrage.[14] Above all else, the pig has remained a symbol of systemic oppressive white authority in Black political discourse and less the bad boy with gender troubles.

The Pig and the Second Wave

Amid the counterculture movements of the 1960s, the Orwellian pig revealed his misogynist self as a second wave of feminism began a more radical quest to call out the all-too-familiar authoritarianism embedded in its very own left-leaning political movements and personal relationships. Frustrated by a lack of legal protections, subservient roles within movements, and sexual objectification, a younger generation of feminists pushed beyond questioning what Betty Friedan called in her iconic second-wave publication *The Feminist Mystique* (1963) "the problem that has no name," which plagued disillusioned suburban housewives, and sought a revolution in ideas and attitudes that would bring social justice to women in work, religion, politics, and the most intimate aspects of familial life. In an era in which feminists declared that "the personal is political," everything from who did the dishes to who had an orgasm was up for a debate about "power, authority, and control," and by the 1970s there were more feminists interested in radical change. "By challenging the ostensible divide between the public world of politics and the private world of family, sexuality, and motherhood, feminists were demanding nothing short of a total reappraisal of the meaning of life."[15]

As the women's and gay liberation movements, to varying degrees, championed men who were sensitive, caring, and in touch with their emotions, men who stood in diametric opposition to these values—who were rugged, aggressive, and violent—increasingly dominated popular films. By the 1970s, not only were those softer images rare, but men in film as a whole had become more disturbed and troubled. John Bodnar's study *Blue-Collar Hollywood* reveals a shift in the image of the working-class white man, from the all-American boy who after World War II could protect his nation, home, and family to the post-Vietnam complex and disturbed individual who does not think twice about taking matters into his own hands. Films like *Joe* (1970), *Dirty Harry* (1971), and *Taxi Driver* (1976), for example, feature "angry men" and "mean streets."[16] The chauvinist pig was never just a barrel of laughs. A 1974 feminist publication titled *Women's Lip: Male Chauvinist Reading Matter* attests to bitter remarks about "dumb broads" and "castrating bitches," as well as misogynist threats that outrageously claimed, "Women liked to be raped," and, "like gongs," all women "should be struck regularly."[17]

For feminists, however, the pig was not typically a distant enemy or occupying force but rather intertwined in the most intimate of familial and potentially volatile relationships. In fact, what made feminism so profound yet so confusing was that the pig was often one's comrade, one's ally, one's husband or lover. For feminists coming of age in the 1960s, tired of liberal restraint that demanded middle-class acquiescence, the ability to call men out as pigs was sweet revenge. Gloria Steinem recalls, "Years of being *chicks, dogs,* and *cows* may have led to some understandable desire to turn the tables, but it also taught us what dehumanization feels like. Police had been *pigs* in the sixties—as in 'Off the Pigs!'—so all prejudiced men became the same for a while." By the late 1970s the male chauvinist pig would peak in feminist discourse.[18] Indeed, the pig was everywhere. From politics and professions, the pigs ran rampant. Behind every great woman, it seemed, stood a male chauvinist pig. Looking back with regret, Steinem felt feminists made a mistake in calling their adversaries pigs. "The invention of *male chauvinist pig*, a hybrid produced by trying to combine feminism with leftist rhetoric, which was often antifeminist in itself[,] . . . [suggested] a willingness to reduce adversaries to something less than human as a first step toward justifying violence against them."[19] Whether or not *pig* was the most humane epithet, it did reinforce the idea that mainstream feminism was white.

At its peak in popular feminist discourse, *pig* was rarely used in Black America's print media as a reference to men of color. This absence reinforced the pig's whiteness. And because pigs were such powerful symbols of white oppression, calling out chauvinists as pigs could make feminism seem racially exclusive and misguided. In an extensive 1971 *Ebony* article and one of the few mainstream Black publications that made any use at all of the expression *male chauvinist pig*, essayist Helen King juxtaposed "the Black woman and women's lib," as an outsider looking in at what she defined as a white woman's problem. According to King, "It was not long, before the feminists met with loud-mouthed opposition from white men who felt their manhood was being challenged and who call the protest 'frivolous.'" However, when it came to the lives of white women, their problems with white men did seem trivial. "Let the Chauvinist Pigs see how they enjoy Babysitting for a change!" was the rallying cry that King described as "just a bunch of bored white women with nothing to do" in "suburbia" with their "gadget kitchens."[20]

In the 1970s, and at a moment when feminism was most readily identified in the media with white middle-class women who were positioning themselves for political and popular attention, King questioned the motivation for using a term like *pig* and suggested that such feminist vernacular that relied on calling out sexist men as pigs represented what scholar Eric Lott would later describe in studies of white appropriation of Black music and culture as a kind of "love and theft."[21] More to the point, she chastised "feminists [who] quickly adopted slogans and symbols of the Black liberation movement like 'Right On!' and the clenched fist."[22]

At the same time, the uneasy cultural transmission of politicized slogans also resurrected tensions between liberation movements privileging different objectives. Psychologist Charles W. Thomas, who was one of many experts featured in her essay, suggested that feminism was purposely designed "to attract attention away from the black liberation movement." According to Thomas, "The women's movement is a diversion in the same way the environment movement is a diversion. Like the environment thing [the pollution controversy] college kids are flocking into, feminism appeals to middle-class whites because, in part, it is an activist way to ignore racism." In his professional opinion, it seemed not just feminists but white liberals writ large were engaging in "avoidance behavior."[23]

Importantly, feminism has a long and uneasy history that has turned on race privilege. The first wave of feminism, which culminated in 1920 with the ratification of the Nineteenth Amendment, giving women the right to vote, was a reminder that some women were more equal than others as a groundswell of self-declared feminists touted Black disenfranchisement and xenophobia.[24] One of King's interviewees feared understandably that "this movement won't be any different from the Woman Suffrage thing. White women won the right to vote way back then but black people including women, didn't win this right until more than 100 years later."[25] The history of feminists, along with their contemporary antagonist, the male chauvinist pig, who was so rarely used as an epithet in Black discourse, reinforced the racial angst that shaped feminism's fault lines and ideas that white feminist complaints were trivial.

Calling out chauvinist pigs without understanding racial hierarchy and state power further revealed the limits of sisterhood. Naomi Jaffe, who joined SDS [Students for a Democratic Society], the Weather Underground, as well as feminist organizations like WITCH (Women's International Terrorist Conspiracy from Hell), found that "attempts to be part of early second wave feminism and an antiracist struggle were untenable." Things came to a head in 1971 during New York State's Attica Prison rebellion, in which excessive state force resulted in the death of thirty-one prisoners and nine guards. Tragically, Jaffe recalls the cynical responses of some white feminists who had no empathy for the rioting "'male chauvinists' who died at Attica," men Jaffe saw as her brothers, not as sworn enemies.[26] In 1974, Marcia Ann Gillespie, editor in chief of *Essence*, a magazine that catered to Black women, offered her support of feminism even as she distanced herself from the derogatory expression. She charged, "Black Women need economic equality, but it doesn't apply for me to call a black man a male chauvinist pig." Here the discourse of the pig signaled too strongly an all-out battle reminiscent of the police altercations so dominant in the 1960s and early 1970s. Which is perhaps why Gillespie added, "Our anger is not at our men. I don't think they have been the enemy."[27] Critiques of hegemonic feminist goals that ignored racial injustice were crucial to complex political debates and issues of social justice. These critiques brought into sharp relief the whitewashing of popular feminism that masked the struggles of women of color.

The male chauvinist pig's relatively scarce appearance in Black media should not imply that somehow women of color were not committed to ending social injustices that turned on patriarchy. Mainstream political figures like Aileen Hernandez, president of the National Organization for Women, Congresswoman Barbara Jordan, and 1972 presidential candidate Shirley Chisholm were constant reminders that despite the media's attraction to white feminist icons, women of color also sought an end to racism and sexism on the national stage and in very public ways. Helen King made room for such voices, including that of Chisholm, who maintained in unmistakable language that "black people can't be free until women are."[28] By her very presence on the political stage, the Democratic presidential candidate complicated any narrative that tried to too neatly present feminism as an exclusively white female concern.[29] Interestingly, in one rare reference to male chauvinist pigs in the *Chicago Defender*, a newspaper that catered largely to a Black readership, an editorial warned its readership in June 1972 that anyone who did not appreciate the education Chisholm was offering the country was "a male chauvinist pig," implying without hesitation that such a label could apply to anyone who dismissed the ideas, social policies, and courage of this first Black female presidential candidate.[30]

Rather than searching for evidence that women of color called out the sexism in their own lives by labeling men pigs,[31] historian Nancy Hewitt reminds us that too narrow of a focus on traditional political definitions, including in this case an epithet or moniker, can result in stultifying and artificial distinctions and understandings of what has been labeled as second-wave or true feminist expression. Therefore she cautions one to avoid "the script of feminist history—that each wave overwhelms and exceeds its predecessor—lends itself all too easily to whiggish interpretations of ever more radical, all-encompassing, and ideologically sophisticated movements."[32] She also wonders whether "it may be impossible to jettison the concept of feminist waves" and suggests different kinds of waves that are not so distinct, offering the concept of radio waves and "different lengths and frequencies." Heard locally and globally, "radio waves echo Elsa Barkley Brown's description of gumbo ya-ya—everyone talking at once—and remind us that feminist ideas are 'in the air' even when people are not actively listening."[33]

In this case, understanding "different lengths and frequencies" reveals the complicated ways in which the chauvinist pig cannot be fully understand as a type without placing him in conversation with other misogynist villains who had their own distinct racial roots. After all, the male chauvinist pig was one of several antifeminist figures outed in the 1960s and 1970s, many of whom were not white but represented *suspect* cultures and the kind that patriarchy deemed particularly sinister. In other words, the pig was a pig, but he was ensconced in the kind of whiteness and respectability that appeared to temper his mood and misdeeds.

The Macho Man

In a high-stakes campaign to dismantle white supremacy, calling out the invisibility of Black women and the sexism in Black Power was seen as a violation of solidarity and a threat to the efficacy of the movement. Looking back at the late 1970s, despite a long history of women of color sorting out the politics of race and gender on their own terms, Black feminism was still seen as not just a contradiction in terms but a threat. And it was at this moment, in 1978, that Michele Wallace's *Black Macho and the Myth of the Superwoman* exposed the raw contradictions in liberation movements that painfully ignored women's struggles with Black patriarchy and ignited a firestorm of controversy. Paying careful attention to the onslaught of emasculating rhetoric directed toward men of color in the mid-1960s, Wallace lamented, "The black man had two pressing tasks before him: a white woman in every bed and black woman under every heel." As the provocative title of her book suggests, Wallace relied heavily on the concept of machismo in her critique of Black men but made it a point to note that *pig* is reserved for the white police state.[34]

In the 1970s, not everyone objected to the label *macho*. After all, it offered a measure of masculine cool without the sting of equating someone of color with raging police brutality or racially infused animal tropes. In her autobiography, Black Panther Assata Shakur, who complains about the "macho culture that was an official body in the BPP," also salutes individual Panther leaders such as Huey Newton and Bobby Seale who could stand up to the powers that were, in her words, "baaad." Such nuances could be lost in mainstream media, especially given the degree to which one could be both for and against aspects of the same movement.[35] Steve Estes, in his study of "race, manhood, and the civil rights movement," notes that at times the party's "'black macho' attitudes implied that this masculinist rhetoric and posturing had a lack of substantive programs" and was detrimental to the workaday goals and ambitions of the Panther Party.[36]

Of course, the legacy of calling out Black machismo is mixed. Estes identifies Wallace's analysis as one that offers a powerful reflection of a history of hypermasculine rhetoric and intrinsic problems with the Black liberation movement, but in hindsight a view that lacks nuance. Estes suggests that Wallace, for example, "ignores much of the party's grassroots political activism and willingness to address issues of sexism and homophobia within the organization."[37] He insists that "as revolutionary mothers, Panther women were often sexual partners of Panther men. The ideals of revolutionary manhood and free love that reigned in the late 1960s had both liberating and deleterious effects on sexual relations in the party." Estes argues that at least "in theory, having multiple sexual partners avoided the chauvinistic aspects of 'ownership' that traditional monogamy often entailed. However, as the Panthers and other movement groups soon learned, chauvinism was not as easily 'smashed' as monogamy."[38] Even Wallace herself would offer self-reflection in a new 1990 introduction entitled "How I Saw It Then, How I See It Now." Of course, Wallace could not fully realize how, in the decades to come, Black feminism would become such a tour de force. "This Black feminist classic," in the words of Jamilah Lemieux, "was a precursor to Black Lives Matter." This movement has not only been often led by women but has once again censured the police as pigs.[39]

When it comes to the legacy of machismo, however, xenophobic discussions of violence and aggression have placed blame heavily on Latin cultures. In the early 1970s José G. Cruz, who published a series of popular adventure and romance comics, produced *El nefasto machismo* (Tragic machismo). The comic book was designed to help Mexicans understand the damaging aspects of machismo and to expose the uncompromising and outlandish acts of bravado and violence specifically associated with men of Mexican descent. According to *El nefasto machismo*, Mexican men had become infamous for squandering their money on drink, gambling their lives away, beating their women and children, and participating in a host of other illicit and unusually violent acts like murder, driving recklessly, abusing drugs, irresponsibly procreating, stealing, and what was described as all-around "mayhem."[40]

In the United States, Mexican and Mexican American men whose labor was inextricably bound to low pay and dirty work in mines and fields in the nineteenth-century Southwest had been deemed morally suspect and intrinsically more brutish than Anglo patriarchs. Derogatory racial epithets like *greaser*, for example, reaffirmed the notion that Mexicans, in particular men, were not simply lazy but also morally unclean and hence untrustworthy. However, the demand for household labor conveniently cast Mexican women as docile and domestic. In the Anglo imagination, women of Mexican descent were thus readily employable as maids, cooks, and caregivers in white households thanks to a cultural machismo that inculcated them with subservient feminine traits that fit the labor demands of white households.[41]

The stereotypes associated with Latinos were also gaining strength in the early 1970s as a neorestrictionist movement began to take shape. In the 1950s and 1960s attitudes toward immigration were relatively lax and hence support for a restrictionist immigration policy was weak. By the late 1960s and just as machismo was beginning to attract more attention, the international boundary with Mexico was portrayed as "out of control," immigration was increasingly described as an "invasion," and the language employed to describe immigrants shifted from "wetback" to "illegals" or "aliens." This shift in part was the product of the liberation movements of the preceding decades, which attacked terms like *wetback* as racist. It also reflected the growing concern that the United States was facing a "boundary enforcement crisis." Joseph Nevins has shown that between 1973 and 1980 the coverage of these topics expanded 650 percent. These stories often dealt with the larger issue of a struggling U.S. economy and the growing concerns about job competition with immigrants and focused on the perceived violence and criminality that was typically ascribed to Latinx immigrants.[42]

Feminism also powerfully shaped this understanding of what it meant to be "macho." Dictionaries of slang trace the origins of *macho*, which implied courage embodied in "foolhardy displays" of masculinity, to the middle of the twentieth century.[43] But its increased popularity would not be visible until the women's movement fully emerged and the economy began to contract.[44] In a 1974 defense of *macho*, freelance writer Steve Ditlea suggested that the "word owes currency to the very movement which has been seeking to abolish it. In writing about the ways in which male dominated society has victimized women, feminists in the last few years have popularized the Spanish notion of macho."[45]

The typical ways in which white women used machismo in the mass media also highlighted violence and aggressive behavior. For example, in a 1973 interview Gloria Steinem argued, "The whole masculine machismo element still worships violence and teaches that's the way to get ahead." In 1974, the *San Francisco Chronicle* asked a number of women, "Do certain types rub you the wrong way?" A bank teller, Linda Stewart, described the "guy who really comes on strong" and is "always on the make" and "trying to sell himself as being really butch" and as the "really aggressive macho type." "There's something about that type," she added, "that I can't stand."[46] Homemaker Judy de

Jong described the macho type in a similar fashion: "Muscular. Strong hands and arms. Demanding [and] Domineering."[47]

Even as white feminists embraced the term to condemn these behaviors, critics claimed that they struggled to apply it to white men. Judith Martin of the Washington Post News Service complained that the word *macho* conjured up an image that was far too violent for Americans. At a meeting of the American Association for the Advancement of Science, Martin noted that sociologist Jessie Bernard's use of *macho* seemed to "denote aggressive behavior." *Macho* "sounds mean," she protested. "Macho is the man who will grind his heel into a woman's face if the dinner isn't done right, whereas what they're really talking about is the nice American man who will just whine about it all evening." Martin failed to explain who this nice man was, but she presented him as so stereotypically middle class that he did not fit the Latinx stereotype from which the term derived.[48] Suzanne Freedman, who was an artist in San Francisco and a self-proclaimed feminist, made an even more explicit argument about white men and machismo. Freedman had little patience for "men who are afraid of women getting together, of uniting or forming a solidarity, because we're going to rock their boat." But her understanding of a "typical male chauvinist was a Venezuelan we met who said 'Women are good for sex, to raise children, and to do housework.'" When Freedman pointed a disparaging finger to the Venezuelan, she invoked the image of the "Latin lover" or patriarch who refused to do women's work and a trope of hot-blooded masculinity that was also identified with Italians who carried the mark of being hypersexed and prone to violence and insensitivity.[49]

The connection between machismo and violence was freighted with racial implications. In the early 1970s, Sonia Lopez was a faculty member teaching courses in Mexican American studies at San Diego State and involved in the Chicana movement. When asked in a 1972 interview whether machismo was more of a problem in Mexican culture, she interrupted and insisted there was no difference between Mexican machismo and Anglo male chauvinism. "You hear more about machismo because you have anthropologists and sociologists, social scientists and so forth you know pointing out and writing about it a lot more than they do about male chauvinism," she pointed out, "but it's the same thing. A male you know that has to be constantly oppressing the woman." When asked whether Mexican men were more violent, she reaffirmed that the only cultural difference rested in terminology, not behavior. She was even more emphatic: "It's the same thing." The language may be different, but "it is the same thing except in one culture it is called male chauvinism and in the other it is called machismo. The same thing about the double standard for the woman, the man being the head of the household. . . . It's in both cultures. . . . But it is the same thing. There is no difference."[50]

More recently, historian Inés Hernández-Avila has argued that the distinction made between machismo and chauvinism continues to exacerbate tensions between feminists. In her words, "It has marked the battleground between white feminists and feminists of color."[51] To be sure, feminists, including writers at *Ms.* magazine, used *machismo* to describe white male behavior, but it usually implied violent or hyperaggressive behavior.[52] Chicana scholar Emma Pérez sees that "many Anglos, particularly white feminists, insist that the men of our culture created machismo and they conveniently forget that the men of their race make the rules." Which is why Hernández-Avila concludes that "a male chauvinist pig is a male chauvinist pig is a male chauvinist pig, in whatever culture he is from, and in whatever language you might use to name him."[53] Images of violence conjured up not only Black machismo but also a darker side to the chauvinist pig embedded in an interwoven history of racism. In other words, the chauvinist pig was typically white but could also be relegated to an in-between racial identity thought to be inherently violent, making the chauvinist pig appear relatively harmless.

The only time machismo appeared to be less of a threat was when it was turned into a joke that reinforced racial stereotypes. In 1979, *Saturday Night Live*'s cast engaged in some racial cross-dressing to gently mock white men's inability to be seen as macho. Bill Murray played a game show host named Paco Venezuela who, along with two contestants, Graciela Cortez (Gilda Radner) and Jorge Lopez (Ricky Nelson), attempted to answer the question, "Quien es mas macho?" The show's format was simple. The competitors were shown pictures of Hollywood stars and asked to decide which of the men was "muy macho." The skit begins with Paco revealing pictures of two Hollywood stars: Fernando Lamas, an Argentine American actor and director who routinely played the Latin lover, and Ricardo Montalbán, a Mexican actor best known for his role as Mr. Roark on the television series *Fantasy Island* (1977–84), as well as in a series of luxury car commercials. The two contestants hesitate to respond, but only for a few seconds, then Jorge rings in and answers "Montalbán." "Porquoi?" asks Paco, prompting Jorge to explain, "Cordoba es automóvil muy macho," a reference to Montalbán's infamous appearance in Chrysler Cordoba television advertisements that featured "rich Corinthian leather"—a phrase that was used in routine spoofs thanks to his masculine tone and distinct accent. In what is a humorously arbitrary moment, Paco responds, "Non es falso, Fernando Lamas es un poquito mas macho" (That's false. Fernando Lamas is a little bit more macho).[54]

Paco then turns to Graciela as pictures of three white men appear on the screen. She looks confused, as the far more challenging bonus round requires her to choose between David Janssen, Lloyd Bridges, and Jack Lord, famous for playing a fugitive (Janssen), an action-adventure star (Bridges), and a detective (Lord). While it was Bridges who was collectively seen as "muy macho," the contestant's confusion, coupled with a nod to brawn over brains, reinforced the degree to which hypermasculine prowess was a racist trope. Not only was the male chauvinist pig white, he was domesticated and thus assumed to be more a nuisance than a threat.

In the same year Michele Wallace published her critique *Black Macho* (1978), the Village People's "Macho Man" queered norms, topped the disco charts, and highlighted looks and attitudes that played on a double entendre and the ambiguity of the musical group's sexual identity. The Village People denied any connection to gay culture in their public relations and played only "straight" clubs, but their song lyrics told another story.[55] "Macho Man" suggested that the real man's bravado defined his gender, not his sexual ambiguity. Much of the song dealt with the look and attitude of the macho man, who was "willing to make a stand," and his body—the "big thick muscles," the "broad shoulders," and the hairy chest. Yet while the macho man had the kind of body [that was] always in demand," what helped make him so macho was that he was "ready to get down with anyone he can."[56] In a 1978 *Rolling Stone* exposé on "machomania," the author questioned the Village People as "America's Male ideal" and exposed the band as anything but heteronormative.[57]

The image associated with the Village People had its roots in what has become known as the gay macho, a "distinctive look among young gay men in the 1970s, defined most notably by leather jackets and jeans, short hair, and a lean, sculpted body from the increasingly popular workout regimes on the new Nautilus weight machines, a body built specifically for the disco scene and a body that was meant for dancing shirtless."[58] Even though gay men have been defying notions of effeminacy throughout most of the twentieth century, scholar Alice Echols argues it was not until after World War II that the stereotype began to change. As George Chauncey notes in his history of New York, gay men in the mid-1940s became increasingly uncomfortable with charges of effeminacy and began adopting a more masculine flair that included blue jeans, leather jackets, and masculine prowess.[59] Such sensual styles anticipated Hollywood actors Marlon Brando and James Dean and the popular embrace of a hypermale sexuality in 1950s popular culture. By the mid-1960s, Echols adds, "masculine gay men were becoming a discernable presence even beyond the community."[60]

Playing up masculine norms to the point of exaggeration was also a form of mockery. While Echols explains that gay machismo was a masculinity that made, in Andrew Holleran's words, "gay men utterly indistinguishable from straight boys"[61] and one that was "meticulous" and "lacked the casualness that marked the self-presentation of straight men,"[62] she also brings into question whether it was masculinity that was "best understood as a parody of conventional or a mimicking of normative masculinity."[63] What made gay machismo so funny was that it was a joke that some men (especially heterosexual men) did not get. Perhaps today we might find it quirkier than Americans did in the 1970s, but even then it was hard not to laugh at the men on stage, in popular culture, and at discos across the country gyrating to the tune of "Macho Man" or any of the other Village People's hits. The potential for humor in both the lyrics and the stage presence of the Village People, who dressed as some of the era's most masculine and erotic male icons (construction worker, soldier, biker/leather man, police officer, Indian, sailor, cowboy), was ever present, if not part of the act—both campy and comical.[64]

In one of the more popular Hollywood films of the era, however, comic relief was not quite so conspicuous. *Saturday Night Fever* (1977) helped to define the disco era, along with its star John Travolta. Travolta plays Tony Manero, a young Italian American who spends his days toiling at the local paint store for minimum wage and his nights at the local disco, where he is the star attraction in his now-famous white suit as he strikes a sensual pose and dances alone (though sometimes with a partner). Manero and his gang of misfits lack goals and direction, perhaps a consequence of the bleak deindustrialization that serves as the backdrop to the film, but they look for meaning outside work—at the disco, on the dance floor, or through Manero's dancing, which has the potential to collectively uplift the masculinity of all straight white men, when they are not trying to prove it by poking fun at or brutalizing women, gays, and Puerto Ricans.[65]

The film is at times disturbingly raw but also invokes a bit of comedy in large part because the film's characters simply don't get the joke. The hip-swiveling moves, the "don't touch my hair" sneer, and the dress and style are so self-consciously serious, as is the assertion of heterosexual posturing, that the movie inadvertently ignores the boundaries between straight and gay even though it so desperately tries to reassert them.[66]

Similar scenes were reproduced in discos across the country. Historian Randy McBee grew up in a white working-class suburb on the north side of

Kansas City, Missouri, in the 1970s and recalls a disco at a theme park near his home. When "Macho Man" came on the loudspeaker, the floor would immediately clear to make way for individual men taking their turn at a solo dance performance. Each performance typically lasted a minute or two and was followed by that of another man and then another who each engaged in what McBee describes as a cross between a Russian squat dance or Cossack dance and a pale imitation of breakdancing "before we knew what break-dancing was." With far less physical dexterity or grace than seen on television or at the movies, these white working-class macho men were not trying to be funny, but "those of us who lacked the courage or brains to refuse to take part couldn't help but snicker."[67]

By the latter 1970s, various definitions of *macho* would contribute to the rise of the "Disco Sucks" movement. While scholar Walter Hughes reminds us that the phrase reflected the fear and anxiety surrounding gay culture and led to violence, including antidisco rallies that saw participants eagerly destroying disco records, the phrase also further distinguished the chauvinist from macho and highlights the extent to which humor has shaped our understanding of American masculinity.[68] "Disco Sucks" was both a symbol of the growing bitterness surrounding gender nonconformity and a joke that played with a double entendre—it criticized an entire genre of music and highlighted oral sex as the singular issue defining gay identities. The focus on gay men did not erase the link between machismo, Latino men, and violence, but collectively the macho man made the chauvinist pig appear all the more heteronormative and white—something that mitigated his harsher manners and mannerisms.

As men stumbled to both define what it really meant to be macho and live up to their own definition, they reinforced the ambiguity surrounding sexual identity. In an example of satire that relied on race to mitigate the dangers of machismo, the *San Francisco Chronicle* in 1974 sent their "question man" onto the street to ask a group of white San Franciscans, "Are you macho?" The mixed responses turned on implications that questioned a man's heteronormativity but not his whiteness. Pat Dietz, a political scientist undergrad, wasn't quite sure about the word's meaning. "Do you mean am I queer or something like that?" he asked, adding, "I've never heard of macho but if that means am I okay, then, yes . . . I'm not gay or queer. I'm just regular." Laborer John Villeggiante claimed that he was macho because "my girl friend tells me I am," and "if you like girls better than guys," he explained, "then you're macho." Steve Simpson, a musician, also claimed he was macho because of his attraction to women. "I usually don't notice guys as much as I notice girls," he insisted, although he was quite convinced that he knew whether someone was gay and had apparently spent some time thinking about gay men. "I've seen a couple of questionable types already today." "They're all over," he added, and said, "I can spot them pretty easily. The way he walks. The way he dresses. The way he acts. There's just no mistaking them."[69]

Other men struggled to defend machismo but only because they desperately wanted to make it a reformation of heterosexuality. In an article entitled "In Praise of Macho," columnist Charles McCabe argued that a small club he patronized in San Francisco epitomized the meaning of macho because it provided a chance for all-male companionship.[70] The patrons were generally working men, and like a typical man's club, it was a "world where, for the time being, women literally do not exist." McCabe likened it to "halftime in a football game, or an extended seventh-inning stretch"—a world, he proudly exclaimed, "of the 'macho.'" McCabe argued that his club was similar to the all-male experiences these men enjoyed in their day-to-day lives. "Most of the clientele, like the firemen and the cops, spend their life working with men. They are completely male-oriented. This luncheon hour is just a continuation of their male life. The women and kids and in-laws come into their life in the evening and on holidays."[71]

McCabe found his club attractive because it was a place where working men could repair themselves physically and emotionally after a long day of wage work and a place where they could let loose and be unruly. As far as McCabe could recall, women were not even "talked about" in his favorite hangout. Still, he was just as quick to emphasize that he "prefer[red] the company of women to men, by a long shot," a predilection he described as a weakness that was "healthily corrected by a visit to this place," as if he (and men in general) had been deluded into believing that their heterosexual lives outside their club were more important than the company of men they preferred in their club, where their female counterparts were neither in attendance nor talked about.[72] At the least, his misgivings about his preference for women reflected his ambivalence about the responsibilities he associated with married life—children, in-laws, and so on. It also reflected his fear about how outsiders might interpret the same-sex relationships that profoundly shaped his club experience.

Thanks to his race and heterosexual posturing, the male chauvinist pig, whether or not he defended a macho lifestyle, often felt at home wallowing in his normative ways. Amid the revelry of his favorite hangout, McCabe's heterosexuality may have appeared distant or peripheral, but that heterosexuality still defined the meaning of those same-sex bonds and the boundaries that separated these men, a point McCabe was anxious to make. The alternative, being gay (or the fear of it), was simply too great of a challenge to the nature of the all-male camaraderie he embraced and what he defined as his very macho world.[73] For the most part, McCabe and other male chauvinist pigs stood apart from the kind of machismo that was bound to a violent eroticism that was presumably intrinsic to Latino culture. To be sure, these masculine tropes fluctuated and at times overlapped, but when understood in connection to each other, they contributed to the whitening of feminism that, in turn, made the image of the male chauvinist pig appear relatively benign alongside the other misogynist villains of the era.

IN AN AGE OF CIVIL RIGHTS and antiwar revolutions, the Orwellian pig's taxonomy came to represent America's apartheid, racial privilege, and violence. Being called a pig revealed how age-old animal tropes long used against subjugated groups could be appropriated and used against the state and the status quo. As satirist Molly Ivins explained, the male chauvinist pig was a "marriage of several strains of male chauvinism" that were inseparable from "good ol' boyism" that rested on white supremacy and the macho man who lacked both self-control and whiteness. In other words, while some men of color were defined as pigs, the genealogy of the chauvinist pig more often than not assumed whiteness. Magazines, newspapers, films, and day-to-day political banter, along with the trajectory of feminist concerns, reinforced an image of the male chauvinist pig as white.

Just as the male chauvinist pig turned on race, so too did feminism. Above all else, news headlines and popular culture in the 1970s reinforced an ongoing battle of the sexes in which white and middle-class feminists took center stage, battling a male chauvinist pig who could enjoy the benefits of white privilege untainted by sexual ambiguity or out-of-control rage. All of which made it seem as though the chauvinist pig was more like a domesticated barnyard animal than a wild beast. He might be a nuisance, but unlike the macho man, the male chauvinist pig at least wouldn't give you a black eye.

CHAPTER THREE

Are You a Chauvinist Pig?
Mixed Political Consciousness and the Mass Media

In the spring of 1971, a *San Francisco Chronicle* reporter, Novella O'Hara, stopped the occasional passerby on a busy street and asked, "Are you a male chauvinist pig?" Men were often unsure about how to answer O'Hara's question, even admitting, "I don't know if I am or not." Others appeared contradictory as they advocated for women's "lib" but still wanted to "feel like a man."[1] At times, even self-declared male chauvinists spoke about equality and offered opinions surprisingly similar to their feminist adversaries'. Tracing discussions and definitions of the male chauvinist from the streets of San Francisco to the level of national discourse reveals above all else a collective ambiguity over his identity and definition. In other words, there was little agreement on who or what defined a male chauvinist pig, making him more complex than a simple stereotype. Thanks to a measure of sympathy that feminists typically did not receive in the media, the ardent male chauvinist pig appeared to be something other than an unthinking political beast.

To be sure, the male chauvinist possessed a mixed political consciousness that should not be easily dismissed. At times he could simply be equated to a staunch "antifeminist," yet at other times he could not. Not all men who opposed feminism were proudly male chauvinist pigs. And some male chauvinists were not necessarily opposed to feminism. Chauvinisms, much like feminisms, are reflections of a fluidity of thoughts and actions that are in constant flux. Think of the grandfather who demands his wife fix his dinner yet pays for his granddaughter's medical school or a white Midwestern populist who voted for Shirley Chisholm in 1972 yet became a Reagan Democrat in 1980. People are complex, and so too was the male chauvinist pig. Individuals possess a political consciousness that is far from fixed or unchangeable. Indeed, what may appear to be political contradictions in the seventies should not be dismissed as irrational thought, but instead reveal that rationality is best understood in personal or subjective terms. Whether or not they called themselves feminist or even adamant chauvinists, individuals' words and actions played with the theoretical underpinnings of both feminist visions and chauvinist reactions, making such labels at times hard to pin down.

San Francisco's Question Man

Between 1964 and 1982, O'Hara's *San Francisco Chronicle* column entitled Question Man stood as an ironic reminder of the degree to which the media remained a masculine domain. One of O'Hara's fellow reporters recalled "that she had a way of putting total strangers instantly at ease" by simply saying, "'Hey, you ought to be in the *Chronicle*,' and she'd ask her question, and people would answer."[2] In April 1971, against the backdrop of the nation's volatile political atmosphere, O'Hara, in what must have been her characteristically affable way, asked men as they walked past whether they were male chauvinist pigs. The responses published in the *Chronicle* reflected the thoughts of predominantly white San Franciscans who worked in various occupations and were often unsure how to answer the question.

Some supported what they understood as the tenets of feminism even as they worried it might disrupt gendered norms. Tom La Torre, for example, labored as a cook and sported long hair, a do-rag, and a moustache, complete with aviator sunglasses. He admitted, "I'm part male chauvinist pig," but continued, "I certainly think a woman is a free person. She should be paid the same as a man," an issue feminists found crucial. He also expressed concerns over what he feared might lead to the demise of what it meant to be a man. "They tried switching roles in Denmark or Sweden," and as he put it, this was something that "wouldn't work for me."[3] Fears that feminism would undermine gender distinctions and norms explain why La Torre defined himself as part chauvinist, though these same issues were far from settled among feminists.[4] His own uncertainties reflected popular speculation about the meanings and long-term impact of a younger generation of women's liberationists. Depending on one's politics, La Torre could have been considered a feminist ally or the epitome of a male chauvinist pig.

O'Hara uncovered in San Francisco the same kind of gender anxiety that media scholar Bonnie Dow found in the television coverage of feminism in the late 1960s and early 1970s. According to Dow, feminism engendered the fears of inverted sex roles thanks in part to news anchors like ABC's Howard Smith, who always insisted that "feminism meant defeminization" as he mocked the movement.[5] Even iconic feminist leaders like Betty Friedan, who served as the president of the National Organization for Women (NOW) and was troubled by her own homophobia, were worried about inverted sex roles or, as Dow puts it, feared just as much as chauvinists that "*women might stop acting like women*."[6] Such remarks were inextricably bound to generational splits in the movement and theoretical differences but also a broader sexual revolution that included gay liberation. La Torre's reference to Sweden as a country where they tried switching gender roles may even have been a consequence of a collective memory of Christine Jorgensen, a World War II GI who in 1953 traveled to Denmark for what became the most infamous gender reassignment surgeries of the era. At the time, Jorgensen was embraced as a symbol of scientific triumph yet still considered an anomaly and a joke.[7]

On the other hand, although the 1970s are today seen as a crucial decade in the nation's shift to the conservative right, political outcomes seemed far from certain at the time. The common man, presumed to be white and working class, was not right-wing or left-wing, but as historian Jefferson Cowie brilliantly points out, he reflected the multifaceted politics of the decade in which he came of age. The 1970s unfolded against the backdrop of a war in Vietnam and a reemerging labor movement that brought the experiences of a very unsettled white, working-class manhood into sharp relief. Cowie argues that it was in the 1970s that the hard hats and blue collars came to dominate popular consciousness and gave rise to television characters like *All in the Family*'s Archie Bunker—the beloved bigot.[8] Yet as Cowie unpacks a workingman's consciousness, he argues that it was "simultaneously profound and strange, militant and absurd, traditional and new, male and female, insurgent and reactionary as well as white, black, and brown."[9] Here Cowie turns to Michael Harrington, who in the middle of the decade declared that America was shifting "vigorously left, right, center, all at the same time." Urban jazz poet Gil Scott-Heron may have best captured the politically volatile and charged ambiguity of the decade that was cast in terms of masculinity: referring to the sheriff in the television Western *Gunsmoke* and the troubadour of the antiwar movement, he writes, "America doesn't know whether it wants to be Matt Dillon or Bob Dylan."[10]

O'Hara's interviews also serve as a reminder that claims regarding who is the victim and who is the perpetrator depend on perceptions of social positionality. It is important to keep in mind that the statements made by the men and women O'Hara interviewed could be powerfully based on one category of identity, such as male, but relatively less powerful when considered from a different angle—for example, as a blue-collar employee, white woman, or gay male. If one rejects a *static* binary reading of power as up or down or dominant or resistant, it is possible to see the male chauvinist pig as more complex and see political consciousness as fluid and not permanently set. All of which offers insight into why it was at times challenging for men and women to answer when asked what it meant to be a chauvinist pig.

When O'Hara asked Bill Henley, a vehicle dispatcher, whether he was a male chauvinist pig, he smiled for his photo as he declared he was not a male chauvinist pig. Despite his insistence, however, he was just as troubled that feminism could upset what he felt were natural distinctions between men and women. For Henley, there was nothing sexist about his belief that men and women held, for example, different attitudes toward love and marriage. According to Henley, "A man would prefer to split, to play the field. Women like those ties. They're more susceptible to fall in love."[11] In the 1970s, there would soon be women identified as cultural feminists who would agree with Henley's remarks that implied women's moral distinctiveness. The belief that women were naturally more loving and nurturing and innately different from their brutish male counterparts has richly defined some of the tenets of feminist thought.[12] Did those same such assumptions make Henley a male chauvinist pig? In his own words, he "wouldn't like to think so."[13]

A belief in inherent gender dissimilarities was also why some of O'Hara's interviewees seemed so confused by her question. "I don't know if I am or not," Chuck Frandrup, an engineer, informed O'Hara. "I think a woman has a role just like a man has a role. It's just different. Women have a natural function, as a woman, which they should not relinquish." Similarly, when asked whether he was a male chauvinist pig, youthful-looking Martin Solov, who worked as a landscape architect, described himself as a "nice guy" who was "pretty much for Women's lib." Solov also believed in "the equality in jobs" and was "for economic equality." However, he too, like Frandrup, did not "think they should lose their roles as women." After all, Solov implied, a female responsibility was "making a man feel like a man," a quip most feminists might insist made Frandrup an unequivocal chauvinist.[14]

When asked whether he was a male chauvinist pig, Steve Adams, who worked as a household goods mover and wore a T-shirt, beard, and shaggy haircut, declared, "I hope not. My old lady thinks I'm pretty fair. She's into the Women's lib thing. She talks about it all the time." He and his "old lady" seemed to be well versed in the tenets of feminism as well as a new generation's sexual and social mores. "We've only been living together a couple of weeks though. We're not married. If we don't like it, we can split."[15] Adams may have been privileging his own perspective on his relationship, but not necessarily. Of course, there were plenty of women who, like Adams's "old lady," embraced a love 'em and leave 'em attitude. Coming of age in the 1960s and 1970s, a new generation of women found sex outside marriage and with numerous partners to be central to their own version of the good life.[16]

As much as women's liberation was tied to a sexual revolution, it was identified with demands of workplace equality. Michel Willey, who appeared to be in his forties and wore glasses and a suit, stumbled at first to answer O'Hara's question regarding whether he was a male chauvinist, switching from "probably" to "actually, I probably am not." He quickly recovered by pointing out that "a couple of the best lawyers I know are female." Similarly, Bob Green, who earned a living as a security cashier and defined chauvinism as "a tendency to judge blocks of people. To generalize," highlighted his female boss to show his support for women's liberation and for women's equality in the workplace. "My boss is a woman," he asserted. And whether he was sincere or looking to curry favor with his employer, he quickly added, "She really knows what's going on. She's superior in her job performance."[17]

Of course, there were plenty of folks who knew exactly what made a man a male chauvinist pig. In November 1971, when O'Hara interviewed women near San Francisco's Civic Center and asked them, "What is a male chauvinist pig?" she found far more poignant answers. Georgia Cornwell, a doctoral student at the University of California, proudly wore a women's liberation button and recalled being mocked by a male chauvinist pig who joked, "A woman is like a vacuum cleaner. You plug them into bed or you plug them into housework." Artist Suzanne Freedman defined male chauvinist pigs in terms of their emotional insecurities. Chauvinist pigs are men "who are afraid of women getting together, of uniting or forming a solidarity, because we're going to rock their boat." Similarly, June Baker, a young white woman who held a professional job in a male-dominated occupation as a city planner, found that "almost all men who grew up in today's culture are male chauvinists." They cannot help it. "There is a male supremacy bias in today's culture." She believed "male chauvinists are men who are afraid to cry, [and] afraid of really confronting their emotions."[18]

When O'Hara asked women to define male chauvinism, however, her informants presented an understanding that sexism was entrenched in American culture. Recreational therapist Patricia Shelton described a male chauvinist pig as "any person [who] views relationships with women from a male dominant point of view." She added, "In most businesses, the male point of view is dominant. Society gives men more chances for promotion and recognition." Pat Cronin defined the male chauvinist pig as "any man [who] treats women as inferiors." And she snapped, "Most men do, in a way." Cronin's answer might be more easily justified given that she worked as a flight attendant at a moment when official job protocol turned on being sexually alluring. "Their ads are vulgar. Their ads equate women with sex," and she complained, "National Airlines is a male chauvinistic airline." It was not just the airline industry. Diane Watson, a personal adviser and president of NOW, called out the *Chronicle* as a "sexist newspaper." After all, "their Help Wanted ads are segregated," and more to the point, "any paper that runs . . . a column entitled Question Man is a male chauvinist newspaper."[19]

The next round of questions on the topic centered more intimate relationships. In December 1971, when O'Hara asked, "Is your husband a male chauvinist?" the responses from self-described housewives were just as mixed as those of the working-class men Cowie so aptly describes. Irene Sexton was one of only two Black women whose interviews were published. She worked as an insurance company employee, but she described herself as a housewife living in Oakland. Sexton was puzzled by the question. "I'm not sure. I don't think he is because if he thought that women were supposed to do only housework and stay at home and everything, well, then I wouldn't be working, I would be at home." Sexton, who was somewhat troubled by the question, added, "I don't want to be a liberated woman because I don't feel I want to do a man's job. I think the woman belongs at home." Dorothy White, a Black working mother who lived in Berkeley and was also an insurance company employee, was no longer living with her husband. "I'm separated, and I'm not sure if he was a male chauvinist or not." Much like Sexton, White fully supported gendered differences in work but also pay. "I don't think men's and women's jobs should be the same. I think a woman's job is easier. They pay us less but our work is much easier." Reflecting deep uncertainty about men's and women's work lives, she admitted, "I would love to be liberated," but at the same time she said, "I like having an easier job than the man."[20]

Leighann Warner, a young, white newlywed from Oakland, admitted, "I don't know because we just got married but we don't go along with Women's Lib." As Warner put it, "Women's Lib, they think they want rights. I know what it is but I don't believe in it." Speaking for her husband, she snapped, "Neither does he." Warner's concerns with feminism were familiar expressions of the gender anxiety that O'Hara's interviews had previously revealed. As Warner put it, "I like being feminine" and having her husband as "the head of our family." She also pointed out, "He doesn't treat me like a man. He treats me like a woman. That's the way I want it."[21] Gail Collins's sweeping statement that "the world had turned, and the conviction that what women needed was protection had given way to a call for an equal playing field"[22] is perhaps a bit of an overreach.

When asked whether her husband was a male chauvinist, housewife and mother Doris Baker was also perplexed. "I'm not exactly sure. I'm not exactly sure what I am married to. . . . I guess maybe he is because I'm not a liberated woman." Baker's embrace of marriage was a nod to the status quo. "I do what he wants me to do because I want to please him." As she explained her own role in the relationship, she distanced herself from the feminist movement, pointing out, "I like things the way they are. I'd never be a Woman's Libber. I like the role of wife and mother. I don't want to change anything." Chris Fairbanks was also a housewife and mother who similarly expressed her opposition to feminism. "My husband is the boss. Does that make him a male chauvinist? If it does, well that's okay with me." As she explained to O'Hara, "I like him to be the boss. I want him to be. I like waiting on him. I like doing housework and being dependent on him. If that means, he's a male chauvinist then, that's fine."[23]

Some housewives considered feminism a challenge to their way of life and sense of respectability. For generations of women, being a housewife who did not have to find work outside the home to support the family was a symbol of their status, but for a younger generation of feminists, being a housewife came to represent second-class citizenship.[24] And this is why Collins suggests, "housewives were not necessarily being paranoid if they felt that the women's movement was looking down on their choices and repudiating the things they valued most."[25] However, if attitudes toward feminism often reflected women's economic roles within the family, that was subject to change.

In the 1970s women were some of the most effective opponents to the women's movement. As Sylvia Ann Hewlett points out, women were crucial when it came to the defeat of important feminist legislation. "It is sobering to realize that the ERA [Equal Rights Amendment] was defeated not by Barry Goldwater, Jerry Falwell, or any combination of male chauvinist pigs, but women who were alienated from a feminist movement because the values of which seemed elitist and disconnected from the lives of ordinary people."[26] And although the anti-ERA movement was primarily a reflection of the efforts of "middle-American women, down-to-earth," who "referred to themselves as 'girls,'" "the diversity and commitment of these women were not something easily captured in a statistical survey." Indeed, one local "chairman" from Vermont had supported Democrat George McGovern for president in 1972.[27] Antifeminist crusader Phyllis Schlafly—a political tour de force who masqueraded as a self-avowed housewife—liked to boast that in the age of so many modern conveniences, it was impossible to suffer from what Friedan called "a problem with no name." On speaking tours, she relied on humor to taunt her opposition. Schlafly often started her speeches by acknowledging her husband and thanking him for giving her his permission to let her speak, something that in her words made the "libbers crazy."[28]

As Gail Collins points out, for feminists attempting to speak for all American women, having to debate not only the male chauvinist pig but also someone who claimed to be the "*true* voice of their sex threw them off balance."[29] Attempting to pass the ERA was a major component of women's liberation; however, the implications of equal rights, much like feminism, appeared uncertain. When asked how the ERA would alter American society, Schlafly struck a nerve when she warned that the amendment's passage would mean wives would have to provide half of the family income, women would serve in the military, unisex bathrooms would become the norm, and gay marriage would be the law of the land.[30]

Even among supporters of the women's movement, O'Hara found that the definition of a male chauvinist pig was somewhat murky because the implications of women's liberation were such a vast and uncharted terrain. In 1971 Martie Carrillo, who worked as a data-processing secretary and as a housewife, supported feminism yet was uncertain about whether her husband was a male chauvinist pig. "I don't think he is. I'm not sure though. I'm not sure what he is." She eventually came to the conclusion that her "husband isn't a male chauvinist," because she was a "Woman's Libber," or at least "in a way." "I'm for Women's Lib because where I work," she explained to O'Hara, "women do the same job as men but women get paid less. For the very same job, women get paid less," and "that's not right." But, she confessed, "I still like a man to pay my way and open doors and things like that."[31]

Having men open doors or perform other courtesies was a reminder that as much as feminism challenged economic and legal inequality, it was also seen as a challenge to what Schlafly described as the "Christian tradition of chivalry."[32] In the spring of 1972, when O'Hara asked San Franciscans, "Is a man a chauvinist if he offers a woman a seat on the bus?" Jeannine Cox, a sales clerk, responded emphatically. "No, I wouldn't feel that way at all. I enjoy being treated like a woman. I would think he was a gentleman." She also pointed out to O'Hara, "I'm not a Woman's Libber," adding, "When a man gives me a seat on the bus, my reaction has always been appreciation." Office clerk Mabel Hannigan could not recall when a man acted so politely. "I'm trying to think. I can't remember a man offering me a seat on the bus, but if he were to, I would think he was very courteous, that he regarded me as a lady. In a big city, I find they just don't care about one another." Elena Holliday agreed. She was a coast guard secretary, and when asked the same question, she replied without hesitation: "Of course not. I ride the bus every day and if a man were to offer me a seat on the bus, I would say he's a gentleman. I wouldn't feel he was being disrespectful or chauvinistic." Her answer also served as a critique of a larger movement, as she pointed out, "I'm not a Women's Libber, I'm not into that at all." Patty Keaver, a government employee, also found the question a troubling reminder of feminism's influence. "No. I wouldn't think he was being a chauvinist. I've had men offer me a seat on the bus and I liked it. I'm not a believer in Women's Lib. I don't think men treat women lower than men anyway."[33]

O'Hara found that when she asked men the same question, it put them on the defensive. Ron Martin, who was an immigration department employee, answered emphatically, "No. I've given my seat to women on the bus and I didn't do it because I'm a male chauvinist. She didn't act like it was an insult. She thanked me. I did it to be nice, not because I'm a male chauvinist, because I'm not." Kenneth Davis, a finger print clerk, however, was much more flippant with O'Hara and impishly responded, "Oink. Oink. I have never given my seat to women on the bus because they never seem to need it." Davis asserted, "I'm not against Women's Liberation. . . . If they liberate me, I'll liberate them," suggesting perhaps that he had as much of a right to be as disgruntled as any woman.[34]

Men's and women's gender politics often turned on a mixed consciousness that questioned the degree to which chauvinist and feminist thoughts and practices followed completely divergent trajectories. Like feminisms, which have been critiqued and celebrated for multifaceted approaches, definitions, and implications, male chauvinism also appeared anything but monolithic. This fluid understanding of political thoughts even meant that the male chauvinist pig and the feminist were not always in diametric opposition to each other or in disagreement on the most divisive topics of the era, a paradox that has gone largely unnoticed given the degree to which second-wave feminism was played out as a battle of the sexes that pitted feminists and chauvinists against each other.

Diagnosing the Male Chauvinist Pig in National Discourse

Attempts to identify the male chauvinist pig were never isolated to San Francisco's Question Man. A shift in focus away from the man in the street to famous personalities and attention-grabbing headlines made the male chauvinist pig appear more cartoonish along with feminist demands. "From the beginning, second wave feminism was simultaneously dismissed and dreaded, co-opted and commodified," argues Dow. "That it accomplished as much as it did, and that it lives on in the countless visible and invisible ways, is a testament to the many lives the movement touched, both through mass media and in spite of it."[35] Even with feminist aim, the male chauvinist pigs appeared benign. Advice columns, personality tests, and other kinds of expert testimonies would dissect the male chauvinist pig and find nothing more than a character flaw in need of diagnoses rather than a symptom of systematic sexism that demanded eradication.

In 1972 psychologist Joyce Brothers diagnosed male sexism with her own "Male Chauvinist Pig Test." The questions were designed to help the ordinary man become self-aware of his often-unconscious piggish traits. The *New York Times* playfully published the didactic list of questions on February 13 under the sardonic headline "Happy Valentine's Day!" The timing of the publication was fitting and humorous since many of the scenarios focused on men's relationships with their wives. Brothers followed up each set of questions with more prodding in an effort to retrain the chauvinist pig. For example, she asked men, what if "you get home, starving. Your wife has to work. Do you start dinner?" And if your answer was no, then "why don't you cook?" Do you "still think the kitchen is woman's domain"? "Worse still, though your wife has a full-time job," do "you expect her to be the sole caretaker of the house"? Other scenarios ranged from asking husbands whether they "do all the driving" to whether women are allowed at their "Sunday TV football gathering."[36]

When it came to the workplace, Brothers continued to corral piggish behavior. "Do you continually refer to women as 'girls' regardless of age?" Brothers pointed out, "a 'girl' is someone who is not an adult," and "a chauvinist is reluctant to let women grow up, to consider women people." After all, Brothers added, "Do you refer to your male friends or colleagues as 'boys'?" Changing workplace vernacular was part of a broader feminist effort to open up male-dominated professions to women, so Brothers also asked men whether, as a father, they would encourage their daughters to go to medical school. "She has excellent grades and recommendations. Do you encourage her?" If the answer is no, then you just might be a male chauvinist pig. Making her point even stronger, Brothers wondered, "Would you discourage your son?" And if you continued to perpetuate a double standard, "maybe you still think women are not 'emotionally suited' for the hard work of this predominantly male profession." Or even worse, at "the extreme, you may still think medical school is a waste for women because they will probably get married." Once again, Brothers reversed the situation and rhetorically asked, "Aren't there plenty of married males in medical school?"[37]

Attempting to force the male chauvinist pig to come to grips with his sexist ways was presented in much the way a psychologist might urge someone to confront an addiction. Admitting you have a problem was the first step toward recovery, and thus quiz questions also included a key complete with diagnoses in hope that even the most hardened chauvinist could be reformed. According to Brothers, if someone managed to score nine points, "you are just too good to be true. Not a trace of chauvinism." But she also wondered, "Are you being honest?" If you attained anywhere from six to eight points, Brothers considered you "fairly liberated and probably unconscious of your chauvinistic tendencies." She had confidence that "most likely you will work on these, if you have come this far." Even if you scored merely three to five points, Brothers still held out "hope for you, but you'll have to make a real effort to accept women as equals." For those low-scoring male chauvinists, Brothers concluded, "you are still too concerned about your masculinity." Last but not least was the "super chauvinist" who failed to answer more than two questions correctly, leading Brothers to mix ridicule with a warning. This "view of women is as modern as Henry VIII's," something Brothers believed would ruin (if it had not already) your "popularity with women."[38]

Similarly, sociologist Warren Farrell, who was a key figure in the men's liberation movement, relied on his own personality test questions to not only put the pig on the path of recovery but also bring him into his movement. Men's liberation emerged in the late 1960s, but it was in the middle of the 1970s that it received much more significant media attention because of its ambivalent relationship to a flourishing women's liberation movement. The men who were part of their own liberation movement viewed themselves as feminist allies but sometimes victims of feminist aims.[39] Farrell, who was identified as the "'Gloria Steinem of Men's Liberation,'" helped to found over sixty chapters and hundreds of men's groups that were, in theory, to operate similarly to women's consciousness-raising groups. However, by the mid-1980s he and his movement were part of larger backlash that asserted feminism had damaged masculinity. In his mind, women had too much power and "exert 'enormous leverage' over slavish men."[40] Yet back in the seventies, while attending NOW meetings and hanging around with white liberal feminists,[41] Farrell believed men would benefit greatly from eliminating gender stereotypes and described "war, the Pentagon, West Point, Hugh Hefner, football and the like" as "among the 'most apparent manifestations' of the 'problem of masculinity.'"[42] Farrell's publication *The Liberated Man* (1974) helped bring the question of men's liberation into the public eye. In many ways a how-to manual, the book included a twenty-seven-question survey that used quite a bit of humor to coax the male chauvinist pig into self-reflection.[43]

The Liberated Man, for example, also set up self-assessment based on hypothetical situations that ranged from child-rearing responsibilities to the predicament of the one-night stand. Some of his questions seemed especially tongue in cheek. For instance, when he asked, What do you call an "attractive woman"? the choices were limited to "Lady," "Doll," "Chick," "Girl," "Honey," and "Broad." In another question, Farrell playfully urged men, "Think of the name of the car you own (e.g., Ford Mustang, Dodge Charger). If your car were called a Ford Pansy or Dodge Daisy how would you feel about owning it?" Some of his survey questions struck a more serious tone, such as when he asked whether men would get a vasectomy or whether they had ever cried in public. Questioning heteronormative assumptions, Farrell also asked men whether they would hire a "more competent" male for a pink-collar position like secretary and wondered, "What if there was a reason to believe he had homosexual tendencies?"[44]

When it came to the implications of male chauvinism, Farrell spoke to its ambiguity. Of course, his aim was somewhat different from those of the pop psychologist who seemed more interested in a reprimand. "The scoring interpretation, like becoming liberated, has few pat, automatic answers," he insisted. Even if you received an exceptionally high score, Farrell warned, "you're fooling yourself, or the men's liberation movement needs you." For Farrell, low scores did not make you a male chauvinist but tragically "unliberated." He also offered a bit of encouragement, because these men were "honest." As he put it to his reader, it may be that you are "more open than you are giving yourself credit for."[45]

Another list of questions for the unliberated man came from feminist male icon and actor Alan Alda, who played an irreverent peace-loving doctor on the hit sitcom M*A*S*H (1972–83). Touted for his good looks, liberal politics, and outspoken support for feminism, Alda was a popular male voice for the feminist cause. His male chauvinist pig questionnaire, however, was published in a 1975 interview with Ms. magazine for an audience more than likely already committed to the cause and appreciative of his signature wit.

1. *Do you have an intense need to win?* When having sex, do you take pride in always finishing before your partner?
2. *Does violence play a big part in your life?* Before you answer, count up how many hours you watched football, ice hockey, and children's cartoons this year on television.
3. *Are you "thing" oriented?* Do you value the parts of a woman's body more than the woman herself?

4. *Do you have an intense need to reduce every difficult situation to charts and figures?* If you were present at a riot, would you tend to count the crowd?
5. *Do you tend to measure things that are really qualitative?* Are you more impressed with how high a male ballet dancer can leap than with what he does while he's up there?
6. *Are you a little too mechanically minded?* Would you like to watch a sunset . . . or would you rather take apart a clock?
7. *Are you easily triggered into competition?* When someone tries to pass you on the highway, do you speed up a little?[46]

Alda's professional diagnosis turned on his own stereotypes about manly behavior, but his aim was to rally the troops by playing the tease. As if in character, he offered first the bad news that a lot of men suffered from what he called "*testosterone poisoning,*" but then he advised men, "*Don't panic.*" After all, "if you answered yes to three or fewer of the above questions, you might be learning to deal with your condition." Regardless, the first step to recovery was to "*try to feel something,*" but, he joked, "not with your hands, you oaf." With a touch of bedside manner, he waggishly prescribed an exercise in which men had to "*see if you can listen while someone is talking*" and then repeat, "You know I think you're right and I'm wrong." Finally, he urged women to wait until the condition improves before you inform any man that "there is no such thing as testosterone poisoning."[47] Alda stood as a feminist ally, but the underlying message was that when it came to reforming a male chauvinist pig, a woman's work is never done.

Of course, some men believed they could reform themselves. The British-born New Yorker and Royal Air Force veteran Michael Korda was a social critic and editor in chief of the publishing company Simon and Schuster. In *Male Chauvinism! How It Works* (1972), he offered a look at the male psyche from the perspective of a self-described former male chauvinist pig. Korda poked fun at the idea that the chauvinist was a threat or even a problem. Sexism, he argued, was grounded in a lack of understanding, and he was living proof that the male chauvinist pig could be rehabilitated.[48] In his own words, "The price of male chauvinism is terrible confusion; the male chauvinist is trying to combine in one person so many contradictory attitudes toward women that he can only end by fearing and hating them."[49] The male chauvinist pig was thus a complex and thinking subject and not the flat, one-dimensional stereotype, or so it seemed.

Korda also proclaimed that chauvinism should not be seen as a fixed condition. It is as fluid as any other emotion. "The same man can, within twenty-four hours, shout at his secretary, make a show of negotiating a contract with a woman lawyer on equal terms, make fun of the same woman to his colleagues, appear at a party with his wife on his arm, looking strong and protective, and return home listening to her criticize him for behaving like an idiot at the party." For Korda, chauvinism was a temporary lapse in judgment, and thus a character flaw that made the violator seem little different from any other asshole.[50]

Had the asshole simply been transformed (thanks to feminism) into a political liability? A 1972 *Playboy* cartoon featured two rather well-to-do men sharing sections of a newspaper as one complained, "This pig business bugs me," and wondered, "Why can't they simply call people horse's asses, as we did?"[51] Philosopher Aaron James has recently argued that "by and large assholes are men." "It is not that women can't be assholes. It is that women are usually classified as a bitch who . . . betrays you behind your back," whereas "the asshole fails to recognize you to your face."[52]

Much like the chauvinist pig, then, the asshole is typically associated with male rather than female privilege. "The asshole refuses to listen to our legitimate complaints, and so he poses a challenge to the idea that we are each recognized as moral equals."[53] James's suggestion that the asshole is not only a man but one who does not "listen to our legitimate complaints" offers a critique that bears resemblance to the feminist critique of the male chauvinist pig of the 1970s. Notably, neither figure was typically rejected as a complete moral outcast.[54] James is critical of the Urban Dictionary's suggestion that an asshole is "the worst kind of person. . . . If you're an asshole, you are disgusting, loathsome, vile, distasteful, wrathful, belligerent, agoraphobic, and more. . . . [Assholes] are the lowest of the low. They transcend all forms of immorality."[55] James insists that "this is overwrought and unhelpful." Instead, he argues, "most are not *that* bad." The asshole has a "sense of entitlement" but is not a psychopath. Rather he is the kind of guy who thinks every day is his special day. "If one is special on one's birthday, the asshole's birthday comes every day."[56] For James there is always someone worse than the asshole.[57] They are not the "Hitlers, Stalins, or Mussolinis" per se or a "murderer, rapist, or tyrant."[58]

Korda's attempt to salvage the male chauvinist pig, while useful, left little room for any sympathy for feminists, whom he cast as the real threat. In front of a San Francisco audience, he made a titillating joke that "every woman, like every black, is a potential revolutionary," and "each man is literally lying on a powder keg."[59] Korda routinely complained about the woman who used her sexuality to manipulate men. He believed women with "any kind of looks" who are "not scared" can get men to do anything they want. In a particularly patronizing remark, he warned women that knew how the game was played, "You listen to them, flirt a little, cry when things go wrong, and say 'gee, I wish you could show me how to do this, you know so much more about it than I do.' It's a snap." Following Korda's twisted logic, male chauvinism was beneficial to women who played on men's desires. And to make matters worse, Korda insisted that this kind of woman "doesn't believe any man is her equal; she is both a female chauvinist and canny exploiter of her own sex and personality."[60]

The Female Chauvinist Pig

Korda was not alone when it came to expressing concerns over the female chauvinist. As the male chauvinist pig was attracting increasing media attention and scrutiny, women with questionable gender politics were also called out for their chauvinistic tendencies. As an epithet, *female chauvinist* increased in print media starting in 1967 and reached a peak in 1974. It would start to decline in the late 1970s and would be soon eclipsed by a much more powerful trope—the feminazi—conjured up in the world of right-wing talk radio and discussed in a later chapter.[61] The feminazi became such a powerful epithet that it further erased from collective memory almost any trace of the older antifeminist tropes like the female chauvinist pig, which had become an almost forgotten tool of mockery. It was more than a decade and a half after Rush Limbaugh and the feminazi made their debut when Ariel Levy in 2005 entitled a popular book-length critique of postfeminism *Female Chauvinist Pigs*, and it almost seemed as if she had coined a new epithet for contemporary feminist troubles. While the concept of the female chauvinist pig still packed a punch, it was relatively tame in comparison to Limbaugh's feminazi.[62] In the 1970s, while the male chauvinist pig could be a temporary ass, the female chauvinist pig was burdened by a legacy of negative feminine attributes that made her appear conniving and manipulative, as well as dogmatic. Misbehaving women and other so-called deviants were inextricably linked to feminine vice, and in the 1970s the female chauvinist pig was no exception.

Much like her male counterpart, the female chauvinist was brought to life because of media attention that defined her through two extreme categories. The female chauvinist pig was identified either as a sanctimonious feminist who assumed a natural sense of superiority and, given the chance, would discriminate against men or as unliberated and unaware, tragically trapped in patriarchal norms. There was some sense that she could be redeemed, but the female chauvinist served primarily as an object of ridicule who brought into question a movement that made a lofty appeal in the name of sisterhood.

Far from famous, Irene Pines submitted her own survey to the editor of the *Miami Times*, which published it in 1972. Pines, who was determined to bring into sharp relief the "true" female chauvinist pig, created her own test that brought women's hypocritical behavior into the spotlight. The female chauvinist pig could be interpreted as the unliberated woman "who had (perhaps subconsciously) absorbed the traditional attitudes of the 'male chauvinist pig.'" For example, she asked, "If you both work, do you believe household chores and childcare should be divided 50-50?" Pines, however, was also troubled by feminists who went too far, so she created "a true test designed to uncover those of us who may have not only freed ourselves from the MCP [male chauvinist pig] attitudes, but who may have (heaven forbid!) stepped over the boundary in the other direction." Hence, her survey asked women, "Are you delighted when your husband tells you that his new boss is a woman, because you now feel that things will be run a lot more efficiently?" And, "Do you believe your husband should give you his full paycheck, since you know you are the more competent to manage the household finances?"[63]

Just a few months later, well-known writer and feminist Anne Roiphe published "Confessions of a Female Chauvinist Sow" in *New York* magazine, expressing concerns with those women who felt they were morally superior to men. We cannot assume, she opined, "that women given power would not create wars." Indeed, "aggression is not . . . a male-sex-linked characteristic." Therefore "us laughing at them, us feeling superior to them, us ridiculing them behind their backs . . . [is] inescapably female chauvinist sowness." Even a "secret sense of superiority" causes women to contribute to their own inequality. Roiphe did not lash out at other feminists but rather admitted her own guilt and susceptibility to what she called "chauvinist pigness."[64] A long-standing belief that women were innately better than men came to be labeled cultural feminism by the middle of the decade and was met with strong opposition from some women liberationists who dismissed it as a form of reverse sexism.

Both Pines and Roiphe were responding to larger tensions brewing between the leaders of the movement. Famous for her 1963 publication *The Feminine Mystique*, which addressed the alienation housewives faced, as well as her uncompromising personality, Betty Friedan became an icon in the women's liberation movement and was a founding member of NOW. According to Bonnie Dow, Friedan and organizations like NOW quickly came to represent an "older generation of women with experience in media, government, and politics and [were] primarily concerned with issues of public discrimination (e.g., education, employment, and pay equity)." However, a new generation of feminists emerged from the countercultural movements whose strategies and goals were considered far more radical.[65]

Journalist and cultural critic Barbara Ehrenreich embraced this more radical turn. "Where she [Friedan] found the 'problem without a name'" to attempt to understand the domestic alienation of the suburban housewife, the new generation "popularized a whole vocabulary of male faults—sexism, male chauvinism, misogyny." The kind of topics and tone Friedan "had skirted, like the sexual division of housework and the uneven distribution of orgasms, now came to the fore as political issues." Ehrenreich celebrated this much more direct message. "Men might be in a new mood of consumerist self-indulgence, but they were warned, women would no longer be indulging them. No more picking up socks, punctual meal service, or cheerful acquiescence to phallocentric sex."[66]

In July 1972 Friedan claimed that cohorts of "'female chauvinists'" who consider men the enemy were exacerbating tensions between the sexes and effectively weakening the movement. Sisterhood could go "too far." Friedan was appalled by feminists who claimed "man is the enemy," promoted a "class warfare against men" and were guilty of reverse chauvinism. According to Friedan, "The assumption that women have any moral or spiritual superiority as a class or that men share some brute insensitivity as a class—this is male chauvinism in the reverse; it is female sexism." Friedan believed that such attitudes would exacerbate tensions between men and women and weaken the movement, but her use of ridicule gave life to the female chauvinist pig and the notion that feminism was deeply flawed. After all, here was a bona fide feminist calling out what she saw as the hypocrisy of a movement that she had inspired but that had now gone too far.[67]

Friedan, possessing a sense of moral absolutism, felt justified lashing out at other feminist leaders who she believed were undermining the movement. When the radical cultural feminist Roxanne Dunbar, the founder of Cell 16 (a Boston-based feminist organization that called on women to separate from men and learn self-defense), met Friedan she recalls being dissed as one of those "scruffy feminists" and blamed for "'giving the movement a bad name.'"[68] However, Gloria Steinem also was "famously the target of

Betty Friedan's rancor." By 1972 Steinem had gone from being a journalist to becoming "the movement's first real celebrity."[69] Steinem, along with New York Democratic representative Bella Abzug, was far more moderate than Dunbar, but Friedan called them out as "female chauvinist boors."[70] As Patricia Bradley points out, "The political splits in the second wave were as real as the anger."[71]

Given the media's tendency to disparage women's liberation, it is not surprising to find that a feminist critique of anything that could be labeled extreme feminism engendered mocking headlines.[72] In other words, for a presumably unsympathetic audience (male or female), feminist splits and theoretical differences could be fun and games. Cultural critic Susan Douglas finds that "by the early 1970s, the catfight had become the dominant news peg about the progress of the women's movement, and the campaign to ratify the Equal Rights Amendment was cast as the catfight par excellence." For Douglas this "staple of American popular culture" was little different from "female mud wrestling or Jell-O wrestling." Moreover, Douglas argues that, "as a metaphor for the struggle between feminism and antifeminism, the catfight provided a symbolic catharsis of woman's internal conflict between the desire for liberation and the longing for security." Douglas also points out that "the catfight served two critically important ideological functions: it put the lie to feminists' claims about sisterhood and reasserted, in its place, competitive individualism in which women, like other Americans, duked it out with each other."[73]

Back in San Francisco in 1973, O'Hara asked women, "Are you a female chauvinist pig?" and found women wanted to distance themselves from anything that smacked of moral superiority. Meagan Stuart spoke in favor of egalitarianism yet claimed that "women's lib" could be a real problem. Stuart worked in the city as an urban intern and equated the feminist movement with female chauvinist pigs. "No, I am not a female chauvinist," she repeated to O'Hara, "that has a very bad connotation," and even more to the point, she declared, "I am not into women's lib. I am into people's lib," suggesting the problem she had with women's liberation was the implication of female condescension, which rubbed her the wrong way. In Stuart's words, "I don't feel chauvinistic," instead, "I feel equal."[74]

In a similar critique of feminism, Cheryl Geyerman, a leasing firm employee, also distanced herself from the female chauvinist by insisting, "Actually, I'm very fair." At the same time, the tenets of feminism appeared to have shaped her views. "As long as the man does the dishes and keeps the house clean, I feel he is doing his share." But again, she pointed out, "I don't feel superior to men. Just that they should vacuum, do the dishes, etc." Louise Horschman, a waitress working in San Francisco, viewed feminism along a broader spectrum: "I am not an extremist when it comes to women's right[s]." Therefore, she claimed, "I am not a female chauvinist." Like Geyerman, who thought men should do their fair share of housework, Herschman was "in favor of both the mother and father participating in raising the children." While she did not fully define what she meant by "extremist," she, like Geyerman, had already embraced flexible gender roles, but presumably not cultural feminism's moral self-righteousness.[75]

O'Hara also found that the female chauvinist was defined not by her attitude but by her circumstances. Marcia Brittain, who was a home economist in San Francisco, insisted that she was not a female chauvinist because she supported the concept of "equal pay for equal work." Not married and on her own, she considered herself "already liberated." Her primary concern was with housewives—a group she felt "should get out and get involved." Marilyn Prezkop, a stay-at-home wife and mother, admitted that she was "a little bit [of a chauvinist] because I am in the traditional role of housewife." For Prezkop, not having a career and earning her own living was what placed her at odds with feminism.[76] Bonnie Dow points to a developing "feminist lifestyle" that was identified with movement leaders like Gloria Steinem and in popular 1970s television shows that often featured a single woman like Mary Tyler Moore, which proposed that a woman could make her way in the world independent of a man. Dow argues this "lifestyle feminism was driven by an identity not an ideology."[77] However, neither identity nor ideology is static. Prezkop, for example, found it important to point out, "I used to have a career," but now things were different and "since I am not liberated, I would tend to be more for liberation."[78]

Living separately from a man and having a wage-earning job was part of what it meant to be liberated for some women. When asked whether she was a female chauvinist pig, Lavon Hunter, a high school teacher living in San Francisco, also blurred a lifestyle with a political stance on feminism. She explained, "I just went through a divorce," and asserted that because she was living alone, that was proof enough that she was "not a female chauvinist," adding, "I'm definitely a liberated woman." Hunter believed "women have fewer advantages than men" and felt women's liberation still had a long way to go. Yet she too was quick to point out that she was not a chauvinist because, as she put it, "I don't feel superior. I feel equal to men."[79]

Linda Thornton appeared to be one of the youngest women O'Hara interviewed, and she most passionately distanced herself from feminism. She was unemployed, looked up to her brothers, and when asked whether she was a female chauvinist pig, quipped, "Are you kidding? I don't like stuff like that. I don't want to be like them." Feminism, it seemed, was a threat to her strong sense of solidarity with the men she hung out with. "My brothers are bikers and I know a lot of bikers and I like the way they are." Not willing to disrupt that relationship or be labeled a female chauvinist, she informed O'Hara, "I want to do things for the guy."[80]

Movement splits meant that the female chauvinist pig could be labeled as such and all too easily turned into a one-dimensional trope of a woman unwilling to compromise. Bitterness toward feminism set the stage, as we shall see in a later chapter, for a far more damaging trope—that of the feminazi. At the time, the popularity of the female chauvinist pig erased the possibility of having a mixed consciousness, as it brought into question any claim to sisterhood. Being too passionate could make you a narcissist who not only ignored men's rights but intentionally suppressed them. In sharp contrast, women who failed to be sufficiently feminist were hopeless victims of internalized sexism and suffered from false consciousness.

Political contradictions should not be dismissed as irrational thought, but instead reveal that rationality is best understood in personal or subjective terms. Whether or not they called themselves feminists or even staunch chauvinists, individuals' words and actions played with the theoretical underpinnings of both feminist visions and chauvinist reactions, making such labels at times hopelessly confusing in the early 1970s. Thus chauvinisms, to borrow from scholar Janet Halley's discussion of feminisms, offer a "simultaneous incommensurate presence of many theories"[81] and a multiplicity of waves, some of which tended to crest and profoundly shape 1970s political discussions at the local and national levels. Personality tests, along with O'Hara's man-in-the-street interviews, reaffirmed ambiguities rather than absolutes. Unfortunately, the female chauvinist pig helped to perpetuate a tarnished image of women who, regardless of political stance, turned into an unpopular stereotype and not a catchy brand.

FOR FEMINISTS, THE MALE CHAUVINIST PIG may have been understandably easy to reject, but he was not always some unthinking boor but rather possessed political thoughts that were far from static. Since men's and women's gender politics were unsettled, neither words nor deeds placed the chauvinist and feminist on completely different paths. Recall feminisms have been critiqued and celebrated for their multiplicity and so too male chauvinisms offers a mix of definitions and directions. Such fluidity meant that the male chauvinist pig and the feminist were not always at political odds with one another, something often overlooked in an era defined by the battle of the sexes.

At the same time, the female chauvinist was roundly condemned in the mass media while her male counterpart engendered mockery but also empathic laughs. After all, it seemed, he was at least trying to reform his chauvinistic tendencies. And whenever he was outed through personality tests and other gimmicky surveys, the male chauvinist pig routinely offered comic relief. Tainted by feminine vice, the female chauvinist pig was a target of ridicule and was readily associated with a strong moral absolutism that, as a trope, failed to be reappropriated by the women's movement. Instead, the female chauvinist pig lurked in the shadows as a warning to women who possessed bad gender politics, while the far more popular pig found his place in a broader political shift that would give rise to modern conservatism and another wave of feminist backlash.

CHAPTER FOUR

Branding the Pig
Playboys, Conservatives, and the Common Man

In 1959 the first episode of *Playboy's Penthouse* (1959–60), a Chicago-based television show, provided its audience a glimpse into Hugh Hefner's audacious party life. The audience was treated to stand-up comedian Lenny Bruce as one of Hefner's first guests. After popping open a bottle of champagne and admiring "some pretty chicks," the infamous comedian began to ponder the show's sponsor and potentially conservative viewership.[1]

For Hefner, the show was a reflection of *Playboy's* brand. "We're trying to build a personality of the show out of the magazine itself and make the thing a sort of sophisticated weekly get-together with people we dig and who dig us." While Bruce agreed that *Playboy* was "chic," "sophisticated," and "filled with cars, coats, [and] sports cars," he brought into sharp relief *Playboy's* bourgeois limitations. "Suppose your viewer can't afford the sports car, the sports coat? You're not interested in the people who don't have any money?" Bruce teased. Without hesitation, a self-assured Hefner insisted, "That's right," setting up the comedian's punch line: "You people out there are just going to have to wait 'til your own magazine comes along." Perhaps *Reader's Digest*, Bruce jested, or better yet *Field and Stream*, with "the playmate for December" striking a pose with "a duck in her mouth."[2]

Bruce and Hefner, along with their sense of humor, would come to be identified with the New Left. Both men were icons of the free speech movement and other liberal causes. A willingness to challenge the status quo, coupled with a bourgeois aesthetic, defined what it meant to be a playboy, and the figure stood in sharp relief to both the country bumpkin Bruce alluded to and button-down conservatives of the Cold War era. Jokes about a *Field and Stream* playmate accentuate the degree to which *Playboy* saw itself as part of the counterculture in which progressive politics mixed with scantily clad women, sex, and naughty jokes. As Hefner put it, *Playboy* was not trying to please everyone but rather only those whom "we dig and who dig us." In fact, the cultural and class conflict that so vividly played out in Hefner's exclusive penthouse party would come to shape the shifting political alliances in the decades to come.

In the 1950s and 1960s, the playboy stood apart from the so-called hillbillies and rednecks, as well as the moralizing crusaders of the Republican Party, yet *Playboy*'s glossy nudes, intriguing interviews, and cartoons found broad appeal. Millions of American men read the magazine and aspired to be part of Hefner's "fraternity of male rebels."[3] A joke about a hillbilly playmate, although condescending, served as a reminder that "tits and ass" humor provided even those with obvious cultural and political differences some opportunity for common ground. After all, raunchy jokes about women and sex crossed all kinds of cultural divides and could make the redneck and the playboy indistinguishable from each other as well as from the quintessential male chauvinist pig.

To be sure, sexism and misogyny pervaded the political spectrum. And despite the profound influence of the women's liberation movement on progressive politics, male chauvinist pigs ran rampant throughout the Democratic Party. The male chauvinist pig, however, would come to play a far more prominent role in modern conservatism by offering the kind of cultural cachet needed to broaden its base. For Republicans with a holier-than-thou agenda, the male chauvinist pig was a godsend. Feminism was easily cast as a threat to traditional family values, making the male chauvinist pig a brazen symbol of American pride with just the right touch of rebelliousness. Indeed, embracing the male chauvinist pig as a badge of honor meant even the most humdrum conservative could claim a measure of masculine bravado. Although he was no Lenny Bruce or JFK, the male chauvinist pig, as a conservative brand, bolstered his and his party's political virility in much the way the male chauvinist pig label successfully marketed everything from sporty shoes to neckties. To be sure, conservativism's infamous Southern Strategy turned on racist policies and rhetoric, but sexism dressed up as a domesticated barnyard animal that cracked inappropriate jokes was just what the Republican Party needed to win over the common man.[4]

Playboy Humor

Playboy's penchant for mocking women's looks and turning women into objects quickly made the magazine a prime target for second-wave feminists. In 1963, Gloria Steinem went undercover as a Playboy bunny and famously revealed the darker side of a not-so-glamorous work culture. Two years later, another journalist, Diana Lurie, offered a similar critique of *Playboy* as a propagator of exploitation.[5] That same year, Miss America pageant protesters

Mr. Playboy, Hugh Hefner, surrounded by Playboy bunnies at his Chicago club in 1963. Hefner, along with his magazine, television shows, and clubs, created a lifestyle brand. Used by permission of Photofest.

burned copies of *Playboy* along with *Ladies' Home Journal*, while unveiling a banner declaring women's liberation.[6]

Hugh Hefner was just as problematic as his magazine. In 1970 on *The Dick Cavett Show*, Susan Brownmiller, who became a catalyst for profound legal changes in definitions and understandings of rape, passionately debated Hefner, critiqued the image that *Playboy* projected, and accused Hefner of reducing women to something less than "full human beings." With biting wit, she asked Hefner, what if he were "to come out here with a cottontail attached to

[his] rear end"? Hefner, who momentarily was speechless and searching for a response, smugly relit his pipe.[7] *Playboy* was simply too prominent of a symbol of women's objectification to escape feminist critique, and the magazine and the man behind it played a conspicuous role in defining the male chauvinist pig.

The playboy's chauvinism was certainly defined by a male gaze that struggled to make sense of women's liberation. However, it was also a chauvinism that grew out of Hefner's humor and *Playboy*'s support of the comic stage. In fact, humor was fundamental to the magazine and the playboy lifestyle. In the inaugural 1953 issue, Hefner announced, "IF YOU'RE A MAN between the ages of 18 and 80, PLAYBOY is meant for you. If you like your entertainment served up with humor, sophistication and spice, PLAYBOY will become a very special favorite." Hefner had been an aspiring cartoonist and promised his readers that "within the pages of PLAYBOY you will find articles, fiction, picture stories, cartoons, [and] humor." At the time, Hefner may not have fully realized the impact of such comedy. According to his first editorial, his magazine's sense of humor and erotic photos were designed merely as an escape for his readers. "Affairs of the state will be out of our province," he explained, and added, "We don't expect to solve any world problems or prove any great moral truths. If we are able to give the American male a few extra laughs and a little diversion from the anxieties of the atomic age then we'll feel we've justified our existence."[8] As the Hefner empire permeated American culture, the Playboy bunny became an icon, but so too did the oversexed playboy and his raunchy sense of humor.

Playboy also helped transform the comedy circuit. On the one hand, Playboy clubs "provided a bridge between old school resorts of the Catskill mountains and the comedy club explosion of the 1980s."[9] On the other hand, not since vaudeville had comedians found such a reliable source of income. According to former stand-up and author Kliph Nesteroff, signing a contract with a Playboy club meant for the first time that "a struggling comedian could . . . get a year's salary, accommodations, travel expenses and a steady crowd." In fact, it was "the most significant circuit for stand-up comics." The Playboy franchise featured comedians ranging from George Carlin to Jackie Vernon. "The Playboy club," notes Nesteroff, "is best remembered for waitresses wearing bunny outfits, but the role it played in the history of stand up should stand as its primary significance."[10]

By the 1960s *Playboy* was at the forefront of turning humor into a countercultural tour de force. The Playboy clubs' popularity peaked from the early 1960s to the mid-1970s, which were also the "transitional years for

American standup."[11] Yet Hefner did more than expand the number of venues for stand-up comedians. He "encouraged a new style of comedy" and used political satire as a useful ally to challenge Cold War conformity.[12] One of those allies was "controversial, political left-wing funnyman 'Professor' Irwin Corey,"[13] who created the character of an eccentric professor of nonsense. In the *Playboy* spotlight, his career flourished, as did his various antics. He was notorious for trespassing into the Bunny Room and chasing the women who worked as the club's Playboy bunnies, but on the other hand he had a long legacy as a political lefty.[14] Before he was a stand-up, in the late 1930s Corey helped write "a musical comedy about a union organizer" entitled *Pins and Needles*, and he was blacklisted for his left-wing activism. In 1960 he even campaigned for the Oval Office on Hefner's Playboy ticket.[15] He was not that serious of a candidate and certainly more interested in being "funny than President."[16] But mixing left-wing politics with humor was his signature trait. One observer noted that on one wall in his home "hangs a letter from Lenny Bruce, along with a photograph of Mr. Corey hugging Fidel Castro, during a visit to Cuba to donate medicine for children."[17] Thus, *Playboy* not only helped to legitimize the male chauvinist pig, it mainstreamed comedy as part of the pig's brand.

The "Reddening of America" and the Chauvinist

The counterpart to Hefner's urban sophisticate that Bruce so readily mocked assumed a number of different names: Okie, redneck, country bumpkin, and hillbilly, to name a few. Their origins varied somewhat, but all of them struggled with a past that was associated with racial violence. The redneck, for example, emerged in the 1880s and 1890s against the growing battle over populism and the rise of Jim Crow. It was a term with obvious class connotations and was linked to dirt farmers who were just as economically disadvantaged as the Black sharecroppers who were the targets of the redneck's bitterness and violence. Over the next six decades the redneck would maintain a distinct role in southern culture and attract national attention, especially as the civil rights movement called out the southern status quo.[18]

The redneck was the archetype of southern violence and intolerance. According to historian Patrick Huber, "The pejorative term *redneck* has chiefly slurred a rural, poor white man of the American South and particularly one who holds conservative, racist, or reactionary views." The redneck reflected both "an economically exploited and yet racially privileged group." In television shows, movies, and novels, Huber notes, the redneck was often "a greasy-haired, tobacco-chewing, poor southern white man with a sixth-grade education and a beer gut." He adds that the redneck could be found living in "a double-wide trailer with his homely, obese wife—who is probably also a first cousin—and their brood of grubby, sallow-faced children and a couple of scrawny coon dogs." He was typically depicted as "a rent farmer, a gas station attendant, or a factory worker, if he works at all." The redneck was readily identified "guzzling six-packs, listening to country music, and hanging out with his buddies in pool halls and honky-tonks, that is when he is not fishing, poaching deer, cruising in his pickup truck, going to stock car races, beating his wife, or attending Klan rallies." Rednecks were assumed to despise "blacks, Jews, and hippies, union organizers, aristocratic southern whites, Yankees, and for good measure, 'foreigners' in general."[19]

Middle-class respectability turned on condemning the hillbilly and his uncouth aesthetics. Nadine Hubbs argues that a narrative of middle-class refinement and sophistication relied on the "hillbilly," "trucker," or "country music joke." The working-class redneck was often turned into carnivalesque caricatures or what she calls "Jed-face"—a tongue-in-cheek reference to the popular 1960s–1970s sitcom *The Beverly Hillbillies* (1966–71) and the show's backward patriarch, Jed Clampett, played by Buddy Ebsen.[20] On politically left variety shows like *The Smothers Brothers Comedy Hour* (1967–69), mocking white southerners was always good for a laugh.[21] For example, when country singer Glen Campbell appeared on the show singing a heartfelt ballad, "a herd of pigs burst onto the stage, quickly enveloping Campbell and his backup dancers." According to Sarah Eskridge, "The pig prank during Campbell's musical performance was not an isolated incident of regional rubbing." The show took on all kinds of "hot button issues of the day including religion, race and the War in Vietnam." In one of its edgier skits, and one that poked fun at the South, Tom Smothers plays a white southern preacher who performs an interracial marriage between a white woman and Black man, and instead of asking for the wedding rings, he asks for "the rope, please." The writers of the show continued to butt heads with CBS censors, and the show was canceled after only three seasons, despite its popularity.[22]

Just as shows like *The Beverly Hillbillies* and *The Smothers Brothers* were lampooning small-town, rural America, the South was undergoing significant economic and political change that would profoundly affect the region and the country. The phrase "the reddening of America" has repeatedly been used to describe the southernization of American culture and the rise of the Sunbelt South—the stretch of land from southern Virginia south to Florida and then west across Texas to Southern California. In the midst of the nation's deindustrialization and the decline of the industrial heartland, the Sunbelt South boomed. Increases in oil prices and the embargo of 1973 bolstered the area's growth, as did the region's oil-rich resources in Texas, Louisiana, and Oklahoma. Federal dollars were also pouring into the South, as were jobs, as corporations looked for a cheaper and nonunion labor force. The economic growth of the Sunbelt South was accompanied by population growth and greater political power. In this climate, not only did the South gain more congressional seats and electoral power, but the Democratic hold on the region collapsed.[23]

The growth in the South and its newfound Republican political power also gave rise to what was described as "redneck chic," a trend white Americans across the country embraced that included a predilection for Levi's and cowboy boots, Lone Star and Pabst beer, Waylon Jennings and Willie Nelson, and fried pork chops, grits, greens, and biscuits and gravy. The racist baggage from the previous century wasn't completely gone, but it had certainly faded into the background and was overshadowed by a good ol' boy who espoused the virtues of hard work, honesty, patriotism, and even a certain sex appeal that attracted television and movies alike. Similar to the playboy, the male chauvinist pig and the redneck enjoyed a sense of humor that came to be identified with an erotic sense of self.[24]

The 1970s produced numerous television shows and films that featured southern characters with plenty of good ol' boy charm and sex appeal. Burt Reynolds, who was most notorious in the early 1970s for posing nude for *Cosmopolitan* magazine, had his biggest box office hit in the 1977 film *Smokey and the Bandit*. With his signature mustache, Reynolds stars as the handsome bootlegger Bo "Bandit" Darville, decked out in audacious cowboy hat, bright red cowboy shirt, and giant belt buckle. With the help of his black Pontiac Trans-Am, he rescues the girl (in this case a runaway bride played by Sally Field) and eludes the law by jumping over a washed-out bridge, leaving behind crashed police cars. In 1977 *Smokey and the Bandit* was one of the highest-grossing films of the year, second only to *Star Wars*. The film would lead to sequels and inspire a television series that featured other titillating rednecks.[25]

The 1970s also produced the hit television show *The Dukes of Hazzard*. The show is set in the fictional community of Hazzard County, Georgia, and focuses on the exploits of the Duke boys, Bo and Luke (John Schneider and Tom Wopat). The handsome duo drive a gravity-defying stock car they affectionately call the General Lee.[26] The Duke boys are "reformed moonshiners" and are a tad more innocent than the Bandit. These antiheroes stand on the side of justice, and like the Bandit, are intent on exposing corrupt local officials as the fool. Bo and Luke may be rednecks, yet as the show's theme song reminded its viewers week in and week out, they are "just good ol' boys, never mean'n no harm."[27]

Rounding out the decade was the feature film *Urban Cowboy*, starring John Travolta. Travolta was one of the hottest male sex symbols of the era, having discarded the white three-piece polyester suit and disco moves that made him famous in *Saturday Night Fever* (1977) for a Texas honkytonk. In *Urban Cowboy*, Travolta now plays an oil refinery worker named Bud who hangs out at the local honkytonk, rides a mechanical bull, and has a love-hate relationship with his girlfriend-wife Sissy (Debra Winger). It seemed the common man with dirt under his nails could shake, to a certain degree, a lingering image of backwardness as long as he had devilish good looks and southern charm.[28]

Posing next to his muscle car or riding a mechanical bull was in fact part of the sex appeal and just what the redneck needed to shore up his masculinity in these rapidly changing times. It was an image that defied the stereotypical image of a dirt farmer as characteristically suspicious and highlighted the themes of decency, common sense, and hard work. These men also exuded a swagger that was distinctly rural and working class. The workplace was rarely the primary setting for these shows. It was generally somewhere in the background, but the struggle to make ends meet was often prominent. It seemed that cowboys and rednecks were the kind of men who worked hard and played even harder. However, they were not playboys, for that was a lifestyle way out of reach. Nonetheless the country boy now had a sense of style and a lifestyle that offered a measure of masculine prowess, rebelliousness, and mystique without all of the posturing associated with the political left.

Depictions of women in these settings were strikingly similar to those in *Playboy* and displayed the humor that was associated with the chauvinist pig. Far removed from the bourgeois world of exclusive clubs and fancy liquors, the redneck, like the male chauvinist pig, could tap into an inversion of an urbane playboy with his backward sense of humor. Hit variety shows like *Hee Haw* (1969–71 on CBS), for example, made a mockery of good taste with their embrace of the country hick and backward, cornpone comedy. The show's producer Bernie Brillstein thought, why not create "a country 'Laugh-In'"?[29] As a showcase for country music legends such as Buck Owens and Roy Clark, the variety show was set in the fictional community of Kornfield

Kounty and featured a variety of skits, sing-a-longs, and country music acts as a mainstream alternative to the high-society guests who made cameos on Hefner's television venture *Playboy after Dark*.[30] *Hee Haw* also featured as part of the regular décor buxom, albeit country, girls in cut-offs and other scanty outfits who, much like their more urbane counterparts, always seemed more than willing to go for a roll in the hay. It was a show where women were as conspicuous as they were inconsequential, if they were not playing the butt of the joke. *Hee Haw*'s backdrop may have seemed a world apart from the exclusive setting of a Playboy club, yet it too was designed to offer an accessible and much more ironic vision of the good life. In so doing, the redneck became a player as well, but with far less serious posturing. Instead, it fit with what Nadine Hubbs sees as the ascendency of 1970s "self-ironic redneck pride."[31]

The chauvinism in this redneck pride was also prominent, if not one of the defining characteristics. *Urban Cowboy*, for example, certainly offered less humor than the other popular cultural examples if we can discount the unexpected chuckles of watching grown and drunken men thrown helplessly off of a mechanical bull into a pit of mattresses. John Travolta's character, Bud, moves to Houston at the beginning of the film to work with his uncle at an oil refining facility, but it is at night at the local honkytonk where his masculinity is proven. Bud is quickly introduced to a bar called Gilley's, which is where he first meets his soon-to-be wife Sissy and the mechanical bull that stands between them. It is clear when the pair first sets eyes on the bull that Sissy is as determined as Bud to ride it. Later that night and after Bud has successfully mounted the bull, he declares, "it's too dangerous" and "it ain't for girls." Unbeknownst to Bud, Sissy starts practicing the art of bull riding behind his back. When he sees her riding the bull for the first time at Gilley's, he is incensed and insists on riding the bull multiple times to prove that he is the better rider. The argument about the mechanical bull continues later that night at their trailer, and when Sissy claims that Bud was angry just because she was a better bull rider, he punches her in the face (for the second time in the movie). Sissy leaves Bud and moves in with an ex-con rodeo rider who has been teaching her how to ride.

The tension between the two is finally resolved when Bud wins the bull-riding contest at Gilley's during the film's climax and when Sissy accepts the conventional gender roles Bud has embraced. At a critical moment in the film, Sissy stops by Bud's trailer to try and resolve their differences. When she realizes he's not there, she cleans the entire trailer and leaves dinner and a letter of apology. Bud returns later that day surprised to find dinner and a clean home, but his new girlfriend keeps the truth from Bud and she tears up the note Sissy left behind. It's only later in the film, after he wins the bull-riding contest, that his then-girlfriend realizes he still loves Sissy and admits to the wrongdoing. By this point Bud has conquered the bull and proved to himself and to any doubters (including Sissy) that he is the best rider, and the wife he loves understands the conventional role she is expected to play.

Along with movies, Nadine Hubbs notes, country music exuded a similar sense of redneck pride, and the genre was undergoing profound change in the post–World War II period. According to Melton McLaurin, country music has passed through three stages since World War II. The first phase ended in the mid-1950s and offered songs about a quaint and peaceful South full of happy, down-home, plain folk. The next period, McLaurin argues, which spanned the civil rights era from the mid-1950s to the early 1960s, highlighted a nostalgia for the old days that included a critique of the region's social problems and poverty. The third era, beginning with the 1970s, featured a more defiant and resurgent South. Examples include Loretta Lynn's 1970 hit "Coal Miner's Daughter," which revealed an "unabashed pride in her humble origins" and her region's culture, and Merle Haggard's "Okie from Muskogee." These songs embraced a populist, conservative political philosophy that tried to remain free from overt racial messages. They expressed anti-city sentiments, complained explicitly about welfare and other government programs that challenged ideas of hard work and individualism, and critiqued liberals, bureaucrats, and trendy northerners.[32]

And like the good old boys who began to have an impact on American popular culture, country music was grounded in a chauvinist longing for a prefeminist golden age. In 1972, for example, country singer Artie Kaplan released a twelve-minute song titled "Confessions of a Chauvinist Pig," in which he chronicles the romantic escapades of "Mr. Average Male Chauvinist Pig"—a "whine" that received scathing reviews.[33] Writing for the *New York Times*, for example, Nancy Elrich noted that lyrics such as, "Sharon was a frenna mine / She would do it anytime . . . Barbara was a friend of mine / Snap my fingers and they would come / Any time I wanted some," conjured up "so flimsy a stereotype that the MCP [male chauvinist pig] doesn't even inspire loathing."[34] Although Kaplan never attracted the notoriety of other country acts, he found the male chauvinist pig to be an attractive marketing niche that highlighted his country roots and a small-town, rural backwardness that made the chauvinist pig seem like part of the musical and rural landscape.

In 1973 another country musician and humorist, Kinky Friedman, released his own salute to male chauvinism with a little ditty he entitled "Get

Your Biscuits in the Oven and Your Buns in the Bed." The song begins by calling out "uppity women" he can't understand who "go and try to act like a man." With his cheeky smirks and grins, Friedman tells women to stay home and skip the "shrink" so they can use their time to "occupy the kitchen" and "liberate the sink." Feminism, Friedman crooned, turned everything upside down, for "now the air is dirty and the sex is clean." And this is why he insisted, "If you can't love a male chauvinist / You'd better cross me off your shopping list."[35]

Friedman spent much of his career mixing his love of music with satire. Inspired by "hero Mark Twain" and the "spiritual elbow room" of his home state of Texas, Friedman and his country western band the Texas Jewboys happily offended "Texans, Jews, and Feminists" with songs like "We Reserve the Right to Refuse Service to You" and "They Ain't Makin Jews like Jesus Anymore." While Friedman played up his defiance for self-categorization, touting both his Jewish background and a defiant love of country music, he had no trouble perpetuating stereotypes about political adversaries like feminists, who became for him the target of his tease. In 1974 when the National Organization for Women named Friedman male chauvinist pig of the year, he was thrilled. Decades later Friedman would relish this honor and what he recalls as an infamous 1973 incident at the State University of New York at Buffalo when he and his band were booed off the stage and chased from the campus by angry college coeds.[36]

The chauvinism that Friedman exploited was similar to Hefner's own. For both, chauvinism was a consequence of feminism, and feminism was equated with a loss of prerogative, sexual discretion, and the radicalization of women that went too far. Men's frustration was often articulated through humorous ditties, jokes, and jabs that made their complaints more palatable as they made feminists the butt of the joke.

Hefner, Chauvinism, and the *Playboy* Mystique

Hefner was a prominent early exemplar of male chauvinism, but growing numbers of contenders overshadowed him by the early 1970s. Thanks to a litany of X-rated films and increasingly explicit magazines, Hefner's naughty jokes and centerfolds came to seem almost quaint as the publishing landscape evolved. As *Playboy's* popularity peaked in the early 1970s, it was increasingly considered mainstream.

By the early 1970s, films like *Deep Throat* (1973) offered elaborately produced porn with a plot and became, in the words of Whitney Strub, a "middle-class phenomenon" that "ushered in the new phenomenon of 'porno chic.'"[37] In a 1975 interview with *Playboy*, even feminist icon Billie Jean King was far from offended when asked whether she ever watched porn. In fact, she replied rather nonchalantly, "Larry [her husband] and I went together to see *Deep Throat* but left halfway through it. I wanted to see it all, but Larry wanted to leave." When asked whether she liked it, she quipped, "It was OK, but too repetitive." King admitted that she would "probably go to see more porn films if I had the time because I'm curious," adding humorously, "I guess I want to try everything once. Well, maybe not everything—so don't ask what I haven't tried yet."[38] In the 1970s *Playboy* also faced competition from raunchier publications like *Hustler* and *Penthouse*, igniting what the porn industry called the Pubic Wars. *Playboy*, however, quickly backed away from the cruder images identified with working men's porn and, in so doing, retained its respectability and centrality to mainstream American political culture.[39]

At the same time, *Playboy* came of age in the post–World War II era, which experienced unprecedented prosperity and the rise of an ethic of consumption that is very visible in the pages of *Playboy*, but there was also a growing uneasiness with this Cold War consensus that sparked widespread critique and protest that was central to *Playboy* and Hefner's image. In other words, Hefner and *Playboy* dabbled in left-leaning politics even as they became two of the defining images of women's sexual objectification and second-wave feminists' fight against it. Hefner, for example, was an outspoken proponent of free speech, and he supported one of the most infamous comedians of the era, Lenny Bruce, who was arrested repeatedly starting in 1961 for violating obscenity laws. By 1966 he was blacklisted from almost every club in the United States, and he died from a drug overdose the same year. In those difficult years leading up to his death, Hefner had hired lawyers to defend Bruce in court and published his biography, *How to Talk Dirty and Influence People*—a title that mocked the 1936 Dale Carnegie publication *How to Win Friends and Influence People*. *How to Talk Dirty* was first serialized in *Playboy* magazine and then published as a book in 1965.[40]

Years later Bruce would remain a pivotal icon indispensable to the legacy of the counterculture. For example, actor Eric Bogosian, who came of age first listening to Bruce on albums in the 1970s, noted that *How to Talk Dirty* "was part of a secret collection of sacred texts that unlocked the doors of hipness and rebellion." "In 1970s, if you were hip to Lenny Bruce, you were *hip*." And what made him "dark, cool, [and] hip" was attitude. "He was a genius of Attitude. If you dig Lenny, you dig the Attitude." For Bogosian, Bruce was one of "the Saints of the New Attitude. . . . That included John Lennon,

Bob Dylan, Jim Morrison, Abbie Hoffman," and what Bogosian admitted was "basically a lot of white men." His improvisational style of stand-up "hooked into the Jazz mentality" and was a crucial link "between post-War African American culture and the 'counter culture' of the '60s and 70s."[41] In much the same way that Beat poets like Allen Ginsberg, William Burroughs, and Jack Kerouac rejected the sterility of white suburbia,[42] Bruce's so-called sick humor carved out a niche for him as one of the kings of comedy. He was the "hep cat" who constantly broke obscenity laws, fought the police, and battled for the right to speak profane truth to power in the courts even as he earned a reputation as a bit of a chauvinist. After all, Bruce loved to make naughty jokes, including one about Eleanor Roosevelt's "nice tits."[43]

Hefner also had no problem challenging the country's racial segregation. Famed comedian and civil rights activist Dick Gregory, for example, insisted that his big break came when Hefner was willing to defy segregation and hire him to work the Playboy club.[44] When Gregory began doing stand-up at the club, he not only earned significantly more money than he would elsewhere, but he now had a platform to speak truth to white audiences. "Never before until Hefner brought me in had a black comedian been committed to work white nightclubs," Gregory insisted. "You could sing and you could dance, but you couldn't stand flat-footed and talk. So when Hefner brought me in, that broke the whole barrier."[45] Decades later, *Rolling Stone* magazine would describe Gregory as one of the most influential comedians of all time, whose fight for civil rights got him thrown into jail during Bloody Sunday (Selma 1965) and shot during the Watts Riot (Los Angeles 1965), as well as inspiring his run for the presidency in the volatile year of 1968.[46]

Hefner also challenged charges of chauvinism because the gender politics in *Playboy* often defied easy categorization.[47] When *Playboy*'s seasoned essayist Morton Hunt titled his provocative 1970 editorial on feminism "Up against the Wall Male Chauvinist Pig!," he revealed a measure of empathy for feminists, or at least those whom he found to be "reasonable." His article was a spin on an essay by Cell 16 founder Roxanne Dunbar entitled "Up against the Wall, Mother!" in which she called for feminist separatism and denounced the patriarchal family for turning women into slaves and children.[48] Hunt's intention was not so much to dismiss feminism but to educate men about the women's liberation movement's more moderate demands. "Behind the few hundred extremists," Hunt argued, "there are from 5,000 to 10,000—no one knows the actual figure of vociferous but less extreme women who belong to all sorts of liberation groups; and behind these are millions of nonjoiners . . . with a host of grievances."[49] They want "better jobs, abortion reform, [and] more child-care centers for working mothers," something Hunt and presumably his readership understood. Hunt added that radical "calls for the abolition of marriage, the transfer of child rearing from the home to communal centers and the elimination of all sex differences in clothing, education, home life, politics and manners" went too far because radical feminists from the New Left were not trying to reform gender politics but wanted a complete "overthrow of male-dominated, sexist, family-based, capitalist-militarist society."[50] Hefner and his associates were liberal reformers and not radicals, content with addressing the excesses of a free market but not in support of undermining white, male privilege. In other words, the gender politics they espoused often reflected the liberal mainstream opinions of much of *Playboy*'s readership.

Three months later *Playboy* published a number of letters in response to Hunt's editorial that reflected a range of attitudes that mixed confusion with concern. Jordan Scher from Chicago joked that Hunt "presents as balanced a picture as a male 'pig' can write." With more than a hint of disapproval directed toward feminists, whom he preferred to call "masculinists," he acknowledged that "women undoubtedly suffer from the restrictions of this society, [but] so do men." Questioning many of their tactics and ideas, he, like Hunt, did find that "some of their goals are legitimate" and even "wish[ed] them luck." Another Hunt supporter appreciated his take on the "spectrum of dissent and dissatisfaction that prevails among women today." Leon Salzmon was from New Orleans' Tulane University School of Medicine and was similarly put off by the "absurdity of the women's liberation extremists . . . who can conceive of no solution less radical than abolishing the past two billion years of evolution and returning the human species to the condition of neutered-sex amoebae." There were some more specific concerns, such as those expressed by Sergeant R. L. Meadows from Beaufort, South Carolina, who had just returned from serving in Vietnam. He wanted to ask feminists, "How long would they want to be 'one of the boys' when it entails sleeping on rocks or in rice paddies or listening all night to the shells and wondering if one has your name on it?" And Don Wilson from Troy, Alabama, simply wanted to know, "Do liberated women also liberate their men from alimony payments?" However, it was radicalism that was most troubling for Alan Stone, who lived in Hollywood. Indicating that he was no longer a "male chauvinist" who engaged in the kind of "chivalry that follows from that attitude," he declared himself ready to take matters into his own hands. "When the militant feminists start their guerrilla insurrection, I will have no hesitation about blasting them the way I would a mob of similarly violent male revolutionaries."[51]

Women who wrote to *Playboy* and had their letters published tended to offer a much harsher critique. Mary Weiner from Woodacre, California, was the exception. She agreed with Hunt and noted that thanks to technology that has reduced domestic work, wives have plenty of time to "pursue intellectual, artistic or other self-fulfilling experiences." In contrast, Elvira M. Wilbur from East Lansing, Michigan, found that it was his "kind of liberalism that provokes angry rebellion." Nora Weingarten from Dayton, Ohio, snapped, "The only good thing about Hunt's essay was the title, *Up Against the Wall, Male Chauvinist Pig!*, which accurately stated by whom, and for whom, it was written." Jesse Bernard, PhD, from Washington, DC, accused him of producing a "piece almost within shouting distance of the 20th Century." On the one hand, she gave him an "A for recognizing the injustice of economic discrimination . . . but an 'F' for not coming to grips with the more basic issue of sexism (a term I prefer to the more pejorative male chauvinism)." She opined that "Hunt is so unconscious of his own sexism" that he has embraced the "Victorian notion that women should invest 50 years of their lives in the world of the home." Hunt, however, got the last word and replied directly to Bernard, suggesting that it was quite possible she had not even read his article because he never made such a claim. Rather he assumed mothers of young children might find it hard to balance both children and a career. Morton insisted that his only "crime" was that he was "a liberal." In fact, he insisted, "I am pro-feminist. On the record, I am a liberal in my outlook on the role of women in modern life." And "nothing infuriates radicals more than a liberal; they see him as an enemy infinitely worse than the reactionaries."[52] All in all, the responses *Playboy* received from readers only confirmed both the intensity of the debates about chauvinism and feminism and the fact that there was little consensus about their meaning and their future.

As seriously as Hunt and *Playboy*'s readers took their discussion of the meaning of feminism, the magazine preferred humor to serious debate. In 1972, *Playboy* published a collection of its illustrations in a book entitled *The Male Chauvinist Pig*. *Playboy* subscribers would be quite familiar with the cartoons that typically depicted women seemingly unaware that they were revealing themselves while posing in a compromising situation. But *Playboy* also found that it could offer a measure of self-deprecation. For example, one cartoon spoke to the hypocrisy of a male-centered counterculture with a shaggy-haired, guitar-strumming hippie lazily stretched out on a mattress while his girlfriend marches out of the room to fetch him some weed. The caption, "'Roll me a joint! Roll me a joint!' A woman's work is never done!"[53]

Feminist comedians also made their way onto the stage at the Playboy club. The duo of Patty Harrison and Robin Tyler managed this feat. Rather than following in the self-humiliating tradition of Phyllis Diller or Joan Rivers (who also appeared at Playboy clubs), Harrison and Tyler disrupted the old-school male stand-up routine by "satiriz[ing] oppressive institutions." They labeled themselves a "sister act" to mask their lesbian relationship but didn't shrink from their feminist politics. According to Tyler, "We took all the jokes that had ever been done on women and we did them on men." By the late 1970s, Tyler, now openly a lesbian, had released her first comedy album, and she reminded her male listeners that they should take it easy. She had been putting up with "tits and ass humor" for years, and in her words, "you're not going to pull the foreskin over our eyes!" She added, if men get too insecure, "just do a crotch-check, it'll still be there."[54] Back in 1972, the "self-described feminists and revolutionaries" were depicted as being "at ease with the irony of their position—making money for the ultimate male chauvinist symbol . . . the Playboy Club." Tyler declared that the comic duo "will get the revolutionary message across . . . by any means necessary." In 1972 John Wasserman, writing for the *San Francisco Chronicle*, described their act as "revolutionary" and "speculated that this college circuit comedy duo . . . was the new Lenny Bruce."[55]

Chauvinism, for Hefner and his associates, was always complicated and always something with which the editor and his staff struggled. The political tension of the Cold War out of which *Playboy* emerged was shifting, and as second-wave feminism gained ground, behavior like Hefner's and his magazine appeared increasingly anachronistic, especially on the left, where feminists' demands were gaining the most traction. The progressive policies and practices that Hefner immersed himself in did not legitimize his chauvinism or make it any less harmful. But it is hard to ignore the way in which liberal views complicated how contemporaries understood and sometimes overlooked the chauvinism he was guilty of promoting.[56] At the least, Hefner's political sensibility contributed to the debate about what constituted chauvinism and perhaps made the trope of the chauvinist pig thus appear more benign.

The Male Chauvinist Pig and the Redneck
Find Their Political Niche

At the same time as chauvinism was becoming increasingly difficult for Hefner (and the Left in general) to defend, the Right was becoming more and more comfortable with its own piggish mystique. Chauvinistic behavior was just as prominent among Democrats, but for Republicans such bravado increasingly fit their political stance. In 1972 author Cornelia Langer Noland, the daughter of a former Republican senator, created a provocative list of "Washington's Biggest Male Chauvinist Pigs" that contained a number of "Prime Porkers" who embraced everything from bad gender politics to womanizing, including the Kennedys. Yet there were conservatives like President Richard Nixon, who she labeled "the blue ribbon hog" for his opposition to abortion rights and women's issues.[57] Indeed, being a pig helped him shape a political persona. When asked about his own thoughts on women's liberation, the president quipped, "Let me make one thing perfectly clear, I wouldn't want to wake up next to a lady pipe-fitter."[58] Nixon was no comic, but he seemed surprisingly comfortable taking a stab at humor to poke fun at women's lib.

Nixon was not the only Republican politician who tried to defuse a complicated political moment or question with the age-old trick of mocking feminism. Evidence suggests that as feminists successfully focused attention on chauvinists and criticized the behavior, growing numbers of men, including conservatives, seemed more eager about embracing the label than they would have been otherwise. Nixon's speechwriter and Ronald Reagan's inspiration was George Gilder, whose most influential publication, *Wealth and Poverty* (1981), "exalted capitalism as the fulfillment of the Christian mission on Earth" and helped chart Reagan's philosophical embrace of supply-side economics.[59] At the time of its publication, Gilder haughtily recalled in an interview how his wife, a Vassar graduate, "burst into tears" reading a portion that was too intellectually challenging for her, crying again out of frustration even after (according to Gilder) he had simplified the discussion for the average reader.[60] Gilder was without question a male chauvinist, and his dubious claim to fame came when *Time* magazine in 1973 named him "Chauvinist Pig of the Year." For a pig seeking affirmation, it must have been the icing on the cake when the National Organization for Women gave him the same award the following year.[61]

Gilder was certainly not a playboy, but he had longed for female attention. As *New Yorker* contributor Larissa MacFarquhar explains, "Despite his relentless pursuits, Gilder never really attracted the sort of female attention he craved until the early seventies, when he discovered his vocation as an anti-feminist." In fact, after one debate in which he expressed his opposition to federally funded day care, he recalls, "'what seemed like hundreds' of women rushed forward onto the stage to argue with him."[62] In the early 1970s he was a shy bachelor, and perhaps this is why, decades later, he considered it a source of "pride" that he was called out as the nation's leading male chauvinist pig, "noting that the previous year's recipient was Norman Mailer." A maverick like Beat novelist Mailer was in many ways Gilder's alter ego, and Gilder's receipt of the award shortly after Mailer suggests that the persona of the male chauvinist pig could offer an unlikely bachelor a kind of mystique. When *Time* magazine described thirty-five-year-old Gilder as "a shy, conservative bachelor and the nation's leading male-chauvinist-pig author,"[63] MacFarquhar notes, Gilder was already a "feminist target" because the publication of *Sexual Suicide* (1973) "elevated him, in the eyes of the women's movement to veritable Satan." Of course, it also gave him a measure of bravado as the feminist fight against conventional behavior reached its peak.[64] As feminist author Susan Faludi notes, Gilder found his literary career as the nation's leading male chauvinist, as well as the attention from women he had always craved.[65]

Gilder, of course, was looking for more than five minutes of fame. His derogatory comments about women were inseparable from boorish insights on the larger political economy. In *Sexual Suicide* he touted his belief that men are healthier and wealthier only if they married and have fulfilled their destiny as providers. According to MacFarquhar, Gilder's argument that men somehow need "the taming and ego-bolstering influence of a wife and family to support" or they will become "barbarous savages" now reads like "political camp, but at the time it caused a tremendous row."[66] Gilder not only identified divorce as a "'deadly event for men' in which they lose everything, including their children,"[67] but he also assumed that being a wife was the best arrangement for women. When it came to wage work, women did not face discrimination; rather, they failed to advance because they were *naturally* "less aggressive and less hard-working."[68] In later publications and interviews, Gilder famously blamed the poor for their own plight and expressed little interest in the trials and tribulations facing single mothers.

Along with women, Gilder condemned what he saw as the deficiencies of Black culture, making him the kind of pig who rolled around in race privilege. In 1978, he published *Visible Man: A True Story of Post-racist America*—an inversion of Ralph Ellison's *Invisible Man*—in which Gilder offered a warped account of a talented African American man and ex-marine named Sam, whose potential is undermined thanks to the welfare state.[69] One *Kirkus* review described the book as just as "insidious and nasty" as his previous work, with a focus on "ADC [Aid to Dependent Children] mothers [who] hold all the aces" and the "cushy" lifestyle they lead.[70] None of this was new. In 1965, Democratic senator Daniel Moynihan became infamous for blaming urban crime and wayward youths on what he imagined as in-verted gender roles within enslaved communities that had created a matri-archal legacy leading to the so-called dysfunctional Black family. Women of color who were blamed for not effectively raising their children or watching their pocketbooks would, it seemed, be forever linked with the "welfare mess."[71]

As cultural critics Susan Douglas and Meredith Michaels point out, "It was Ronald Reagan, the king of the 'welfare queen' anecdotes, who was the politician most responsible for promoting the gendering of welfare in the popular imagination." According to Douglas and Michaels, "He specialized in the exaggerated, outrageous tale that was almost always unsubstanti-ated, usually false, yet so sensational that it merited repeated recounting." Most striking, the pronouns had changed with Reagan's speechmaking, and now increasingly in the 1970s welfare was female: "She has eighty names, thirty addresses, twelve social security cards. . . . She's got Medicaid, get-ting food stamps and she is collecting welfare under each of her names," Reagan insisted. Switching the cause and effects of poverty meant ignoring the problems associated with spending millions on the Vietnam War. And it was much simpler to take aim at Black mothers on welfare, something that set off a series of tax revolts that would further devastate the lives of those living on the margins, as well as those clinging to the middle class.[72]

The Right's equally enthusiastic embrace of chauvinism was not simply a knee-jerk reaction to feminism's growing influence or because its challenge to conventional masculinity was inextricably bound to race. It reflected a broader political development that was a consequence of a regional shift in power to the Sunbelt South and the resulting backlash against the libera-tion movements of the previous decades. This backlash that would gain ground throughout the 1970s and 1980s, promoting Republican electoral success and becoming ever more focused on feminism. The political con-stituency that allowed the Democrats to dominate politics at the federal level from the 1930s to the 1960s was breaking apart, and as southern whites were moving into the Republican camp, their influence on the party was conspicuous.

The redneck was one of the most powerful images to emerge out of the political realignment of the period and an obvious representation of an ide-ological shift. "The redneck," as Jefferson Cowie explains, "maintains a paradoxical combination of rebellion and patriotic nationalism—the state is his enemy, the nation his mystical identity." In short, he hated his gov-ernment and loved his country, a theme that would resonate among Republicans over the next few decades and one that would figure prominently in many campaigns and policy goals. At the root of the redneck's bitterness and hatred was the economic malaise from which the country was suffering, but it was often articulated as a growing unease with a government that he had become disillusioned with and a government he blamed for pandering to women and minorities.[73] The redneck already had a long-standing relationship to racism that was muted in favor of conversations about hard work and patriotism. He represented the mood of a country that was not simply disillusioned about government but increasingly opposed to it. And he was a chauvinist who wallowed in his own self-righteous ideas about gender that were increasingly anachronistic in the face of feminism.

Nixon recognized the redneck's appeal as part of his Southern Strategy to try to break up the Democratic constituency that included southern whites and trade unionists. He acted on that appeal by reaching out to these men when he invited Merle Haggard (and similar musicians) to the White House to mitigate, if not mask, his elite sense of aesthetics and top-down policy making. In so doing, he sought support from his "silent majority," many of whom saw themselves as victims and as God-fearing men with a fondness for country music that promoted their values. It was a strategy staunch segregationist George Wallace had embraced in the 1950s to warm up the crowd before campaign rallies as he attempted to pull together a constituency that is remembered for its anti-Black positions, and one Nixon found just as appealing in the face of a broader Left that included feminists. According to Cowie, "In the thirties, the Left had Okie troubadour Woody Guthrie; in the seventies, the Right had Merle Haggard and the number one hit on the backlash Billboard, 'Okie from Muskogee.'"[74] Cowie reveals how an assertion of race privilege was precariously perched on a slippery class identity that came to embrace anti-Left patriotism through music. As Haggard's song goes, "We don't smoke marijuana in Muskogee / . . . / We don't burn our draft cards down on Main Street / We like livin' right and being free."[75]

By looking at this period through the lens of gender, the prominence of chauvinism in this ideological shift comes into sharp relief. Haggard's expression of a "class consciousness" reawakened in the 1970s is well understood, yet there is more to be said about gender. Muskogee, Oklahoma (the inspiration for Haggard's song), was "a place not only where even squares can have a ball" but also where "leather boots are still in style for manly foot wear"—not sandals or other symbols of a counterculture—and thus was imagined as an important place where left-wing, gender-bending aesthetics had yet to gain a foothold.[76] A more explicit example comes from another

In an attempt to appeal to white southern voters, President Richard Nixon invited country western singer Merle Haggard to the White House in 1973. Used by permission of Photofest.

Haggard song, titled "Are the Good Times Really Over," in which he invokes the days "when the country was strong / back before Elvis and before the Vietnam war came along." It was a time before welfare when "a man could still work and still would" and before microwave ovens, "when a girl could still cook and still would." In the song Haggard laments, "Is the best of the free life behind us now / Are the good times really over for good?"[77]

The Republican attempt to court the white working class in the 1960s and 1970s generally ignored the economic issues with which working men and women were struggling as unemployment reached double digits and as wages stagnated. Instead the Republicans worked to escape their reputation for elitism and as the party of big business, and they did it with humor and by co-opting the populist images associated with the Democrats: flags, country music, racially charged topics like the death penalty and law and order, and of course chauvinism. "Blue-collar conservatism," Cowie and other historians have argued, "works for one simple reason: class in America today is a cultural category, not an economic one."[78] Humor was particularly effective at downplaying the distance that had developed between establishment Republicans and ordinary working Americans, and chauvinism countered the growing clamor about the problems of conventional masculinity as too aggressive.

Poking fun at the Left or making women's "libbers" the butt of the joke was critical to the Right's success in the 1970s. A simple oink or whine allowed men to blame women or feminists for whatever problems the chauvinist could imagine, and little explanation was needed. While playboys like Hefner considered themselves politically hip, conservatives needed the male chauvinist pig's cachet. It is no surprise that chauvinist pig memorabilia could be just the thing to heal a bruised ego. After his defeat to soon-to-be inaugurated Jimmy Carter, President Gerald Ford might have been a lame duck, but he was also, at least in his daughter's eyes, a favorite male chauvinist pig. In 1976 Ford's Christmas gift made headlines when his daughter, Susan, gave him a black bath robe embroidered with a white pig and the initials "'MCP,' standing for 'Male Chauvinist Pig.'" It was an amusing gift in the exchange of presents among the first family as they celebrated the holiday with churchgoing, turkey dinner, and skiing at a Rocky Mountain resort. Although the gift was more than likely a not-so-serious gesture by a devoted daughter who understood more intimately the meaning of her father's recent loss, the celebrated robe afforded journalists a means to discuss Ford's mixed stance on feminism — Ford was a president who "has been a proponent of the Equal Rights Amendment, but continues to play golf at Burning Tree Country Club in Bethesda, Md., which excludes women." Avoiding any larger political implications, the spokesman for the Ford family had no immediate explanation for nineteen-year-old Susan's gift, except that "she thought it was cute."[79]

Most important of all, the male chauvinist pig helped make modern conservatives appear just naughty enough to disrupt the lingering image of the old-school conservative as an out-of-touch square. As a potent symbol of masculinity and an animal version of the self, the male chauvinist pig offered men a sense of domesticated naughtiness that was easy to tap into even if you lacked a Kennedy mystique or counterculture cool. The desire to be a playboy or invoke some redneck boyish charm helped define the male chauvinist pig and inspire the conservative's or any square's political libido.[80]

WHEN IN 1972 AUTHOR CORNELIA LANGER NOLAND created her list of "Washington's Biggest Male Chauvinist Pigs" that included a number of "Prime Porkers" who embraced everything from bad gender politics to womanizing, she called them out not simply because of their opposition to the feminist issues of the day but because they were guilty of a hedonism and an unrelenting *Playboy* mentality in which women, like missiles and third-world countries, were another means to assert one's Cold War free market self. These liberals were stereotypically chauvinists because they attempted to emulate a cavalier Kennedy lifestyle. In her understanding of chauvinism, the Kennedys stood as the archetype of what a chauvinist looked like. "Nobody," Noland argued, "has done more to foster the role of women as 'decorative object' than the three Kennedy brothers." "Their wives," she complained, "were expected to have children, involve themselves in religious pursuits and keep up appearances while the men pursued their machismo."[81]

Noland would go on to critique prominent Republicans like Nixon. But when she wrote the piece in 1972, she could not have imagined how the political landscape would evolve and how it was shaping our understanding of male chauvinism. The economic malaise of the late 1960s and early 1970s, coupled with the rise of the Sunbelt South and its move into the Republican fold, weakened the Democratic constituency that had dominated electoral politics at the federal level for several decades. The Sunbelt South's influence on American culture was profound and gave rise to a redneck chic that promoted a conservative political ideology, figured into the backlash against the liberation movements of the preceding decades, and promoted a sexy swagger that defied age-old stereotypes about backwards rednecks, downplayed race, and elevated chauvinism.

We cannot ignore the extent to which the battle over sexism continued to rage on the left. Yet the men associated with the prominent political realignment of the period co-opted not only much of what the Democrats had used to attract the working class but also a political edge that used humor to challenge their reputation for elitism and used chauvinism to displace the blame for the problems working-class men faced and the ineffective economic policies pursued by Republicans. The conservatives' reach for the workingman's consciousness centered particularly on southern whites, and they did it through culture rather than economic substance.

Ironically, as this political movement was gaining ground in the 1970s, feminists' calling out men as male chauvinist pigs began to ebb. While this shift reflected to a certain degree the emergence of a postfeminist moment that pulled back from previous strategies and tactics, it also reflected a much more conscious appropriation of chauvinism by the Right for political gain. As we will see in the chapter that follows, no one was better at this than Rush Limbaugh.

CHAPTER FIVE

Modern Conservatism's Missing Link

Rush Limbaugh, Feminazis, and the Rise of Donald Trump

In 1995 writer and documentary filmmaker Stephen Talbot described stalwart conservative talk radio host Rush Limbaugh as a cultural phenomenon who "energized 20 million voters with rock 'n' roll and bad-boy jokes." Talbot warned that Limbaugh was spearheading a new conservative trend that was "becoming more political, strategic—and dangerous." Limbaugh, he insisted, was "the national precinct captain for the Republican Party" or "like an electronic ward boss." On his radio show five days a week, "Limbaugh explains the issues, offers the conservative GOP spin, rallies the faithful, and turns out voters" with ridicule and mockery, "leavened by bursts of rock 'n' roll, and moments of self-deprecating humor." Limbaugh created a powerful affect. His singular achievement, Talbot insists, was destroying "the notion that 'funny conservative is an oxymoron.'"[1]

In 1992 Limbaugh influence's among Republican leaders was undeniable. KFBK-AM in Sacramento had hired Limbaugh in 1984, when "they were looking for a kinder gentler conservative." Talbot explains, "Rush played the angry white guy with a sense of humor. It seems obvious now, but no one tried it before." Limbaugh seemed to be touting the American dream. Even though Talbot found it an "astonishing reality of American political life" that "a college dropout, fired from four jobs, twice divorced, obese, and insecure," "has become one of the most influential forces in the country," it was becoming increasingly clear across the political divide that Limbaugh was no joke.[2]

Talbot's characterization of Limbaugh reflected both the pedigree and legacy of the male chauvinist pig who came to represent the average, albeit white, American along with his wounded sense of nationalistic pride. Limbaugh, the college dropout, appeared to be a self-made man as well as the new maverick of modern conservativism. And for his fan base who felt they were the victims of limousine liberals, the Clinton presidency, and narcissistic feminists, his mockery, no matter how vicious, was speaking truth to power.

Of course, Limbaugh was not self-made. Instead, he rode the wave of deregulation that allowed conservative and corporate giants to mass-produce his image along with a new and troubling trope—the feminazi. With a single catchphrase, feminism became an indispensable enemy for the Right. For conservatives who considered themselves at the mercy of feminism and the Left, Limbaugh's willingness to eschew political correctness was a breath of fresh air with daunting effect.[3] As Limbaugh continued to rise to national attention, so too did his ability to powerfully discredit feminism.

Limbaugh and his particular brand of ridicule would come to serve as the missing link between the more endearing male chauvinist pig of the 1970s, Archie Bunker, and his far more disturbing incarnation, Donald Trump, the quintessential womanizer whose role in bringing playboys over to the revanchist Right cannot be underestimated. The most famous male chauvinist pigs during the 1970s and at the peak of the second wave were a washed-up tennis player and a sitcom caricature, both of whom were seemingly losing power and more readily dismissed as a joke. By the 1990s, the nation's shift to the right was undeniable, and the most infamous misogynist pig was now an unconventional bad boy who had taken command of conservative airwaves. In the 1970s, feminists often despised the male chauvinist but also found him to be just an anachronistic patriarch who seemed out of touch, and hence easier to ignore. By the early 1990s and after nearly two decades of a conservative resurgence that was shifting the country to the right, there was no way of ignoring the chauvinist anymore.

Limbaugh was critical to a conservative comeback and a backlash that took particular aim at feminists and people of color. His notorious use of humor and ridiculing taunts profoundly helped Republicans take control of Congress in the Clinton years and later during Donald Trump's ascendency to the White House. With the excuse that his opponent just needed to lighten up, Limbaugh redefined acceptable conservative discourse and paved the way for an unlikely presidential candidate who, in early 2016, few took seriously. Yet as Trump played the rebellious playboy and Washington outsider, he tapped into the male chauvinist pig's long-lasting appeal, which all too easily set up the Democratic nominee, Hillary Clinton, as the second-wave feminist who couldn't take a joke, let alone make one.

Rush Limbaugh as the Missing Link: From Square to Stand-Up

Limbaugh had been in radio since the early 1970s, but his meteoric rise in the mass media came when he launched his nationally syndicated program in August 1988. The numbers he attracted are hard to fathom. "By 1991 he had 350 stations, 1.8 million listeners each quarter hour, and 7.1 million listeners a week," which is why his adversaries declared him "the most dangerous man in America."[4] Just four years after Limbaugh debuted on the national political scene in 1988, President Ronald Reagan honored him as "the Number One voice for conservatism in our Country."[5] In 1995 the Republican freshmen inducted him as an honorary member of the 104th Congress, because of the crucial role he played in conservative campaign victories.[6]

Even decades later Limbaugh is still a force with which to be reckoned. Rush has spawned imitators, but in the Trump era he remains the most popular conservative political commentator.[7] Regardless of the competition, in 2010 his fifteen million weekly listeners made him the king of conservative talk show hosts.[8] Phyllis Schlafly, famous for playing the righteous homemaker and for her tenacious efforts to halt the ratification of the Equal Rights Amendment in the 1970s, adored Rush. Thinking about his profound influence in 2008, Schlafly concluded, as did his critics, that he was a tour de force. "Without a script, Limbaugh continues to hold an audience for three hours, five days a week. In her opinion, "he entertains, informs and teaches with plenty of solid, fact-based arguments that, for many Americans, is the only conservative message they hear."[9]

Limbaugh has also come to represent the American dream, appearing to be anything but privileged. "A college dropout, Limbaugh is completely self-educated and a self-made man," Schlafly noted approvingly.[10] Author John Wilson insisted that there was nothing unattainable about Limbaugh's pedigree, something Wilson felt made him somewhat resentful. "Limbaugh's lack of formal education has haunted him for decades. As a college dropout, he has always felt jealous of his better-educated peers, which is why he mocks the Ivy League graduates and anyone else who is well educated."[11] His southern Missouri roots, complete with his uncouth banter, made him appear to be a good ol' boy who stood in bold relief to the liberal elite.

Limbaugh's lucky break came from his father's business ventures, while his wicked sense of humor reflected his mother's influence. Despite his father's pressure to become a lawyer and to "follow in the family tradition," Limbaugh, "who always hated school," found support from his mother to "become a Top 40 disc jockey." Rush's father was a "Goldwater Republican" who undoubtedly shaped Limbaugh's ideology. But it was his mother, Millie, who humbly admitted, "He got his good sense from his dad and his nonsense from me." Millie's parents were Democrats, and her dream was to be a jazz singer: "'I was paid to be a singer for about four months of my life,' she recalls with a smile, 'and that's been the biggest joy of my life, besides my family.'" Following his mother's interest in public performance, sixteen-year-old Rush found his calling on "an after-school show on a tiny radio station partly owned by his father," and thus he was not quite the self-made man some imagined him to be.[12]

In much the same way George Gilder longed for attention in early 1970s when he was first crowned male chauvinist pig of the year, Limbaugh had a reputation as "the square, the nerd, the guy girls refused to kiss." Talbot insists, "Rush also bears the profound insecurity of a lonely socially awkward fat boy who skipped his senior prom." Limbaugh's first two marriages were ended by disgruntled wives. "His mother confesses, 'I can't imagine what it would be like to be married to him,'" even admitting, "I think he needs a wife subservient to him." Millie acknowledged that on the air her son has a strong sense of "superiority"—one of the male chauvinist pig's more undeniable traits.[13]

In an era that preached Christian family values, Limbaugh's politically incorrect, shock-jock theatrics offered conservative politics much greater reach. There is a rich history of "strident right-wing voices on the radio . . . —Father Coughlin, Joe Pyne, Morton Downey Jr.—but they were mean-spirited and shrill," notes Talbot.[14] There was also the feel-good conservative commentary of radio storytellers like Paul Harvey, whose "velvety voice" could move "seamlessly from a story to commentary to a carefully placed advertisement." From the 1970s into the 1990s, Harvey was the mild-mannered voice of conservative talk radio.[15] Harvey would, however, fade to the background and his gentle aesthetic would be all too easily eclipsed. "Before Limbaugh," Schlafly recalled, "there wasn't interesting talk radio. There were only sour liberals who pontificated to a shrinking audience. Limbaugh turned AM radio into a lively genre where liberals are completely outclassed because they are boring, just regurgitating tired notions that are a proven failure and can't be intelligently defended."[16]

Limbaugh's vaudevillian tone also provided a welcome measure of comic relief in an era when many on-air conservatives preached nothing but hell and damnation. Cultural critic Kembrew McLeod argues that in the 1970s Christian conservatives' "massive communication network" made "its first order of business . . . to scare the hell out of believers."[17] Historian Robert Self similarly contends that by the 1970s and 1980s, "televangelists re-created the psychic melodrama and emotional stagecraft of the tent crusade in their studio churches." Fear-mongering televangelists like Jimmy Swaggart declared, "Satan is laying a diabolical plot to destroy the citadel of democracy in the world," and helped exacerbate America's culture wars. For those looking to inspire a "mixture of religious collective anger at the secular world," the televangelist who offered "moral certainty" was "a winning combination."[18]

Limbaugh invoked a fiery style reminiscent of the newly politicized pulpit, yet his profound influence in conservative politics came not from moralizing threats of damnation but rather from mockery and belly laughs. Thus, for a fan base already familiar with impassioned ministers and television evangelists' fire and brimstone, comic relief from an uncouth redneck turned shock jock was a novelty, to say the least. Writing for the *New York Times* in 1990, Lewis Grossberger described Limbaugh as a "political vaudevillian."[19] Of course, Limbaugh's humor, or "nonsense," as his mother put it, was never intended as a temporary escape from political discourse but rather as a far more effective means to whip up and inspire the conservative base.

Journalist and author of *Rush Limbaugh: Army of One* Zev Chafets had a similar reaction to Limbaugh when he first heard him on the radio. Chafets admits, "Listening to Rush became a guilty pleasure. I didn't agree with everything—in fact, I disagreed with a lot—but agreeing wasn't the point. He was doing something really interesting. Ridicule has always been a weapon used by the left against the right. Limbaugh had somehow seized the cannon and turned it around. I relished his bravado, laughed at his outrageous satire, and admired his willingness to go against the intellectual grain."[20] Of course, Limbaugh also benefited from a popular backlash against feminism that in the late 1980s included, for example, "the ascendency of virulently misogynist comics like Andrew Dice Clay—who called women 'pigs' and 'sluts.'"[21]

Modern conservativism owes much to its most popular joker, Ronald Reagan. Reagan was both a "storyteller and collector of jokes," noted *New York Times* journalist James Reston, and thus a double threat for his opponents on the campaign trail. To be sure, he targeted his political adversaries with humor, "but it's gentle. He mocks but never wounds, and increasingly, he pokes fun at himself, particularly at his age." For example, amid serious trade concerns, Reagan set up his audience like a seasoned stand-up: "'The United States,' he said, 'had a merchandise trade deficit in almost all the years between 1790 and 1875.' Then he added, deadpan: 'I remember them well. Of course, I was only a boy at the time.'" Which is why Reston characterized Reagan as "his own court jester."[22] Daniel Wickberg similarly argues that Reagan, who was by far the oldest politician to run for president at the time, had a "reputation as 'the great communicator' . . . undergirded by a use of self-deprecating humor, particularly in regard to his age."[23]

Reagan, however, had a long habit of ignoring comedy's golden rule—a problem compounded by both his political rhetoric and his retaliatory actions. As historian Kyle Longley points out, in the 1960s Reagan "denounced the Civil Rights Act of 1964 and the Voting Rights Act of 1965 while running radio ads referring to urban areas as 'jungles.'" When it came to housing, he supported what he claimed was an individual's right "to discriminate against Negroes" and infamously targeted Black activists like Angela Davis as he joked about "Africans and cannibalism." As Richard Nixon noted, Reagan knew how to manipulate "the emotional distress of those who fear or resent the Negro, and who expect Reagan somehow to keep him 'in his place.'"[24] In 1966, during his run for governor, Reagan also condemned the University of California, Berkeley, and its "small minority of beatniks, radicals, and filthy speech advocates," who had ruined the school. On one hand, he joked about hippies who "act like Tarzan, look like Jane, and smell like Cheetah,"[25] and on the other hand, with newfound authority, he ordered a violent police response to student protesters on the Berkeley campus. In May 1969, "nearly 800 officers responded, dressed in riot gear, many with badges obscured to hide their identity, went after the protestors with nightsticks swinging. As the protesters retreated, officers fired tear gas canisters and '00' buckshot at the crowd's backs as they tried to escape." One student was killed and 128 were admitted to a hospital. When Reagan was asked about his use of force against the student protesters, he quipped, "It's very naïve to assume that you should send anyone into that kind of conflict with a flyswatter."[26]

Limbaugh, then, was not the first to use ridicule to find his political niche. But his success as a national radio personality not only amplified the message of modern conservatism but thrived thanks to the tenets of deregulation.[27] Talk radio's great transformation would begin in 1987 when the Federal Communications Commission stopped enforcing the Fairness Doctrine that had required radio shows since 1949 to present contrasting political opinions and give them equal amounts of time. Through the early 1990s, talk radio still provided a diverse range of stations airing liberal, moderate, and conservative opinions. But the Telecommunications Act of 1996 allowed for rampant deregulation that undermined the small "mom and pop" stations that had populated and diversified the airwaves. As fewer industry giants came to own hundreds of radio stations, the stage was set for Limbaugh and the ascendency of talk radio's waves of ridicule and exclusionary laughs.[28]

Conservatism has thrived to a large degree by perpetuating damaging racial tropes. As historian David Roediger argues, Limbaugh's "populist, 'y'all come' whiteness" was a particularly troubling stand-in for class politics. Like Gilder and Reagan, Limbaugh would come to blame the plight of the common man on Black communities and particularly the so-called welfare queen. Insults masked as simply jokes that overly sensitive liberals needed to get over allowed Limbaugh to pander to his fans by relying on a "white look" or gaze that distorted images of people of color.[29] During televised airings of his radio program, for example, Limbaugh would appear in a small box in a lower corner of the screen before an overwhelmingly white studio audience, often ridiculing anyone of color. With unremitting mockery, Roediger insists, Limbaugh undermined the very "idea of Black expertise with a panoply of rolled eyes, raised eyebrows, nods, snickers, and chortles." And then, "at the clip's end, the camera surveys the studio audience's satisfaction."[30] With little risk of ever encountering a heckler, the "white entertainer, white studio audience and white viewers" created an ideological echo chamber that furthered Limbaugh's popularity with an ability "to endow his look with awful power."[31] And when liberals and progressives complained that Limbaugh was not funny, it was further proof that there was something wrong with the Left. They were now the moralizing stooge.

Mocking people of color and women has been an American tradition, but Limbaugh was "the Master of Racial Poison." "Let's face it, we didn't have slavery in this country for over 100 years because it was a bad thing," Limbaugh sniped. "Quite the opposite; slavery built the South. It had its merits. For one thing, the streets were safer after dark." Just as perverse, "Limbaugh said of the man who confessed to the assassination of Martin Luther King Jr.: 'You know who deserves a posthumous Medal of Honor? James Earl Ray. We miss you, James. Godspeed." Instead of apologizing for his racist taunts, he dismissively noted, "Blacks are 12 percent of the population. Who the hell cares?"[32] However, for his predominantly white audience, a joke is just a joke.

Chafets recalls that Martin Luther King Jr. had once said, "Sunday morning at 11 o'clock was the most segregated hour in America," but the popularity of Limbaugh and his almost exclusively white audience offered a cynical update. In an interview with NPR's David Greene in 2010, Chafets insisted that "between noon and three, Monday through Friday, when the Limbaugh show is on, is the most politically segregated hours in America." Thinking about Limbaugh's impact, he declared, "The country is really divided into people who listen to Limbaugh or who don't listen to Limbaugh,"[33] something that foreshadowed the volatile age of Trump.

In many ways, that novel idea that conservatives had the best sense of humor came into sharp relief in 1987 with the publication of philosopher Allan Bloom's *Closing of the American Mind: How Higher Education Has Failed Democracy and Impoverished the Souls of Today's Students*. His book inspired an attack on political correctness that would shape politics for decades to come.[34] For conservatives who considered themselves victims of feminism and the Left, a willingness to eschew political correctness was a breath of fresh air.[35] Calling out liberals for what seemed like nitpicky political sensibilities engendered heated debates that peaked over the next decade yet never completely faded away, and made conservatives appear as the new champions of free speech.[36]

With Limbaugh disguising his misogynist and racist jokes as free speech, he and his fandom ignored the degree to which humor is inextricably bound to power dynamics and social positions. Limbaugh's insults were mixed with the kind of buffoonery that created waves of affect that bolstered a conservative hubris as he declared open season on political activists from a broad range of social movements. No one was off limits, because his threats were always veiled as simply jokes. In much the way stand-ups work the crowd, Limbaugh galvanized the conservative base with mockery and ridicule and in so doing turned squares into bad boys who once again set up feminists as the laughingstock.

The humorless feminist remained one of the more attractive tropes for Limbaugh and a particularly easy target. The male chauvinist pig of the 1970s may have faded as an epithet, but he was reincarnated as a talk show host whose aggressive sets and punch lines were fueled by making fun of feminism. And for Phyllis Schlafly the ascendency of Limbaugh was long overdue. In 2008, Schlafly still liked to joke, "When I lecture on college campuses, it's easy to identify feminists. They don't laugh; they don't have a sense of humor." Recalling "the pre-Rush years," she complained about an anonymous conservative writer whom she admired except when it came to humor. She even wrote him a letter of complaint: "I'll accept wives and mothers-in-law as fair game, but we need some jokes about feminists." In her mind, he, like too many conservative pundits, was a "coward," because "he never included a single joke ridiculing the feminists." But then came the game changer, and Schlafly found herself in awe of the "fearless Rush Limbaugh who dared to poke fun at the feminazis and point out their silliness, intolerance, pompous self-importance, inconsistencies, and obnoxious whining about sexism." Limbaugh, Schlafly enthused, "even dared to say, 'feminism was established so as to allow unattractive women access to the mainstream of society.'"[37] Mocking feminism had been fun and games, but turning the feminist into public enemy number one demanded a trope that was both a joke and a threat.

The Rise of the Feminazi

One of Limbaugh's most lasting and influential routines entailed rebranding feminists as feminazis. And unlike the male chauvinist pig, whose anti-feminist jabs could all too easily be appropriated as a humorous badge of honor, the feminazi was a much more sinister trope that conjured up the fear of feminism and the atrocity of fascism. Limbaugh introduced the epithet in 1989, and it would continue to be used for decades.[38] According to Limbaugh, an economics professor and friend at the University of California, Davis, Tom Hazlett, coined the term *feminazi* to "describe any female who is intolerant of any point of view that challenges militant feminism."[39] Hazlett was not the first to associate feminism with fascism, however. Sociologist Ferdinand Lundberg and psychologist Marynia Farnham, in their 1947 study *Modern Woman, the Lost Sex*,[40] linked feminism with ideological intolerance. "Lumping feminism, anarchism, anti-Semitism, Communism, and racism, by claiming they all preach hatred and violence," Kate Millett explains, "it made a broadside attack on revolutionary movements, which it bundled together with Nazism and the Ku Klux Klan."[41] However, it was Limbaugh's volatile use of mockery that made *feminazi* such a powerful moniker.

Although Limbaugh claims his usage of the term *feminazi* was merely directed toward only "the most obnoxious feminists," who in his words were "obsessed" with abortion, he effectively reduced feminism to the moral equivalent of Nazis, something that inspired an "open season" of hate while perpetuating his own popularity as an old-school chauvinist pig who used naughty jokes to take on the liberal elite.[42] On one end of the spectrum were the feminists who claim "they don't need men to be happy," Limbaugh chortled. "Nothing matters but me, says the Feminazi."[43] And on the other end of the spectrum were feminists "obsessed with perpetuating a modern day holocaust" and who fiendishly like to "celebrate" abortions.[44] Although Limbaugh argues that his use of the term *feminazi* was intended to single out feminists who advocated women's reproductive rights, it quickly expanded and became synonymous with almost any woman who dared take a progressive stance placing people, ideas, and organizations in dangerous political crosshairs. In Limbaugh's America, the feminazi became an indispensable enemy for a widening conservative base.[45]

Over the course of a career built on ridiculing feminists, Limbaugh's obsession with Hillary Clinton stood out. When Talbot was producing his documentary in 1995, he described Limbaugh fans as "20 million people telling each other how they hate Hillary."[46] Historian Sara Evans also contends that

Limbaugh, more than anyone, "led the attack on Hillary Clinton and what he viewed as the liberal takeover" during Bill Clinton's presidency.[47] As a First Lady who refused to stay in her place, Hillary Clinton was turned into a plethora of punch lines that brought into question her femininity and the president's administrative prowess. For example, "What happened when Bill Clinton got a shot of testosterone? He turned into Hillary." Another jab turned into a popular bumper sticker that proclaimed: "IMPEACH CLINTON! And her husband, too!"[48]

Like the male chauvinist pig of the 1970s, Limbaugh's rhetoric surrounding Hillary managed to be both demeaning and disturbingly flirtatious. Looking back after more than a decade's worth of anti-Hillary jokes, journalist Suzi Parker categorizes "Limbaugh's archives" as a "treasure trove of all things Hillary." When she ran for president, Limbaugh famously asked, "Do the American people want to watch a female president age before their very eyes?" With an ironic twist, Parker suggests that Limbaugh has always been infatuated with Hillary "like the highschooler who wants the smart girl, knows he can't have her, so he makes fun of her to hide his crush." Limbaugh has even claimed that Hillary seduced him on an elevator. Going so far as to reenacting a made-up fantasy, he mimics Hillary's attempt to seduce him: "Would you, would you make a real woman out of me?" As she started to take off *his* clothes, Limbaugh stopped her and, like the quintessential patriarch, insisted that she "fold them." Much like the male chauvinist pig who never got to step foot in the Playboy mansion, let alone get the girl next door, Limbaugh found that old-school misogynist humor could bolster his (and his party's) political virility.[49] Limbaugh should have been a potent reminder for the Left that a joke is never just a joke, but a visceral force to be reckoned with.

Jokes are inextricably bound to power and social position, which is why punching up and not down is comedy's golden rule. Yet Limbaugh made his career by egregiously violating any and all rules. When it came to Chelsea Clinton, the president's teenage daughter, for example, satirist Molly Ivins protested that Limbaugh went too far. "Limbaugh put up a picture of Socks, the White House cat, and asked, 'Did you know there's a White House dog?' Then he put up a picture of Chelsea Clinton, who was 13 years old at the time and as far as I know had never done any harm to anyone." This was the kind of humor that gave Limbaugh his high ratings but "trouble[d]" Ivins. "Satire is a weapon and it can be quite cruel." Instead of taking aim at power, Ivins noted with a shudder, Limbaugh "consistently targets dead people, little girls and the homeless—none of whom are in a particularly good position to answer back."[50]

Limbaugh's popularity was often blamed on the naïveté of poor, uneducated whites. Ivins opined, "A large segment of Limbaugh's audience consists of white males, 18 to 34 years old, without a college education." As she put it, the typical Limbaugh fan was, "basically, a guy I know and grew up with named Bubba," "because Limbaugh gives him someone to blame for the fact that Bubba is getting screwed." However, Ivins was sympathetic: "He's working harder, getting paid less in constant dollars and falling further and further behind." On the other hand, she could not resist stereotypes. "Not only is Bubba never gonna be able to buy a house, he can barely afford a trailer. Hell, he can barely afford the payments on the pickup." Ivins assumed that the rise of Limbaugh reflected a "generation of young white men without much education and very little future. This economy no longer has a place for them." But they don't lash out at "the corporations [that] have moved their jobs to Singapore." Instead, she lamented, Limbaugh manipulates and stokes their resentment. After all, "because Bubba understands he's being shafted, even if he doesn't know why or how or by whom, he listens to Limbaugh," someone who "offers him scapegoats. It's the 'feminazis.' It's the minorities. It's the limousine liberals. It's all the people with the wacky social programs to help some silly, self-proclaimed bunch of victims," she protested. It appears as though Limbaugh is not violating comedy's golden rule only because "Bubba feels like a victim himself—and he is—but he never got any sympathy from liberals."[51] In other words, Bubba and all the other Limbaugh fans, according to Ivins, suffered from a bad case of false consciousness.[52]

Limbaugh certainly knew how to manipulate an audience that reached deep into the middle and upper class. Like a skilled comedian warming up the audience, Limbaugh showered his loyal following with flattery: "Is this the best-looking audience in television or what?" To be sure, they were smartly dressed. It was never simply the poor or working class who regularly listened to Limbaugh. Talbot remarks that "they are not trailer park trash, survivalists in battle fatigues, or rednecked Klansmen" but rather decked out in suits and ties, with a few in military uniform. "Most of them are white men—whiter than the Republican delegation in Congress— between 18 and 54." And "women are welcome," Talbot chides, "as long as they behave." Indeed, "Rush may be blaring from the AM radio in Bubba's battered pickup as he bounces down some backwoods road on the way to an NRA meeting. But Bubba is only part of Rush's audience." Although Talbot describes Ivins as "a national treasure," in this case he admits, "she's behind the curve about the typical Rush Limbaugh listener." Talbot points out that "it might reassure Democrats to think of Rush's fans as poorly educated, gay-bashing morons. But dittoheads [self-identified Rush fans] are not just marginalized hatemongers; they are a mainstream political force, and as such they are far more threatening." Perhaps just as telling is their attitude. Far from being bitter, at least "on the surface," dittoheads "appear happy, deliriously happy. And why not? Their side is winning."[53]

If in the 1970s *All in the Family*'s Archie Bunker offered comic relief for a liberal audience, by the 1990s, symbolically, the bigot was no longer the butt of the joke but a rising star of talk radio whose use of mockery could rally political forces. For his adversaries, Limbaugh appeared to be a bully, a blowhard, and anything but funny.[54] For his loyal following, however, Limbaugh was in touch with the common man in ways that eluded liberals. And by relying on humor, he could assume the position of the bad boy, mitigating the moralizing aesthetics of an era entrenched in family values, which, in turn, broadened the reach of the Republican Party.

The rising modern conservatism, with its moralizing refrain and Christian condemnations, desperately needed a clown or court jester to mask and manipulate conservative scare tactics with humor and waves of laughter. Against the backdrop of the political landscape that came to be defined as postfeminist, the 1980s and decades to come witnessed tremendous feminist gains but an intense backlash, much of which had to do with the rise of Limbaugh and humor's messy affects. Yet it was possible for feminists to be funny, assertive, and powerful. In fact, it was exactly that combination that was needed to put the pig in his place.

Feminist Fun and Ann Richards

Challenging the boundaries of bourgeois respectability with populist wit was also Texas Democrat Ann Richards's signature move. In 1988, at the Democratic National Convention that nominated Democrat Michael Dukakis in an election that witnessed incumbent vice president George H. W. Bush ultimately win, Richards delivered a punch line that thrust her into the national limelight. As Jan Reid explains in her biography of Richards, she was a gifted speaker, and that "saucy, plain-spoken keynote address, borrowing from the great tradition of vernacular Southern oratory," set in motion an iconic campaign for Texas governor. Nevertheless, the most memorable one-liner came when she took a jab at the vice president's privileged upbringing: "Poor George," she quipped, "he can't help it. He was born with a silver *foot* in his mouth."[55] Although Richards was herself a jokester, that particular one-liner came her ways thanks to a long friendship she had with the comedian Lily Tomlin, whose partner and collaborator, Jane Wagner, "offered the line that would make Ann Richards a household name."[56]

In 1983 Richards became the first woman to win a state office in Texas in half a century. Not only was she now the state treasurer, but she also had won more votes than any other candidate in a statewide campaign. She was re-elected in 1986. However, her most impressive victory came when she defeated oil tycoon and misogynist good old boy Clayton Williams to become governor of the state in 1990.[57] Williams was a notoriously out-of-touch "businessman who liked to brag about his financial success, cracked rape jokes around reporters, and kissed 'just about every woman within arm's reach.'"[58] Her defeat of him, however, was still somewhat of an upset. As Reid explains, Richards won when, "politically, the word 'liberal' was now almost a curse word in Texas; [and] electoral power was swinging fast toward the conservative wing of the Republican party."[59]

Richards knew how to make a joke, and her humor was amplified rather than erased, in part because she also touted a background that put her in touch with the common man, who was always, lest we forget, assumed to be white. When asked about her ethnic background, Richards teased, "I am about three-quarters WASP—that's Waco and Sure Poor." Richards's good-old-gal persona, complete with her own no-holds-barred humor, however, made her stand apart from liberal elites and contradicted the prevailing image of the feminist who was moralizing and lacked humor. After her triumphant victory over Williams, Richards's inauguration paid tribute to southern white constituents with a rendition of Ray Wylie Hubbard's anthem "Up against the Wall, Redneck Mother."[60] The lyrics praise a "mother who has raised her son so well / He's thirty four and drinkin' in a honkytonk / Just kickin' hippies' asses and raisin' hell."

> M is for the mud flaps she gave me for my pickup truck
> O is for the oil I put on my hair
> T is for T-Bird
> H is for Haggard
> E is for Eggs
> And R is for Redneck.[61]

Richards's white southern populism may have seemed right out of a conservative playbook, as did her posturing as a political outsider. When Richards was invited to speak at a White House celebration during the George H. W. Bush presidency, she playfully roasted her inside-the-Beltway

At a 1992 party in her honor, Governor Ann Richards, along with friend and gossip columnist Liz Smith, holds up a T-shirt displaying the governor's iconic *Texas Monthly* magazine cover. The magazine had superimposed Richards's face on a picture of a model dressed in white leather atop a Harley Davidson motorcycle with an intriguing headline that asked, "Can she be the first woman president?" Photo by Jim Smeal, used by permission of Getty Images.

colleagues: "So this is what you all do up here on Saturday nights," she pondered with a wink and grin. "I don't know why anyone would think you're out of touch." Looking out at a well-to-do audience, she scoffed, "As my mama would say, you look as good as a newly-scraped carrot." Continuing with her roast of Bush, she quipped, "In any event, I'm proud to be out with such a high-class crowd. But I've been wondering, Mr. President—to overcome the image of attending a white-tie dinner like this, how many pork rinds do you have to eat?"[62]

In July 1992 Richards's image as a bad girl was enshrined on the cover of *Texas Monthly*. The magazine's art director, D. J. Stout, was inspired after the governor learned to ride a motorcycle and then received a Harley Davidson as a gift. Richards was too busy to pose for the picture, so an undeterred Stout superimposed Richards's smiling face on the body of an attractive model dressed all in white leather, complete with fringed gloves, straddling a "great big Harley hog." With self-deprecating humor, the governor joked that "she hadn't had thighs like that in thirty years" and thanked the art director for "matching her face with a model that had such a 'sexy body.'" The caption, "White Hot Momma: Ann Richards Is Riding High—Can She Be the First Woman President?," also revealed a political potential she uniquely fashioned.[63]

Richards was riding high, and her brand of humor, combined with feisty Texas populism, mitigated—at least for a moment—the more censorious traits attributed to mainstream feminism and white liberal politics. She had, after all, taken on the Trumpian pig of her day and won. Although she lost her reelection bid to George W. Bush in 1994—an outcome tied to an epic Republican revolution that led to sweeping congressional victories across the country and a critical appraisal of the Bill Clinton presidency— her legacy would continue.[64] Richards was hard to forget but also seemingly impossible to duplicate.

For conservatives, controlling Congress turned on controlling humor. Newt Gingrich's Contract with America was a popular pledge to cut taxes and social programs and balance the budget—but Republican midterm victories were owed to the unprecedented influence of talk radio's game-changing satirist, Rush Limbaugh, who also played the feisty populist. In 1994 House Republicans made Limbaugh an honorary member as they celebrated his role in turning the House—after forty years—back to Republican rule. And as representative Barbara Cubin from Wyoming put it, "There's not a femiNazi among us."[65] Although the Left still believed they owned antiestablishment satire and that conservative humor was a contradiction in terms, liberal leaders were more often than not set up as the stooge, something made all too clear with the political awakening of the Trumpian playboy.

2016: The Second-Wave Feminist and the Playboy

By the 1980s and 1990s, after coming of age against the backdrop of Christian conservatism, Donald Trump appeared to be more playboy than right-wing politician. Starting in high school, "he steadily built an image as a young playboy," and "by senior year, his classmates had crowned him 'ladies' man' in the yearbook, a nod to the volume of his dates."[66] As a business mogul, he has maintained a similar lifestyle and for decades was friends with Mr. Playboy himself, Hugh Hefner. In an office "which is as much

Trump's trophy room as workspace," *Rolling Stone* journalist Paul Solotaroff noticed that "every flat surface is adorned by his image: framed magazines, glossies from important publications, none more so, at least for Trump, than the 1990 *Playboy* where 'I was one of the only men to ever get on the cover.'"[67] Three years after his *Playboy* cover appeared, Trump partook in a nationwide search for the next playmate. And in 2000, Trump even had a cameo in a soft-porn Playboy film.[68] Before he was ever concerned with making America great again, Trump's primary focus seemed to be on his phallic self. Even amid the crisis of 9/11, "just hours after the attack," Trump touted the fact that *his* building was now the tallest in Manhattan.[69]

When Trump, who had never toed a party line, became just a decade and a half later the front-runner in the Republican primary, winning the nomination, Hefner mistakenly thought there had been a revolution in conservative thought or what he hailed as "the Conservative Sex Movement." As Hefner saw it, "voters nominated Donald Trump, a thrice-married New York entrepreneur who once owned the Miss USA pageant, over [Ted] Cruz, the son of a pastor," something Hefner celebrated as "a sign of the massive changes in the 'family values party' and proof of . . . a sexual revolution in the Republican Party." But what Hefner portrayed as the playboy's victory over the prude was not a revolution in conservative attitudes but a coronation of the party's latent tendencies. Trump's New York office, which so famously flaunts his *Playboy* magazine cover, also features a litany of accolades from conservative religious groups that found in Trump the apotheosis of the male chauvinist pig.[70]

However, when it came to a presidential campaign trail, there was something new. With ruthless attacks masked as humor, Trump has stood apart from slick politicians with jokes and a refusal to stay on script. Not only did Trump's use of jokes, especially ridicule directed at Beltway liberals, make him *appear* more authentic, his campaign revealed how waves of mockery and laughter can create their own momentum. As one female voter informed *Rolling Stone* magazine at a campaign rally in the fall of 2015, "Finally, someone's saying what we've all wanted to say—we've been pushed too far for years." Another woman supporting Trump described him as refreshing, saying, "I like that he's not politically correct—we don't have time for that here," and likened him to Ronald Reagan. Trump's use of humor and disdain for political correctness made his audience believe that he was speaking their truth to power. While attending the same rally, a former Democratic voter insisted he switched parties because Trump "means what he says, and says what he means."[71] Trump's brashness and unrelenting

Rush Limbaugh and Donald Trump — the movers and shakers of right-wing ridicule — at Turning Point USA's Student Action Summit, West Palm Beach, Florida, 2019. Photo by Nicholas Kamm, used by permission of Getty Images.

wisecracks made him *seem* fearless and hence a truthteller in the minds of his supporters.

Trump's piggish traits are what allowed him to be both the penthouse playboy and the common man. As he donned a red "Make America Great Again" baseball cap, he often seemed no different from the fictional blue-collar bigot Archie Bunker, who generated laughs with his out-of-touch comments, outrageous jokes, and longing for a mythical past. Like Archie, who felt entitled to throw around racist tropes and referred to his wife as "Dingbat" and his son-in-law as "Meathead," Trump, with access to a Twitter account and a 24/7 news cycle, had an extensive list of monikers and insults that he hurled at hundreds of "people, places, and things."[72] For much of the 2016 campaign, journalists, political analysts, and his opponents dismissed Trump as a joke who was more like a sitcom character than a serious political contender.[73] But like Limbaugh, who targeted anyone and everyone from AIDS patients to welfare recipients, so too did Trump litter the campaign trail with hate speech masquerading as humor. Along the 2015–16 campaign trail, Trump's misogynist behavior was reminiscent of that of the male chauvinist pig who rolled around in the privileges of whiteness as he carved out his political niche far right of center.[74]

In May 2011, well before the Me Too movement emerged, *Time* magazine ran a cover story in which journalist Nancy Gibbs boldly asked, "What makes powerful men act like pigs?" Gibbs's essay turned the spotlight on a disturbing pattern of famous political leaders and cultural icons, ranging from France's former head of the International Monetary Fund Dominique Strauss-Kahn, who had just been accused of rape, to golf sensation Tiger Woods, who had an affair and was a reminder that being a playboy as well as a misogynist had a rich history. *Time* magazine raised the levity of the article with a somewhat humorous "misconduct matrix" that mapped out along a horizontal axis which men should be relegated to the "doghouse" and which should be in the "jailhouse." Vertically arranged were more guilty faces that were somewhere between "massively hypocritical" and "just plain stupid." Included were historical figures such as Thomas Jefferson, whose fathering of six children with enslaved Sally Hemings, for example, put him at the top of the hypocrisy index right next to Ted Haggard, the staunchly antigay evangelical who purchased "meth and a massage from a gay male escort."[75] In sharp contrast to *Time*'s 2017 Person of Year cover story, which featured the faces of the silence breakers of the Me Too movement,[76] the 2011 cover featured a rather innocent piglet that appeared in the right-hand corner accompanied by a light-hearted apology to the barnyard species for having cast it as a symbol of man's misdeeds.[77]

Much like the popular questionnaires of the 1970s that attempted to diagnose the male chauvinist pig as a character flaw, Gibbs sought to understand why some men behave so badly, and she turned to psychologist Mark Held to do so. Held argued, "When men have more opportunity they tend to act on that opportunity," and hence "powerful men tend to assess risk differently." Newt Gingrich, John Edwards, and Arnold Schwarzenegger, Held found, were "overachievers" who aggrandize power and have little self-control. Whether it is nature or nurture, Gibbs added, a life of "indulgence and entitlement" means those with wealth and prestige often lack self-control and self-discipline and thus have a history of affairs and sexual abuse that can lead to time behind bars—recall, for example, heavyweight champion Mike Tyson's conviction of rape and film director Roman Polanski's "sex scandal" with a thirteen-year-old girl. Just as puzzling were the wives like Ann Sinclair, who stridently informed French journalists (while Strauss-Kahn was running for president) that she was "'rather proud' of his reputation as a ladies' man, a *chaud lapin* (hot rabbit) who was nicknamed the Great Seducer. 'It's important,'" she explained, "'for a man in politics to be able to seduce.'"[78]

The long-standing tension between taking sexual harassment seriously and brushing it off as a joke set up the 2016 presidential election as a particularly volatile battle of the sexes. Well before "Lock her up" became the mantra of the Republican convention, conservatives had made Hillary Clinton their public enemy number one. Recall back in the 1990s when Limbaugh fans were characterized as "20 million people telling each other how they hate Hillary."[79] Limbaugh had made a career out of attacking the Clintons and, on the eve of the 2016 election, signed a four-year contract with Premiere Networks under the assumption that Hillary Clinton would be the first female president. "It was Limbaugh's constant lambasting of the Clintons in the 1990s that helped propel him into mega-stardom and already his 2016 ratings had spiked 25 percent." And now, on the eve of the election, Eliot Nelson, senior reporter for the HuffPost, quipped, "the band, it seemed, might be getting back together." But as Nelson points out, "it wasn't to be. Instead of having two Presidents Clinton to lob bombs at, Limbaugh instead has a commander in chief who is, arguably, a far better shock jock than he is." To be sure, politicians had dabbled in ridicule and outlandish statements, but no one operating in the realm of formal presidential politics before Trump had made such divisive ridicule a campaign signature. As president of the United States, Trump targeted, Nelson reminds us, "the disabled, immigrants and prisoners of war and also boasted about sexual assault and his ability to execute people in public."[80] Just like Limbaugh's use of his favorite trope, the feminazi, Trump's attacks on Hillary Clinton during the 2016 election felt like a reboot of a 1970s battle of the sexes featuring a second-wave feminist and the male chauvinist pig.[81]

Playing it straight was particularly difficult for women caught in the crosshairs of Trump's wrath. During the early months of the campaign, Fox newscaster Megyn Kelly found herself the target after she confronted candidate Trump in a live debate. After she reminded him of his habit of calling women "fat pigs, dogs, slobs and disgusting animals," she poignantly asked him, "Does that sound like the temperament of a man we should elect as president?" The following day, Trump snapped back with a vengeance and dismissed Kelly as a woman gone crazy because it was that time of the month, crudely suggesting she had "blood coming out of her wherever." Yet each firestorm of controversy he lit simply fueled his campaign.[82] Most famously, in the weeks leading up to the election, footage surfaced of Trump in an NBC parking lot boasting to *Access Hollywood* correspondent Billy Bush in 2005 that when it came to women, his fame and fortune allowed him, in hard-to-forget words, "grab them by the pussy." Trump opponents became even more outraged, but there were plenty of supporters who shrugged it off as just a joke or, as Trump put it, "locker-room talk."[83]

When Trump insisted, "I'm no different from anybody else, and people joke, and I joke," it struck a chord with many of his followers.[84] Of course, his excuse was embedded in a rich history of turning women into the target of ridicule. And Hillary Clinton, one of the most experienced candidates for the presidency in recent memory, became the object of such mockery. When she responded with the same reasoned discourse that we have come to expect of presidential candidates, it did little to convince those who were not part of her base. Thus, in a political campaign that relied on raucous punch lines, she was often the unwitting stooge caught in the trope of the humorless feminist.

Just days before the 2016 presidential election, *Rolling Stone* magazine featured an interview with Cecile Richards, Ann Richards's daughter, who expected Hillary to become the first woman president. "The sexism her mother faced in 1990 is eerily similar to misogyny in the 2016 race." To be sure, this was a battle of the sexes, but not a tennis match or a struggle to sit in Archie Bunker's chair. "This presidential campaign is unprecedented," in the words of Cecile Richards. "Not only are we poised to elect the first woman president in U.S. history, but we've witnessed the most grotesque display of sexism ever seen in a presidential candidate," something that was certainly no coincidence. After all, there is a rich history of misogynist attacks directed toward women who seem to be making political, social, and economic gains, something that further exacerbates men's feeling that they are losing status. Deeply troubled by the campaign, Richards worried that "by bragging about sexual assault, demeaning Miss Universe, female news anchors and others, joking about women's looks and breast size, and brushing it all off as a joke, Donald Trump has not only affected how our children feel about themselves and their country, but he's triggered memories of painful experiences for so many women." And she referred to Clayton Williams as "the Donald Trump of Texas." Just like Trump, "Williams bragged about not paying taxes, which for many Texans was the final straw," and he also "liked to joke about sexual harassment," including rape. But on the eve of the election, Richards, like most progressives, assumed that Trump would be defeated just like Clayton Williams.[85]

When it came to humor and broadening her base, Hillary Clinton was no Ann Richards. An "excruciating Pokémon Go joke" about the popular mobile app that was sweeping the nation failed miserably[86] and was followed months later by an all-too-staged one-liner about Donald's "trumped up

Reaganomics," something that became a political gaff turned cannon fodder for shows like *Saturday Night Live*.[87] Hillary's use of humor repeatedly fell flat in part because she had positioned herself as morally superior to Trump and his supporters, or as she once called them, "a basket full of deplorables." Her remark about his deplorable base backfired to such a degree that it reaffirmed just how much the male chauvinist pig gets to play with different rules. At the same time, Hillary's campaign attempt to "go high," in the words of Michelle Obama,[88] was problematic because of Hillary's long political record, which (like most people in politics) made her hands a bit dirty in ways Michelle's were not. Hillary also found herself situated as the more conventional, prudent wife in order to provide a balance to her own husband's sexual improprieties. Let us not forget that Bill Clinton has been described by many as a sexual predator whom liberals found to be charming, if not endearing, and whose reputation was all too easy to troll when it came to pointing fingers at just who (Bill or Donald) treated women with the least respect.[89]

Of course, well before she ran against Trump, when Hillary did laugh, it came under intense scrutiny, and not just by conservative pundits. For years, mainstream commenters derided Hillary's laugh, something that was cast as everything from a witchy "cackle" to a girlish "giggle." As women have had to overcome a legacy of not being funny, they have had to negotiate the meaning of their laughter through the prism of feminine vice. This does not exactly encourage women to show, let alone respond to, humor in an unscripted fashion. When Hillary ran against Barack Obama, both candidates, as well as Michelle—who also was accused of being angry and militant—had to carefully manage everything from body language to humor. While Barack and Michelle have been praised for their wit and warmth, Hillary struggled. In 2007, Patrick Healy of the *New York Times* asked, "What's behind the laugh?" noting earlier cases in which reporters were dismayed when Hillary, for no apparent reason, let loose a "hearty belly laugh that lasted a few seconds." There was even speculation that she used laughter as a tool of manipulation to avoid answering certain questions. Sometimes Hillary has called reporters out on their double standard. "You guys keep telling me, lighten up, be fun. Now I get a little funny and I'm being psychoanalyzed." Most troubling, however, is what Healy called "the deployment of the Clinton Cackle," something that was considered to be the equivalent of an insult or eye roll. Showing a montage of repetitious Clinton belly laughs on *The Daily Show* made it easy for Jon Stewart to jest that Hillary was a bit "robotic." He also casually suggested that something evil might be lurking. After all, Stewart quipped, "she will be our first president that you can't spill water on."[90]

AGAINST THE BACKDROP OF THE July 2016 Republican convention, an episode of *Real Time with Bill Maher* featured an illuminating discussion between national correspondent Joy Reid, media pundit Dan Savage, and Tony Schwartz, author of Trump's *Art of the Deal*. Political satirist Bill Maher asked Schwartz, who had worked closely with the Republican nominee as his ghostwriter, "Does he [Trump] have a sense of humor?" As Maher listed the names of past presidents who he believes knew how to laugh at themselves, he concluded, "I've never seen it in Donald Trump"—that is to say, the kind of humor that turns on self-deprecation, associated with, for example, the "Great Communicator," Ronald Reagan.

In an aha moment a bit later in the show, the working-class troubadour Michael Moore launched a passionate plea for just "an hour with her [Hillary]" in debate prep. Looking at his host, who also saw the writing on the wall, Moore insisted that together "we would give her the comedy shiv that just needs to go underneath the skin" and "bring him down." Few progressives forecasted Trump's victory, with the exception of Maher.[91] It might seem an all-too-familiar critique and a bit patronizing to suggest that a female political figure needed a lesson in humor, but Reagan made it a habit of collecting jokes and wisecracking Ann Richards turned occasionally to Jane Wagner when she needed a punch line.

Scholars have ignored humor and its messy affects, but it proved a visceral force in the 2016 campaign. After the election, writer and comedian Judd Apatow insisted the funnier candidate always wins. "I said it as a joke, but I think there's something to it. . . . Reagan was funny. Bill Clinton was funny. Bush was funnier than Gore. Obama was funnier than probably anybody who's ever run for office." Apatow even admitted that Trump rarely ever laughs and "has a demented sense of humor," but "Trump is way funnier than Hillary Clinton."[92]

To be sure, not everyone would agree that the funniest politician steals the show. After all, what is funny to some is often offensive to others. Yet ignoring humor and its visceral affects makes contemporary politics hard to explain. When it comes to movements, humor can engender a sense of community and exclusion. It can fuel frustration as well as fun. At the same time, not having a sense of humor—whether or not it is just a matter of perception—can turn even the most commanding politician into the fool.

Epilogue
Who Gets the Last Laugh?

In 2012 Sandra Fluke, a third-year Georgetown law student, testified in front of Congress asking health insurance companies to cover the cost of women's contraceptives. In response, on his nationally syndicated show, Rush Limbaugh called her a "slut" and "prostitute." He flippantly added, "She wants you and me and the taxpayers to pay for her to have sex."[1]

Flash forward eight years to President Donald Trump's 2020 State of the Union Address, just weeks before a pandemic would sweep across the United States. With understandable empathy, Trump began to speak about "the pain when a loved one is diagnosed with a serious illness," as he paid tribute to Limbaugh, who had just announced his diagnosis of advanced lung cancer (Limbaugh passed away in February 2021 while this book was being prepared for publication). As the president thanked him for "decades of tireless devotion to our country," he then, in a much more unexpected move, awarded Limbaugh the Presidential Medal of Freedom.[2] This highest of civilian awards has gone to humanitarians, entertainers, and literary greats ranging from Mother Teresa to Fred Rogers and Toni Morrison.[3] Anointing Limbaugh in this way reaffirmed his importance in the rise of a Trump presidency, yet it also brought into sharp relief both humor's power and its tragic failure.

On the 2016 campaign trail, Trump masterfully played the Washington outsider, something that is relatively easy to do when your political opponents have names like Bush and Clinton. As Trump transitioned from dark-horse Republican nominee to president of the United States, it became increasingly obvious that he felt the sting of ridicule, but only when it was directed at him. Late-night comedy shows like *Saturday Night Live* (*SNL*) became particularly problematic for Trump. For example, "Alec Baldwin mocked the president-elect's impulse control in a sketch that saw him retweeting random high-school students during a national security briefing," and in a surreal moment of life imitating art, "the real Trump" actually "tweeted at 12:13 a.m., about halfway through the episode." According to David Sims of the *Atlantic*, "The irony couldn't have been more plain: In response to a sketch mocking his propensity for impulsive tweeting, the president-elect . . . impulsively tweeted about it." Baldwin's impersonation, Trump insisted, was "totally biased, not funny," and makes the show "unwatchable."[4] Trump is not the first president to be mocked, however.

SNL has aired for over forty years and lampooned eight presidents, none of whom, until recently, seemed to be all that concerned. After all, they understood the dynamics of power that come with the presidency. Chevy Chase portrayed Gerald Ford as "clumsy and accident prone," a caricature Ford gracefully ignored, just like every president who has followed in his footsteps.[5] To be sure, some presidents handle ridicule better than others. "Perhaps no president embraced mockery more than George H.W. Bush," notes journalist Steve Hendrix of the *Washington Post*. Dana Carvey's spot-on impersonation, with his "Not gonna do it, wouldn't be prudent," turned the president and Carvey into friends and collaborators who frequently appeared together, sometimes on television and sometimes for charity events. As Hendrix points out, Carvey and the real Bush were so in sync, it was "difficult to tell who was imitating whom, Bush doing Carvey doing Bush." Bill Clinton also had the ability to roll with the punches. Phil Hartman played the first *SNL* version of the new Democratic president. "In one skit, Clinton, sworn to stay on his diet, dragged his detail into a McDonald's during a jog and proceeded to scarf fries and McRibs from voters' trays as he explained his economic plan and Balkan security." Hendrix points out that even when Darrell Hammond portrayed a "more lecherous" version of Clinton toward the latter part of his presidency, "none of it seem to bother the real president." When it comes to American presidents being mocked, "all of them have reacted the same way—until now."[6]

Of course, as a new president, Trump's objections to *SNL* turned on much more than the antics of Baldwin's impersonation. When contemplating the political influence of shows like *SNL*, journalist and comedian Dean Obeidallah opines that it is female comedians and their cross-gender impersonations that most powerfully disrupted the staffing of the White House and the legitimacy of Trump's inner circle. "Assuming the media reports are accurate," Obeidallah argues, the "SNL depiction of [White House Press Secretary Sean] Spicer got under Trump's skin since a woman was playing Spicer." Obeidallah was not the only one to see the power of humor.[7] CNN also summed things up in an early 2017 headline: "Sean Spicer Has a Problem: Melissa McCarthy."[8] Just weeks into Trump's presidency, the actress's *SNL* parody of the angry, gum-chewing fiend who "don't talk so good" and used his podium as a motorized weapon went viral. In an equally popular skit, McCarthy's Spicer is frustrated with his inability to deal with foreign names, countries, or facts. But this time when journalists question the president's immigration policy, a spiced-up Spicer reaches for a dolly in a patronizing attempt to keep things simple. The implicit racism is central to a joke that features a "nice American girl," Barbie, as the model citizen. As McCarthy's Spicer insists, "We know she's OK because she's blonde," but then out comes Moana, a Polynesian Disney doll, who is greeted with an "Uh oh," "slow your roll, honey." As a TSA doll inappropriately pats down Moana, Spicer's caricature boasts, "We're going to read her emails and if we don't like the answers—which we won't—boom, Guantanamo Bay!"[9] Less than six months after McCarthy first played Spicer on *SNL*, the real press secretary resigned from his post. A few years later, reflecting back on when he first saw McCarthy's parody, Spicer admits thinking, "I'm screwed."[10]

SNL's queen of impersonations, Kate McKinnon, was particularly adept at taking on all the president's men with her cross-gendered caricatures. Attorney General Jeff Sessions provided the cannon fodder for a number of *SNL* skits. McKinnon's Forrest Gump version offers up a hilarious rendition of the "sneaky little liar" who gleefully talks about his life like it's a box of chocolates as he spills secrets to anyone who happens to sit down by him. Boasting, "I'm the attorney general of the whole United States," Sessions admits, after appearing on the cover of the *New York Times* for potential perjury charges, "I had a bad week." As the skit continues, Forrest Gump, a.k.a. Sessions, claims, "I never talked to any Russians ever," to a stranger he meets at the bus stop but quickly confesses to another, "I met with a fellow who turned out to be Russian on account of he was the Russian ambassador." Then the next person he meets turns out to be a smug, shirtless Vladimir Putin, who instructs Sessions in a thick Russian accent, "This meeting never happened." The skit reaches a climax, however, when Oscar winner Octavia Spencer makes a cameo appearance. Playing her character from *The Help*, she reminds Sessions and the audience of his long, egregious record on civil rights as she offers him a slice of her infamous poop-filled pie.[11]

When it comes to just deserts, Trump revealed an inability to take what he dishes out. Thus it is no surprise that he refused to attend the annual White House Correspondents' Dinner, an event that routinely features a comedian who roasts the sitting president. Since the event began, the only other president not to attend the gala was Ronald Reagan in 1981, but he was recovering from an assassination attempt, and even in that condition Reagan managed to phone in some remarks. Not every president has enjoyed being roasted. George W. Bush was far from thrilled with Stephen Colbert's 2006 performance, but he managed to maintain his decorum.[12] Against the backdrop of Trump's presidency, former president George W.

Bush made a point of touting his own sense of humor in a 2017 appearance on *Jimmy Kimmel Live!* The former president noted that he had an awesome joke writer and, in a not-so-subtle swipe at Trump, added, "I love humor. The best humor is when you laugh at yourself," to which Kimmel snapped back, "Tell that to the president."[13]

To be sure, Trump is the kind of pig with thin skin. But when it comes to humor and the battle of the sexes, let's not forget that this is an area where Hillary Clinton certainly struggled. In a 2019 interview with Howard Stern, Clinton admitted that making an appearance on *SNL* was challenging. "It's outside my comfort zone, let me be honest . . . I'm not a comedian by any stretch of the imagination." Thinking about the role of humor in presidential races, especially the debates, Stern wished things could have gone differently. "I used to have this fantasy when I would watch you debate Trump. . . . I wish you would take out a map and say, Donald, point to where Russia is. . . . I wanted you to say, name the president of Yugoslavia." Stern added, "I wonder if he could find Texas on the map?" Clinton agreed that would have been fun, yet when Stern suggested that she was perhaps "too nice" in those debates, their conversation turned toward a double standard that has plagued both comedy and politics.[14]

With so few female role models, Clinton was trained to play it straight. Of course, let us not forget that even when she laughed or made a joke, it was viewed as suspect. For women in politics and so many other careers, you have to keep your cool. Clinton responded to Stern, "I was certainly very careful." And the reason stemmed from the fact that she "grew up at a time if you were gonna get through a door as a woman you did not react to anything." During her early career as a trial lawyer, she recalled men coming into court dressed in camouflage in the middle of a deer hunt just to see the "lady lawyer." And in perhaps the most revealing part of the interview, she recounted "taking the law school exam at a huge hall at Harvard. And there were hundreds of men and there was like maybe fifty women and we were in this room waiting for the test to start." She continued, "I was with some of my women friends who were there with me and all of a sudden these young men start harassing us. 'What are you doing here?'" As Stern looked aghast, Clinton recalled how men would insist, "'You have no right to be here.' It was during the Vietnam War so they were saying things like 'If you get a slot then I'm gonna get sent to Vietnam. I'm gonna die. It's gonna be your fault.' So what did we all do? We just put our head down like okay you take the test. You show you can do it." Coming of age as the first woman in so many settings, you simply cannot show emotion. And as Clinton put it, "I am of that generation where it was the first all of the time." If you are the first woman to do something, "you've gotta stay focused, don't get distracted. Guys are going to be trying to say this and do that. You just keep going." The strategy of not showing your emotions or even letting people get to know you stemmed from "that training."[15]

Of course, this speaks to a double standard that women face, especially those who seek positions of power. Numerous studies have shown that too many people still perceive ambitious women as "unlikable" by definition and not somebody you might have a beer with.[16] As Clinton explained, "In my experience, the balancing act women in politics have to master is challenging at every level, but it gets worse the higher you rise." On one hand, "if we're too tough, we're unlikable. If we're too soft, we're not cut out for the big leagues. If we work too hard, we're neglecting our families." On the other hand, "if we put family first, we're not serious about work. If we have a career but no children, there's something wrong with us, and vice versa. If we want to compete for a higher office, we're too ambitious."[17] And of course if "a woman lands a political punch—and not even a particularly hard one—it's not read as the normal sparring that men do all the time in politics." Invoking one of Trump's misogynist remarks from the 2016 campaign, Clinton concludes, "It makes her a 'nasty woman.'"[18]

Thinking about a moment during one of the debates, Stern was reminded of a common tactic that men use to intimidate female opponents especially. When Trump invaded her space and stood behind her as she spoke, Clinton reflected on her options: "Suppose I had turned around and said, 'Back up you creep. You're not going to intimidate me.' The headlines would have been 'lost her, you know, calm, switches into being angry.'" Then, in an all-too-familiar refrain, "the pundits would have said, 'Well if she can't take Donald Trump, how's she going to take Vladimir Putin?'"[19] It might have been a game changer if she jokingly asked Trump whether he was lost and pointed him back toward his half of the stage, but there is an old adage, "Never wrestle with a pig. You both get dirty and besides, the pig likes it." Looking toward the future of women in public life, Clinton was optimistic. "We are getting to a point where there are enough different role models now so that you don't have to have some preconception of what you have to meet as a stereotype that people impose upon you. But it still is tough and it still is a challenge. . . . There are still these double standards."[20]

For women playing it straight on the political trail, can their female comedic counterparts chip away at a prevailing double standard? A younger generation of women have seen the Me Too movement emerge right along with a golden age of feminist humor.[21] Yet many women coming of age during the second wave would remember the comic stage much like the mass media, an unfriendly resource for women. Of course, comic mischiefs had found their way into grassroots campaigns of the era. Recall the 1968 Miss America pageant in which feminists crowned a sheep and tossed bras into the trash, which remains one of the most powerful symbols of the second wave. However, there was no Tina Fey literally rewriting the script and taking command of a comedy powerhouse like *SNL*, nor was there a Wanda Sykes to call out racism at a White House Correspondents' Dinner. The 1960s and 1970s boasted talented comedians like Lily Tomlin, Carol Burnett, and Moms Mabley who laid the foundation for female comedians to come into the spotlight, but there was still a heavy dose of self-humiliation that came with their generation's comedic success.[22]

As women have challenged the gendered boundaries of respectability and found the spotlight, we have found comedy's potential. As Kirsten Leng points out, "Humorous acts mobilize the imagination to allow an audience member to view the world from a different perspective, and to envision and explore alternate ways of being and living."[23] After the arcane male chauvinist pig antics secured a Trump White House, hundreds of thousands of women took to the streets in American cities and across the globe in protest. Trump's raunchy rhetoric and innuendos were transformed into waves of resistance celebrated with pink-knitted hats and iconic slogans warning that the "pussy grabs back."[24] From queen of late-night television Samantha Bee's *Full Frontal* to Negin Farsad's use of justice comedy to counter Islamophobia, funny women have lead an uproarious attack on Trumpism.[25] Indeed, feminists even subverted Trump's misogynist epithet and proudly proclaimed themselves "nasty women."[26]

In 2020 social media's newest platform, TikTok, served as another reminder of just why women play such an important role in taking down the pig.[27] Former "social worker turned film student" Kylie Scott found her comedic niche on what became known as the Drunk Trump series on TikTok. While listening to the president trying to speak about the coronavirus and then viewing someone miming the president's words while acting as if he were a clueless substitute teacher, Scott got the idea to do her own version. After all, his speeches seem less presidential and more like "the 3 a.m. ramblings of a drunk girl in a club."[28] In fact, it was because Trump "sounds wasted" that Scott found her comedic niche, creating a parody entitled "Drunk in the Club after Covid."[29] Such parodies play with the master's tools not only by separating Trump from the prestige of the presidency but also by reducing him to a woman and hence the kind of person he has long dismissed. Comedian Sarah Cooper puts it best: "I look at it as taking off the emperor's clothes." In her brilliant TikTok "How to Medical," Cooper lip-syncs Trump with a straight face and mimes his words verbatim—"Suppose you brought the light into your body, which you can do, either through the skin or some other way"—all while pointing to various orifices of the body. In so doing, Cooper, who received tremendous praise for this new comedic niche, explains, "I've basically taken away the podium and the suit and the people behind him nodding. . . . That's why it highlights how ridiculous his words are." Of course, as Cooper notes, "Trump—who would, presumably, particularly hate being presented as a woman—is almost beyond being satirized, having made reality unbelievable."[30] And there is "the added frisson of having Mr. Trump—who boasted of sexual assault, ran on xenophobia and referred crudely to African and Caribbean countries—played by a black woman born in Jamaica."[31] Homemade TikToks came to offer sweet revenge in 2020, but let us not forget, Trump plays a very dangerous game of divide and rule.

Looking back on the 2016 inauguration of Trump, Hillary Clinton admits that was the first time she "got really worried." Listening to him address the nation, she thought, "It's not what a president does." You are supposed to "reach out to people who weren't for him or her," but instead of a speech unifying Americans, what he did was "bizarre." As she listened to Trump speak about "carnage in the street and a dark dystopian vision," she recollects, "I was sitting there like, wow, I just couldn't believe it." And this is when "George W. Bush says to me, 'Well, that was some weird shit.'" Understanding that human nature makes it easy to rev up a crowd, she assumed, as leader of the nation, Trump would now mitigate fears and anxiety, not fuel it. But in her words, "he has made it possible for all the worst impulses. It's like Pandora's box. Lift the top off and things start flooding out. That's difficult to get back into the box."[32]

At its best, humor can elicit waves of laughter that work to diminish fear, anxiety, and hatred. Laughter can motivate people to alter social relations that break down barriers based on social identity and even remove the emperor's clothes. But ridicule can be deadly. It can motivate a base to commit acts of violence. Indeed, genocide has also been fueled by racial caricatures. Whether it's a joke spread through the pulpit of a conservative talk show or by the Orwellian pig in chief, the misuse of humor's affect must be brought into sharp relief. When President Trump smirked at the thought of shooting immigrants and turned it into a joke just months before a mass murder by a white nationalist in El Paso, Texas,[33] we are left to wonder, When will the power of the pig's humor come to an end?

Tragically the power of a pig has perverse appeal. Amid Trump's autocratic use of force on American citizens during the Black Lives Matter protests that swept the nation in the wake of the May 25, 2020, police killing of George Floyd, Trump insisted, "if you don't dominate," you will look like a "jerk,"[34] and in so doing, he seemed to embody the mentality of a pig named Derek Chauvin, who, with hand in pocket, used his knee to execute a public lynching.[35] Perhaps the gravest problem with the old-school battle of the sexes is that it relies on humor to lighten the heavy issues of oppression, serving all too tragically to mask hate speech as just a joke.

Acknowledgments

To be sure, there are a few folks whom I would love to thank for inspiring this particular book, but I have chosen not to name names to protect the guilty. Along those
same lines, I want to give a shout-out to all the individuals who have asked me
whether they are a male chauvinist pig. Perhaps you will find your answer here.

Far more indispensable, however, has been the tremendous support from Texas
Tech University and the larger community of which I have been a part for more than
twenty years. The Women Faculty Writing Program, Women's and Gender Studies,
and the Department of History have helped create a work culture that has allowed me
and my research to thrive. Words of encouragement, critical insight, and shared
sources have come from so many students, friends, mentors, and colleagues both
here in Lubbock and elsewhere. I cannot thank enough Jean Allman, Jacynda Am-
mons, Willie Armstrong, Amber Batura, Jameson Baudelaire, Jack Becker, Colleen
Berg, Stefanie Borst, Laura Calkins, Erin Collopy, Kirk Cunningham, Sean Cunningham, Trisha Earl, Lindy Evans, Rob Fink, Tiffany Fink, Leah Frank, Frank Garro,
Mansell Gilmore, Tiffany González, Barbara Hahn, Cathy Jung, Alishba Khan, Melissa
Lambert, Erin-Marie Legacy, Kirsten Leng, Miguel Levario, Jackie Manz, Ian
McDowell, Kristen Messuri, Maxine Milam, Ron Milam, Sarah Myers, Kathy Peiss, Ben
Poole, Reda Rafei, Michael Rangel, Benito Reyes, Dave Roediger, Walt Schaller, Eliza-
beth Sharp, Alan Singer, Colleen Sisneros, Emily Skidmore, Courtney Slavin, Mabel
Sodeinde, Victoria Stambaugh, Lyn Stoll, Mark Stoll, Elissa Stroman, Phil Tiemeyer,
Susan Tomlinson, Giang Trinh, Nguyễn Hồng Uyên, Jessica Waldrop, Robert Weaver,
Elaine Wilson, and Celeste Yoshinobu. I also thank Kim Schreck, who played a par-
ticularly crucial role in the final version of this book. I am especially grateful for her
spot-on suggestions and our friendship, which stretches back to graduate school at
Mizzou and the countless conversations we had out along the MKT Trail.

I am so pleased to have had the opportunity to work with an editor like Brandon
Proia. He has offered such clear vision and has been a steady guide through a revision
process that has run its course against the backdrop of a global pandemic and unrelenting political tumult. I am not sure how this book would have come to fruition
without his skilled editorial insight. The anonymous reviewers were also invaluable
to the process and helped me add more nuances and context that at times reshaped
arguments as well as the trajectory of this book. Dylan White and Jay Mazzocchi at
the University of North Carolina Press also provided much-needed assistance with
the publishing process. And special thanks to Stephen Barichko, Margaretta Yarbor-
ough, and Michelle Witkowski who helped with the final editing process.

Offering love and laughter every step of the way has been my family: Matt Aharonov,
Joe Boetcher, Leslie Chiang, Vickie Fridge, Dylan Garcia, Jeff McBee, Ruth McBee,
Kelsey Merrigan, Pat Merrigan, Terri Merrigan, Haley Merrigan-Garcia, Gabriella

Villalobos, Liza Willett, and Lori Willett. My mother- and father-in-law, Mary and Roy McBee, along with my parents, Joe and Ellen Willett, may not always remember, but they have expressed much amusement with my topic of study over the years, and I always think of them living through the eras that I so often write about. This book would not have been written if those so close to me had not been willing to listen to me discuss my research at length. This is especially true when it comes to my sister, Cynthia Willett, whose own work in philosophy and humor studies has helped sort out so much of my theoretical take and tone on the male chauvinist pig. Her commitment to my success and happiness is matched only by that of my husband and fellow historian, Randy McBee, who has read every page of this book in almost all of its manifestations. Along with the reflections and revelry of our children, Dylan McBee and Chloe Willett, on this topic, your passion for me and my research has influenced every aspect of this book whether you wanted it to or not. And guess what? This time, it is really done.

Notes

Introduction

1. Roxanne Roberts, "I Sat Next to Donald Trump at the Infamous 2011 White House Correspondents' Dinner," *Washington Post*, April 28, 2016, https://www .washingtonpost.com/lifestyle/style/i-sat-next-to-donald-trump-at-the-infamous -2011-white-house-correspondents-dinner/2016/04/27/5cf46b74-0bea-11e6-8ab8 -9ad050f76d7d_story.html; Andrew Rafferty, "That Time When Barack Obama and Seth Meyers Roasted Donald Trump," NBC News, April 29, 2016, https://www.nbcnews .com/storyline/white-house-correspondents-dinner/time-when-barack-obama -seth-meyers-roasted-donald-trump-n565081; Jethro Nededog, "Seth Meyers: 'I Am the Reason' Trump Became President," Business Insider, February 9, 2017, https://www .businessinsider.com/seth-meyers-responsible-for-president-donald-trump-fallon -2017-2; Julia Ioffe, "Seth Meyers Has 'Very Fond' Memories of Roasting Trump," *Atlantic*, June 2018, https://www.theatlantic.com/magazine/archive/2018/06/seth-meyers -trump-oprah/559118/.

2. For a discussion of how historians complicate the use of the wave metaphor in understanding feminism, see Nancy A. Hewitt, introduction to Hewitt, *No Permanent Waves*, 1–12.

3. Whether he was called a male chauvinist or a male chauvinist *pig* (and the sources suggest that these phrases were used interchangeably), adding "pig" to the end of the epithet implied whiteness. For a discussion of the white police force as pigs, see Estes, *I Am a Man!*, 160. For more on the Black Panthers and police confrontations, see Murch, *Living for the City*; Joshua Bloom and Martin, *Black against Empire*; and Jones, *Black Panther Party*. In contrast to the use of *chauvinism*, see the discussions of how race infused understanding of machismo in Domínguez-Ruvalcaba, *Modernity and the Nation*; Ray González, *Muy Macho*; and Mirandé, *Hombres y Machos*.

4. The expression started its ascendency in 1967 and peaked in 1976–77, but never completely faded. See "Male Chauvinist Pig," Google Books Ngram Viewer, accessed August 8, 2020, https://books.google.com/ngrams/graph?content=Male+Chauvinist+ Pig&year_start=1800&year_end=2000&corpus=15&smoothing=3&share=&direct_url =t1%3B%2CMale%20Chauvinist%20Pig%3B%2Cco.

5. On the image of the humorless conservatives, see Dagnes, *Conservative Walks into a Bar*. The serious tone of modern conservatives reflects not only the centrality of religion in the movement but also the degree to which so many fears turned on the rhetoric of protecting children. See, for example, Gillian Frank, "'Civil Rights of Parents'"; and McGirr, *Suburban Warriors*.

6. See Willett and Willett, *Uproarious*, 21–45. On the perpetuation of the humorless feminists, we must turn to the significance of right-wing satirist Rush Limbaugh.

For a discussion of Rush Limbaugh's significance to modern conservatism, see Kornacki, *Red and The Blue*.

7. *Political correctness* as a term began to enter into American discourse in the late 1980s with the publication of philosopher Allan Bloom's 1987 *The Closing of the American Mind*. The phrase peaked in the mid-1990s. See "Political Correctness," Google Books Ngram Viewer, accessed August 8, 2020, https://books.google.com/ngrams/graph?content=Political+Correctness&year_start=1800&corpus=26&smoothing=3&year_end=2019&direct_url=t1%3B%2CPolitical%20Correctness%3B%2Cco#t1%3B%2CPolitical%20Correctness%3B%2Cco.

8. For a broad theoretical understanding of humor's more radical potential, see Willett and Willett, *Uproarious*.

9. On controversies surrounding rape jokes, see Lindy West, "How to Make a Rape Joke," *Jezebel*, July 12, 2012, http://jezebel.com/5925186/how-to-make-a-rape-joke; and Green and Day, "Asking for It."

10. For the larger context of the 2005 *Access Hollywood* tape in which Trump boasts that "when you're a star," "you can do anything to women," even "grab 'em by the pussy," see "Transcript: Donald Trump's Taped Comments about Women," *New York Times* (hereafter *NYT*), October 8, 2016, https://www.nytimes.com/2016/10/08/us/donald-trump-tape-transcript.html.

11. Paul Solotaroff, "Trump Seriously: On the Trail with the GOP's Tough Guy," *Rolling Stone*, September 9, 2015, http://www.rollingstone.com/politics/news/trump-seriously-20150909; Kray, Carroll, and Mandell, *Nasty Women and Bad Hombres*.

12. Zaretsky, *No Direction Home*; McGirr, *Suburban Warriors*; Cowie, "Enigma of Working-Class Conservatism"; Cowie, *Stayin' Alive*; Self, *All in the Family*.

13. Dagnes, *Conservative Walks into a Bar*; Webber, *Joke Is on Us*.

14. Hill Collins and Bilge, *Intersectionality*, 2. On intersectionality, see also Crenshaw, "Mapping the Margins"; and Hill Collins, *Black Feminist Thought*.

15. Willett and Willett, *Uproarious*, esp. chap. 5.

16. Zoglin, *Comedy at the Edge*, chap. 1, esp. 4. Zoglin describes Bruce and other stand-up comics as forgotten icons of 1960s and 70s social and cultural revolution.

17. Zoglin, chap. 2; Richard Zoglin, "How George Carlin Changed Comedy," *Time*, June 23, 2008, http://content.time.com/time/arts/article/0,8599,1817192,00.html.

18. Haggins, *Laughing Mad*; Zoglin, *Comedy at the Edge*, chap. 3.

19. Zoglin, *Comedy at the Edge*.

20. A good example of the political influence of *Saturday Night Live* is Tina Fey's 2008 impersonation of vice-presidential candidate Sarah Palin. See Marx, Sienkiewicz, and Becker, *Saturday Night Live*. *The Smothers Brothers Comedy Hour* was preceded by *The Smothers Brothers Show* (1965–1966). See Eskridge, *Rube Tube*, 146. For more on the history of these shows, see Nesteroff, *Comedians*, chap. 9; and Krefting, *All Joking Aside*, chap. 2.

21. Wickberg, *Senses of Humor*, chap. 5, esp. 197.

22. For examples of politicians who appeared on *Saturday Night Live*, see Marx, Sienkiewicz, and Becker, *Saturday Night Live*. During the 2019 presidential primary, Democrat Kirsten Gillibrand, for example, formally announced she was running for

president during an interview with comedian Stephen Colbert. Jon Campbell, "Kirsten Gillibrand Says She's Running for President in 2020," *Democrat and Chronicle*, January 15, 2019, https://www.democratandchronicle.com/story/news/politics/albany/2019/01/15/kirsten-gillibrand-2020-presidential-run-colbert/2580042002/.

23. Zoglin, *Comedy at the Edge*, 183.

24. On why women and feminists have struggled to be seen as funny, see Yael Cohen, *We Killed*; Mizejewski, *Pretty/Funny*; Mizejewski and Sturtevant, *Hysterical!*; Krefting, *All Joking Aside*; and Douglas, *Where the Girls Are*, 226. See also Douglas, *Enlightened Sexism*; Rowe, *Unruly Woman*; Willett and Willett, *Uproarious*; Barreca, *They Used to Call Me*; Auslander, "'Brought to You by Fem-Rage,'" 316; and Gail Finney, "Introduction: Unity in Difference?," in Finney, *Look Who's Laughing*, 11.

25. Leng, "When Politics Were Fun." Leng reveals a rich legacy of feminist humor in the 1970s but the comic stage was dominated by men.

26. Christopher Hitchens, "Why Women Aren't Funny," *Vanity Fair*, January 2007, https://www.vanityfair.com/culture/2007/01/hitchens200701/. For a discussion of Hitchens's cultural biases, see Mizejewski, *Pretty/Funny*, introduction.

27. Douglas, *Where the Girls Are*, 165. See also Douglas, *Enlightened Sexism*.

28. Dow, *Watching Women's Liberation*, 4; Dow, *Prime-Time Feminism*; Bradley, *Mass Media*.

29. For discussions of how women have long relied on a position as moral arbiter to carve out their own niche in the world of politics, see, for example, Alice Echols, who argues that "the almost sacrosanct position accorded the family in much early feminist literature is understandable, given women's economic dependence upon men and the absence of reliable contraception, and the centrality of motherhood to women's lives." Echols, *Daring to Be Bad*, 13. On working-class feminism, see Stansell, *City of Women*; Gabin, *Feminism in the Labor Movement*; Cobble, *Other Women's Movement*; Enstad, *Ladies of Labor*; Freedman, *No Turning Back*; and Rosen, *World Split Open*. For conservative and religion-infused understandings of women's role as moral arbiter, see Critchlow, *Phyllis Schlafly*; Ginzberg, *Women and the Work*; Kerber, *Women of the Republic*; and Norton, *Liberty's Daughters*.

30. Hewitt, introduction to Hewitt, *No Permanent Waves*, 1–12.

31. Clinton as quoted in Barreca, *They Used to Call Me*, 178.

32. The Miss America protest featured signs such as "Welcome to the Miss America Cattle Auction" and a "Freedom Trash Can," which was proudly displayed as a place to throw out sexist consumer goods like *Playboy* magazine. For more discussion of this protest and other pranks, see Douglas, *Where the Girls Are*, chap. 7, esp. 139–40. For more on WITCH, see McLeod, *Pranksters*, 14, 146–48. Also see Gilmore, *Groundswell*, 22; and Katrina Vanden Heuvel, "Radical Cheerleaders," *Nation*, May 23, 2003, https://www.thenation.com/article/radical-cheerleaders/.

33. Cobble, Gordon, and Henry, *Feminism Unfinished*. See also Bow, *Asian American Feminisms*; Bradley, *Mass Media*; Echols, *Daring to Be Bad*; Evans, *Personal Politics*; Freedman, *No Turning Back*; García, *Chicana Feminist Thought*; Hull, Bell-Scott, and Smith, *All the Women Are White*; and Rosen, *World Split Open*.

34. Rowe, *The Unruly Woman*; Mizejewski, *Pretty/Funny*; Finley, "Black Women's Satire"; Finley, "Raunch and Redress"; Green and Day, "Asking for It"; Haggins, *Laughing*

Mad; Krefting, *All Joking Aside*; Leng, "When Politics Were Fun"; Pérez and Greene, "Debating Rape Jokes"; Hennefeld, *Specters of Slapstick*; Warner, *Acts of Gaiety*.

35. Willett and Willett, *Uproarious*.

36. Ware, *Game, Set, Match*.

37. The male chauvinist pig shared many traits with the playboy, who, along with Hugh Hefner, has been richly studied. See ,for example, Ehrenreich, *Hearts of Men*; Pitzulo, *Bachelors and Bunnies*; and Fraterrigo, *Playboy*.

38. Inspiration on this topic came from a rich array of material located in the Peter Tamony Collection, 1890–1985. See, for example, Novella O'Hara, "Question Man: Are You a Male Chauvinist Pig?," *San Francisco Chronicle*, April 8, 1971, "Male Chauvinist," Tamony Collection, State Historical Society of Missouri, University of Missouri–Columbia.

39. See Allan Bloom, *Closing of the American Mind*. For more on the rise of modern conservatism, see Kruse, *White Flight*; Lassiter, *Silent Majority*; Carter, *Politics of Rage*; McGirr, *Suburban Warriors*; Formisano, *Boston against Bussing*; and Dochuk, *From Bible Belt to Sunbelt*.

Chapter One

1. Bornstein, *Queer and Pleasant Danger*, 17.

2. Mansbridge and Flaster, "Male Chauvinist," 257. Also see Shapiro, "Historical Notes"; Pallavi Prasad, "The Revolutionary Origins of the Term 'Male Chauvinist Pig," *Swaddle*, October 14, 2019; and Morton Hunt, "Up against the Wall Male Chauvinist!," *Playboy*, May, 1970, 94–104, 202–9.

3. Eric Porter, "Affirming and Disaffirming Actions: Remaking Race in the 1970s," in Bailey and Farber, *America in the Seventies*, 69; and Adler, *All in the Family*.

4. Buck Wolf, "Archie Bunker's Last Stand," ABC News, February 22, 2006, https://abcnews.go.com/Entertainment/WolfFiles/story?id=93010&page=1.

5. For an overview of the show, see McCrohan, *Archie and Edith*. See also Bailey and Farber, *America in the Seventies*; Adler, *All in the Family*; and *All in the Family*, season 3, episode 4, "Gloria and the Riddle," written by Norman Lear, aired October 7, 1972, on CBS.

6. "Gloria and the Riddle."

7. "Gloria and the Riddle."

8. De Puymège, "Good Soldier Chauvin," 333–34.

9. In leftist circles, for example, most notably the Communist Party in the United States, members sought solutions to the problems of ridding its own white membership of racism and thus warned of "white chauvinism." White chauvinism was seen as emerging from the ruling class as a fascist strategy of divide and rule. But in daily practice it also implied the conscious and unconscious acceptance of a racist ideology by white workers that constantly had to be held in check. According to Mansbridge and Flaster, the Communist Party adopted Stalin's 1928 usage of the term *chauvinism* to attract the support of the Black worker and call out racists. See Mansbridge and Flaster, "The Cultural Politics of Everyday Discourse," 639-641; See also Tarrow, *Language of Contention*, 123; and Tarrow, *Strangers at the Gate*, 165–66. An Ngram search

of Google Books also reveals that the rise of the term *male chauvinist pig* in published discourse took place during the late 1960s and early 1970s. See "Male Chauvinist Pig," Google Books Ngram Viewer, accessed August 8, 2020, https://books.google.com /ngrams/graph?content=Male+Chauvinist+Pig&year_start=1800&year_end =2000&corpus=15&smoothing=3&share=&direct_url=t1%3B%2CMale%20Chauvinist%20Pig%3B%2Cc0. I thank David Roediger for a conversation pointing to the links between white chauvinism and male chauvinism in the Communist Party. As Roediger pointed out, the experience of Black women who encountered the heavy weight of gendered-infused racism that often made them invisible at political and social events offers another connection between the legacy of white chauvinism and calling out male chauvinists. See also Claudia Jones, "An End to the Neglect of the Problems of the Negro Woman!," in Guy-Sheftall, *Words of Fire*, 116–18; and Hurewitz, *Bohemian Los Angeles*, 221.

10. Fred Shapiro's investigation of the roots of women's movement vocabulary traces *chauvinisme* back to the Napoleonic era and a soldier named Nicolas Chauvin, who was mocked for his "spectacular adoration of the Emperor"—hence "chauvinism" came to "signify extravagant patriotism." Shapiro, "Historical Notes," 3. Also see *Oxford English Dictionary* (2012), s.v. "male chauvinist pig."

11. In 1963 composer Jerome Moross said, "Not that I'm an ardent chauvinist, but I do have a love affair with this country." He was interviewed because his musical history of the Civil War is "in the form of a minstrel show." Quoted in "The Civil War with Tambo and Mr. Bones; Native Forms Singular Development," *NYT*, October 6, 1963, 139. In a 1965 letter to the editor about "Vietnam withdrawal," chauvinism and nationalism remain synonymous: "American prestige in the sense of chauvinist vanity would suffer a blow." Quoted in Norman K. Gottwald, "Vietnam Withdrawal," *NYT*, August 26, 1965, 32. Also see another letter to the editor, from 1966, "To Control Tourist Dollars," which reads in part, "The Administration's chauvinist 'Why Leave America?' position will simply harden into a hickish 'Why Leave Texas?,'" *NYT*, April 24, 1966, E11. Talking about George Herter, a cookbook author, who is "enthusiastic about the native foods of Minnesota," a journalist says, "Chauvinist or not, Mr. Herter has some absorbing thoughts about North America's contribution to European cuisine." Craig Claiborne, "He's Eaten Bear, but Draws the Line at Oysters from Hong Kong Harbor," *NYT*, September 29, 1966, 77. Similarly, in "News Summary and Index; the Major Events of the Day International National Metropolitan," *NYT*, November 28, 1966, 41, a journalist writes, "A Soviet Communist party attack on Peking's 'splitting' and 'chauvinist' policies were regarded as an outline of the principal charges of ideological heresy the Soviet Union will raise against Peking if a world Communist conference is held." And Joseph A. Loftus writes, "The native chauvinist says that budgets are low because of the free recreation here, particularly the lakes west of the city, the climate and the stability." Loftus, "Austin Explains Low Living Cost; Residents Tell Why Texas City Is at Bottom Sales Tax Coming," special to *New York Times*, November 5, 1967, 50.

12. According to the *Oxford English Dictionary*, in 1935 there was a reference to "male chauvinism" in the *Christian Science Monitor*. In 1940, the *New Yorker* featured author J. Mitchell's *Old House a Home* whose feminist protagonist demands equality

and calls another character a male chauvinist. *New Yorker*, April 13, 1940. The expression was relatively uncommon, however, until the late 1960s and 1970s, when it became dominant in American discourse. See *Oxford English Dictionary* (2012), s.v. "male chauvinist pig"; "Male Chauvinist Pig," Google Books Ngram Viewer.

13. Mansbridge and Flaster, "Male Chauvinist," 257. Also see Shapiro, "Historical Notes."

14. The following quotations from 1969 suggest a shift in the meaning of *chauvinism* toward the implication of sexism. "Though whites are at least ashamed of racism, most men are outspoken chauvinists and refuse even to recognize the problem." Ellen Willis, "Women, Revolution, Sexism, Etc., Etc.," *NYT*, March 2, 1969, SM6. "The discussions were a result of a statement by a speaker from the Black Panther party last night. The statement was generally considered by many delegates to be 'male chauvinist.'" John Kifner, "S.D.S. Parley Split as Panthers Score Labor Unit," *NYT*, June 21, 1969, 25. In a review of the book *The Feminized Male*, by Patricia Sexton, a journalist writes of the author, "whom I can title either 'Professor' (for the feminists) or 'Mrs.' (for the male chauvinists)." Richard R. Lingeman, "Books of the Times; (1) Male (2) Female (3) Other," *NYT*, August 12, 1969, 37.

15. Collins, *When Everything Changed*, 184–85.

16. Farber, *Age of Great Dreams*, 254. Fred R. Shapiro credits Morton Hunt for making *male chauvinist pig* a popular expression. See Shapiro, "Historical Notes," 8. For responses to Hunt's article, see, for example, Martin and Lyon, *Lesbian/Woman*, 74; and Gornick, *Woman in Sexist Society*, 171.

17. Ware, *Game, Set, Match*, 1–4.

18. Ware, 4.

19. "Was 1973 'Battle of the Sexes' Tennis Match Thrown?," NPR, August 26, 2013, https://www.npr.org/templates/story/story.php?storyId=215838779.

20. Roberts, *Necessary Spectacle*, 29.

21. "The Happy Hustler: How Bobby Runs and Talks, Talks, Talks," *Time*, September 10, 1973, 54; Ware, *Game, Set, Match*, 3; BlaoSM, "Bobby Riggs on Sixty Minutes," YouTube video, 9:59, posted July 25, 2008, http://www.youtube.com/watch?v=dxHrO8 pwSww&feature=related.

22. "The Happy Hustler: How Bobby Runs and Talks, Talks, Talks," *Time*, September 10, 1973, 54.

23. BlaoSM, "Bobby Riggs on Sixty Minutes"; spuzzlighyeartoo, "Bobby Riggs for Power Tennis Game 1970's," YouTube video, 0:30, posted November, 19, 2012; https://www.youtube.com/watch?v=dkgSv_5qK-Q&list=PLXyxFMK6LkNClIUTPoa9pQ_G9dC_MDP3V&index=38.

24. Wells Twombly, "Riggs-King Match Sheer Nonsense," *San Francisco Examiner*, September 19, 1973; Greer advocated sexual liberation as a condition for women's liberation. Rosen notes that thanks to her own "aura of aggressive sexuality," a feminist described her as a sell-out: "Here was a libber a man could like." Rosen, *World Split Open*, 154.

25. "Was 1973 'Battle of the Sexes'?"; Ware, *Game, Set, Match*.

26. Twombly, "Riggs-King Match Sheer Nonsense." See also an earlier article, Wells Twombly, "Riggs: Male Chauvinist Swine," *San Francisco Examiner*, July 13, 1973.

27. Wells Twombly, "Riggs-King Match Sheer Nonsense," *San Francisco Examiner*, September 19, 1973.

28. Bradley, *Mass Media*, 274.

29. Roberts, *Necessary Spectacle*, 119. Everyone from comedian Phyllis Diller to Bea Arthur (*Maude*, 1972–78) turned Bobby Riggs into the butt of the joke. Bob Parker, "Our World Fall 1973 Part 2," YouTube video, 10:02, posted August 19, 2009, http://www.youtube.com/watch?v=VG8Puzsx800.

30. Roberts, *Necessary Spectacle*, 119–20.

31. Ware, *Game, Set, Match*, 4.

32. Twombly, "Riggs: Male Chauvinist Swine."

33. Ware, *Game, Set, Match*, 4.

34. King, for example, is described as an angry woman despite the obvious examples of shared humor in interviews. Parker, "Our World Fall 1973."

35. IceManNYR, "Sunbeam Curling Iron Ad 1973," YouTube video, 0:29, posted December 20, 2008, http://www.youtube.com/watch?v=J3MygBj8SSs.

36. *The Odd Couple*, season 4, episode 10, "The Pig Who Came to Dinner," written by Neil Simon, aired November 16, 1973, on ABC, http://www.hulu.com/watch/630582.

37. Roberts, *Necessary Spectacle*, 121.

38. In a 1986 television show Billie Jean King is laughing it up with Bobby Riggs years after the match, but there are also excerpts from the 1970s of comedian Phyllis Diller and actress Bea Arthur, using Riggs as a punch line. The commentator also reminds the viewing audience that "the women's movement is said to not be able to take a joke." Parker, "Our World Fall 1973."

39. spuzzlighyeartoo, "Bobby Riggs for Power Tennis Game 1970's."

40. Ware, *Game, Set, Match*, 3.

41. Roberts, *Necessary Spectacle*, 1–2; Ware, *Game, Set, Match*, 1. See also Evans, *Tidal Wave*, 96–97.

42. Steve Cady, "That Happy Hustler Brings His Talkathon to Town," *NYT*, August 25, 1973, 18.

43. Ware, *Game, Set, Match*, 2.

44. Parker, "Our World Fall 1973."

45. Bradley, *Mass Media*, 277.

46. Steinem, *Outrageous Acts*, 171.

47. Steinem, 171.

48. Pallavi Prasad, "The Revolutionary Origins of the Term 'Male Chauvinist Pig,'" *Swaddle*, October 4, 2019, https://theswaddle.com/origins-male-chauvinist-pig-sexism/.

49. Kiverst, *Male Chauvinist's Cookbook*.

50. Pitzulo, *Bachelors and Bunnies*, 72.

51. Pitzulo, 72.

52. Jill Gerston, "For Chauvinist with Everything: Shop Talk," *NYT*, October 6, 1974, 66.

53. Various eBay and Pinterest sites note that the soaps were sold from 1977 to 1979. Every site that had information about these soaps had this same range of

dates. For example, see "Male Chauvinist Pig" on Pinterest, accessed November 15, 2020, https://www.pinterest.co.uk/pin/777011741933965958/ http://members.cox.net /jenglish4/animals.htm. Besides the Avon soaps, other male chauvinist pig items were easily found for sale including mugs, patches, pins and even a radio. For example, see "Male Chauvinist Pig" on Ebay, accessed November 15, 2020, https://www .google.com/search?q=ebay+male+chauvinist+pig&sxsrf=ALeKko3bO3lQHT_zmgR ratvvQJzIzQPjmw:1605460085412&source=univ&tbm=shop&tbo=u&sa=X&ved =2ahUKEwjY9t3whIXtAhUPCKwKHYM_Ba8Q1TV6BQgGEIoC&biw=1172&bih =696: Several of these items are now in the author's possession.

54. R. M. Hurley and Betty Swords, "Male Chauvinist Pig Calendar," 1974, Billy Ireland Cartoon Library and Museum.

55. "Ray Horsch: Sociopathic Villain," podcast 27, 1:41:00, Rialto Report, December 15, 2013, https://www.therialtoreport.com/2013/12/15/ray-horsch-sociopathic -villain-podcast-27/.

56. Shaun Brady, "Locally Made Classic Porn at PhilaMoca," *Metro Philly Daily Newspaper*, January 15, 2014, https://philly.metro.us/locally-made-classic-porn-at -philamoca/.

57. Andy Newman, "Al Goldstein, a Publisher Who Took the Romance Out of Sex, Dies at 77," *NYT*, December 19, 2013, https://www.nytimes.com/2013/12/20/nyregion /al-goldstein-pioneering-pornographer-dies-at-77.html; "Ray Horsch: Sociopathic Villain."

58. Benson, *Household Accounts*; Kelley, *Race Rebels*, 161–82; Peiss, *Zoot Suit*; Enstad, *Ladies of Labor*; Lizabeth Cohen, *Consumers' Republic*.

59. For an example of this iconic slogan on a protest sign, see Gilmore, *Groundswell*, cover.

60. Echols, *Daring to Be Bad*, 26.

61. Brenda Feigen Fasteau and Bonnie Lobel, "Rating the Candidates: Feminists Vote the Rascals In or Out," *Ms.*, Spring 1972, 74–82, 84.

62. Abramson, "Turning Up the Lights," 2, 3, 6.

63. FoundationINTERVIEWS, "Phil Donahue on Gloria Steinem—EMMYTVLEGENDS.ORG," YouTube video, 7:06, posted July 13, 2016, https://www.youtube.com /watch?v=T5Cuo3A-aPg.

64. Willett and Willett, *Uproarious*, 24.

65. "Male Pigs Learned It from Mom," *San Francisco Examiner*, May 11, 1974.

66. News accounts of the study circulated first in 1974 and again two years later. "The Male Chauvinist—Is It Mom's Fault?," *San Francisco Examiner*, February 9, 1976.

67. Tickner, *Spectacle of Women*; Adrienne Lafrance, "The Weird Familiarity of 100-Year-Old Feminism," *Atlantic*, October 26, 2016, https://www.theatlantic.com /technology/archive/2016/10/pepe-the-anti-suffrage-frog/505406/.

68. For a discussion of the feminist killjoy manifesto, see Ahmed, *Living a Feminist Life*.

69. For a discussion of why historians reject yet rely on the use of the concept of the second wave in understanding the women's liberation movement, see Nancy Hewitt, introduction to Hewitt, *No Permanent Waves*, 1–12.

70. Douglas, *Where the Girls Are*, 165. See also Douglas, *Enlightened Sexism*.

71. For discussions of how women have long relied on a position as moral arbiter to carve out their own niche in the world of politics, see Echols, *Daring to Be Bad*, esp. 13. On working-class feminism, see Stansell, *City of Women*; Gabin, *Feminism in the Labor Movement*; Cobble, *Other Women's Movement*; Enstad, *Ladies of Labor*; Freedman, *No Turning Back*; and Rosen, *World Split Open*. For conservative and religion-infused understandings of women's role as moral arbiter, see Critchlow, *Phyllis Schlafly*; Ginzberg, *Women and the Work*; Kerber, *Women of the Republic*; and Norton, *Liberty's Daughters*.

72. On blues singers, see Davis, *Blues Legacies*. On the use of humor in feminist movements, see Leng, "When Politics Were Fun."

73. Finley, "Black Women's Satire," 236.

74. Willett and Willett, *Uproarious*, 26.

75. Finley, "Black Women's Satire," 239.

76. Finley, 240.

77. Finley, 241.

78. Finley, 242.

79. Eric Grundhauser, "The Great Harvard Pee-In of 1973," *Atlas Obscura*, December 23, 2016, https://www.atlasobscura.com/articles/the-great-harvard-peein-of-1973.

80. Kennedy, *Color Me Flo*, 81, 132; Clara J. Bates, "The Harvard Pee-In of 1973," *Crimson*, November 1, 2018, https://www.thecrimson.com/article/2018/11/1/harvard-pee-in-1973/.

81. Echols, *Daring to Be Bad*, 12.

82. Echols, 10.

83. Zaretsky, *No Direction Home*, 15.

84. Stephanie Harrington, "Women Get the Short End of the Shtick," *NYT*, November 18, 1973, 163.

85. Naomi Weisstein, "Why Aren't We Laughing . . . Any More," *Ms.*, November 1973, 89.

86. Weisstein, 88.

87. See also Harrington, "Women Get the Short End," 163. For more on the rich history of female comedians, see, for example, Finley, "Black Women's Satire"; Finley, "Raunch and Redress"; Haggins, *Laughing Mad*; Mizejewski, *Pretty/Funny*; Cohen, *We Killed*; Reed, *Queer Cultural Work*; and Finney, "Introduction."

88. Weisstein, "Why Aren't We Laughing," 49, 50.

89. Weisstein, 49, 50.

90. Willett and Willett, *Uproarious*, chap. 1.

91. Wickberg, *Senses of Humor*.

92. Scott, *Domination*.

93. Wickberg, *Senses of Humor*, 199.

94. Wickberg argues that "Mark Twain, in fact was probably one of the first humorists in this modern sense and the American humorists of his era, with their deadpan ironic delivery which only hinted at the intelligence that lay behind it, probably did much to change the meaning of 'humorist' to its modern sense." Wickberg, *Senses of Humor*, 29.

95. Wickberg, 198, 203.

96. Wickberg, 205.

97. McLeod, *Pranksters*, 16.

98. Wickberg, *Senses of Humor*, 218, 197–98.

99. Ryan Lintelman, "In 1968, When Nixon Said 'Sock It To Me' on 'Laugh-In,' TV Was Never Quite the Same Again," *Smithsonian Magazine*, January 19, 2008, https:// www.smithsonianmag.com/smithsonian-institution/1968-when-nixon-said-sock-it -me-laugh-tv-was-never-quite-same-again-180967869/#:~:text=According%20to%20 television%20historian%20Hal,without%20sounding%20angry%20or%20offended.

100. Dagnes, *Conservative Walks into a Bar*, 108–9.

101. Schulman, *Seventies*, xvi.

102. Reed, *Queer Cultural Work*; Cohen, *We Killed*, 110, 113. Also see "50 Greatest 'Saturday Night Live' Sketches of All Time," *Rolling Stone*, February 3, 2014, http:// www.rollingstone.com/tv/pictures/50-greatest-saturday-night-live-sketches-of-all -time-20140203/point-counterpoint-0207143.

103. Willett, *Irony*, chap. 4.

104. "JUST DESSERT," *Ellensburg (WA) Daily Record*, September 24, 1973, accessed November, 29, 2020, http://news.google.com/newspapers?nid=860&dat=19730924&id =WXVUAAAAIBAJ&sjid=Ao8DAAAAIBAJ&pg=4784,4755879.

105. Allan Sutherland, "John Callahan Obituary," *Guardian*, August 17, 2010, https://www.theguardian.com/artanddesign/2010/aug/17/john-callahan-obituary. For more on the life of cartoonist John Callahan, see Bruce Weber, "John Callahan, Cartoonist, Dies at 59," *NYT*, July 28, 2010, http://www.nytimes.com/2010/07/28/arts /design/28callahan.html?_r=0.

106. Jennifer L. Pozner, "Louis C.K. on Daniel Tosh's Rape Joke: Are Comedy and Feminism Enemies?," Daily Beast, July 18, 2012, http://www.thedailybeast.com /articles/2012/07/18/daniel-tosh-rape-joke-are-comedy-and-feminism-enemies .html.

Chapter Two

1. Molly Ivins, "Lib in Longhorn Country," *NYT*, October 18, 1971, 37.

2. For a discussion of the police as pigs, see Estes, *I Am a Man!*, 160. For more on the Black Panthers and police confrontations, see Murch, *Living for the City*; Joshua Bloom and Martin, *Black against Empire*; and Jones, *Black Panther Party*.

3. Orwell, *Animal Farm*, 134; Pallavi Prasad, "The Revolutionary Origins of the Term 'Male Chauvinist Pig,'" *Swaddle*, October 4, 2019, https://theswaddle.com/origins -male-chauvinist-pig-sexism/.

4. Out of place and hence dirty could easily turn on gender and sex. Women who were considered unclean or unappealing were deemed pigs. See Harris, *Good to Eat*, chap. 4, esp. 71. See also Douglas, *Purity and Danger*, 44. For more on the long history of the pig's relationship to human survival, see Essig, *Lesser Beasts*.

5. Tackett, *When the King Took Flight*, 104. Other animal metaphors used to describe the former queen include an "impure insect," a "tigress," a "she-monkey" a "she-wolf," and a "ferocious panther." See Hunt, "Many Bodies of Marie-Antoinette," 129–30.

6. Prasad, "Revolutionary Origins." See also Mathew J. Mancini, "Pig Law," *Mississippi Encyclopedia*, July 11, 2017, https://mississippiencyclopedia.org/entries/pig-law/.

7. *Oxford English Dictionary* (2012), s.v. "pig"; Shapiro, "Historical Notes," 3, 4; Daniel W. Gade, "II.G.13. Hogs," in *The Cambridge World History of Food*, vol. 2, ed. Kenneth F. Kiple and Kriemhild Coneè Ornelas, http://www.cambridge.org/us/books/kiple/hogs.htm.

8. Marable, *Race, Reform, and Rebellion*.

9. Estes, *I Am a Man!*, 160.

10. "Parting Shots," *Life*, November 14, 1969, 96.

11. For more on the Panthers and police confrontations, see Murch, *Living for the City*; Joshua Bloom and Martin, *Black against Empire*; Major, *Panther Is a Black Cat*; Jones, *Black Panther Party*; Hilliard, *Huey*; and Newton, *Revolutionary Suicide*.

12. "Pigasus the Immortal," *Porkopolis: Considering the Pig, a Single-Minded Bestiary* (blog), September 27, 2008, http://www.porkopolis.org/2008/pigasus/.

13. "SDS Picks Chicago for Its Convention," *Washington Post*, June 12, 1969.

14. See Norm Van Ness, "'Occupy' Protesters Taunt Cops with Donut on String, 'Here Piggy, Piggy," NBC 24 News, March 23, 2012, https://nbc24.com/news/local/occupy-protesters-taunt-cops-with-donut-on-string-here-piggy-piggy; Louise Boyle and Daniel Bates, "'What's His Name? Pig': Ferguson Police Chief Hit with Abuse from Crowd after Refusing to Name Officer Who Shot Michael Brown as Highway Patrol Are Called in Over Fears of ANOTHER Night of Violence," *Daily Mail*, August 14, 2014, http://www.dailymail.co.uk/news/article-2725108/Whats-Pig-Ferguson-police-chief-hit-abuse-crowd-refusing-officer-shot-Michael-Brown-Highway-Patrol-called-fears-ANOTHER-night-violence.html; "Hundreds Demand Justice in Minneapolis after Police Killing of George Floyd," *Guardian*, May 26, 2020, https://www.theguardian.com/us-news/2020/may/26/george-floyd-killing-minneapolis-protest-police; and "Cities on Edge as Fires Burn Near White House," *NYT*, May 31, 2020, https://www.nytimes.com/2020/05/31/us/george-floyd-protests-live-updates.html.

15. Zaretsky, *No Direction Home*, 16; Friedan, *Feminine Mystique*; Shapiro, "Historical Notes," 3, 4; Prasad, "Revolutionary Origins."

16. Bodnar, *Blue-Collar Hollywood*, 184–85.

17. Cahones, *Women's Lip*, 5.

18. According to the Google Books Ngram Viewer, the expression *male chauvinist pig* peaked in 1977. See "Male Chauvinist Pig," Google Books Ngram Viewer, accessed August 8, 2020, https://books.google.com/ngrams/graph?content=male+chauvinist+pig&year_start=1800&year_end=2008&corpus=15&smoothing=3&share=&direct_url=t1%3B%2Cmale%20chauvinist%20pig%3B%2Cc0.

19. Steinem, *Outrageous Acts*, 171. Steinem was relieved that the use of the derogatory insult was part of "a period that has mercifully passed."

20. Helen H. King, "The Black Woman and Women's Lib," *Ebony*, March 1971, 68–71, 74–76, esp. 69.

21. Lott, *Love and Theft*.

22. King, "Black Woman and Women's Lib,"69.

23. King, 69.

24. Blee, *Women in the Klan*.

25. Poet Gwendolyn Brooks charged that "black people have always had to fight for black freedom and this movement won't be any different." Similarly, she quoted writer Carolyn Rogers, who declared that the real problem was "American Apartheid." Feminism not only seemed suspect given the recent violence visited upon Black protesters but also appeared as a threat to the family that was inextricably bound to Black nationalism. "Actress-educator Amina Baraka is a black nationalist who exalts family life, says women's lib is 'part of America's destruction.'" Brooks quoted in King, "Black Woman and Women's Lib," 75.

26. Becky Thompson, "Multiracial Feminism: Recasting the Chronology of Second Wave Feminism," in Hewitt, *No Permanent Waves*, 46.

27. Marcia Ann Gillespie quoted in "About Women," *Los Angeles Times*, May 12, 1974.

28. King, "Black Woman and Women's Lib," 69. In tune with the largely white and bourgeois media coverage, King, like Morton Hunt, also gravitated toward titillating stories of radical organizations like SCUM (Society for Cutting Up Men) and WITCH (Women's International Terrorist Conspiracy from Hell), "whose Karate trained members called themselves the first guerrilla fighters against the oppression of women."

29. Chisholm, *Unbought and Unbossed*.

30. Louis Martin, "Mrs. Chisholm Education America," *Chicago Defender*, June 1972, 3.

31. The absence of such a popular linguistic slur, however, tilted a media-hyped battle of the sexes to such a degree that it appeared not only exclusively white but also trivial. In response to this motif, scholars have spent considerable effort to reveal that the women's liberation movement was not monolithically white or middle class. Myra Marx Ferree and Beth B. Hess, for example, argue that the idea that feminism did not appeal to Black women is just "another myth that has received much media attention." Rather than assuming middle-class women were the only feminists, they find that, "in fact, African-American women have always held more favorable views toward the movement than have their white sisters: 60 percent versus 37 percent in 1970; 77 percent versus 65 percent in 1980; and 85 percent versus 64 percent in 1989." Ferree and Hess, *Controversy and Coalition*, 89. In her literary collection *Words of Fire*, Beverly Guy-Sheftall uses the centuries of Black women's writing that eloquently "documents the emergence of what we now call contemporary black feminism, which is traceable in large part to the frustrations of black women in the male-dominant Civil Rights and black nationalist movements of the sixties." It connects, however, to "the dilemmas black women faced with white women more committed to the eradication of sexism than they were with ending racism." Beverly Guy-Sheftall, preface to Guy-Sheftall, *Words of Fire*, xvi.

32. Nancy A. Hewitt, introduction to Hewitt, *No Permanent Waves*, 4.

33. Hewitt, 8. In this search for "different lengths and frequencies," the larger cultural terrain of music brings much into view.

34. Wallace, *Black Macho*, 31–32. For example, "'You big fat racist pig, draw your gun!' The cop made no move. 'Draw it you cowardly dog!' Huey pumped a round into the chamber of a shotgun." Wallace, 74.

35. Shakur, *Assata*, 222. In 1973 Assata was involved in a controversial shootout on the New Jersey Turnpike, which led to her arrest and notoriety. Her solidarity with the Panthers is unquestionable. Her mysterious prison escape suggests that she had a community of support and her continued exiled life in Cuba turns in part on her identification with the Panthers.

36. Estes, *I Am a Man!*, 171.

37. Estes, 171.

38. Estes, 165.

39. Wallace, *Black Macho*; Jamilah Lemieux, "Black Feminism, Named and Celebrated," *New Republic*, June 1, 2015, https://newrepublic.com/article/121925/black-feminism-named-and-celebrated; Gabby Bess, "Revisiting Michelle Wallace's Essential Black Feminist Text 'Black Macho," *Vice*, July 22, 2015, https://www.vice.com/en_us/article/vdxya3/revisiting-michele-wallaces-essential-black-feminist-text-black-macho.

40. Conrad Manley, "The Machismo Menace: New Target for the Comic Book Crusade," *San Francisco Chronicle*, August 22, 1971. See also Linda Wolfe, "The Machismo Mystique," *New York Magazine*, August 7, 1972.

41. On the history of the greaser, machismo, and other Latino stereotypes, see, for example, Gordon, *Great Arizona Orphan Abduction*; and De León, *They Called Them Greasers*.

42. Nevins, *Operation Gatekeeper*, 61–64, 112–13. See also Perea, *Immigrants Out!*, 13-43.

43. In Spears, *Slang and Euphemism*, *macho* is defined as "masculine; hypermasculine; pertaining to strongly assertive and even foolhardy displays of masculine courage, physique, or tastes." See also Partridge, *Dictionary of Slang*; and Burchfield, *Supplement to the Oxford English Dictionary*.

44. Biskind and Ehrenreich, "Machismo"; Paredes, "United States, Mexico, and Machismo"; Chudakoff, *Age of the Bachelor*; Kimmel, *Manhood in America*; Beth Bailey, "She 'Can Bring Home the Bacon': Negotiating Gender in the 1970s," in Bailey and Farber, *America in the Seventies*; Rosen, *World Split Open*. On working-class masculinity, see also Freeman, "Hardhats"; and Nystrom, *Hard Hats*.

45. Steve Ditlea, "In Defense of Macho," *Mademoiselle*, July 1974, 11–12.

46. Novella O'Hara, "Do Certain Types Rub You the Wrong Way?," Question Man, *San Francisco Chronicle*, May 2, 1974.

47. "Is Your Hairdresser Macho," Question Man, *San Francisco Chronicle*, April 28, 1975.

48. "Mas-cu-line 1: Mean 2: Pungent 3: Fair?," *San Francisco Chronicle*, January 18, 1973.

49. Novella O'Hara, "What Is a Male Chauvinist?," Question Man, *San Francisco Chronicle*, November 24, 1971.

50. Sonia Lopez, interview by Jose Perez, reel-to-reel audio tape, 1973, in "Raising Our Voices: The History of San Diego and San Diego in Sound," San Diego State University, accessed May 16, 2020, http://library.sdsu.edu/scua/raising-our-voices/san-diego-history/chicano.

51. Hernández-Avila, "In Praise of Insubordination," 191–92.

52. Brenda Feigen Fasteau and Bonnie Lobel, "Rating the Candidates: Feminists Vote the Rascals In or Out," *Ms.*, Spring 1972, 74–82, 84.

53. Pérez quoted in Hernández-Avila, "In Praise of Insubordination," 191.

54. "SNL 'Quien Es Mas Macho?' Sketch from 2/17/19 Hosted by Ricky Nelson," *Even in the Future Nothing Works!* (blog), October 23, 2013, http://norewardisworththis .tumblr.com/post/64845798933/snl-quien-es-mas-macho-sketch-from-21719. See also the SNL Archives, accessed May 16, 2020, http://snl.jt.org/.

55. Ken Emerson, "The Village People: America's Male Ideal?," *Rolling Stone*, October 5, 1978, 26–28.

56. Gayle Rubin, "Valley of the Kings," 340–44. See also Primm, "American Bad-Ass." The lyrics to "Macho Man" can be found at https://www.songfacts.com/lyrics /the-village-people/macho-man.

57. Emerson, "Village People."

58. McBee, Born To Be Wild, 200.

59. Chauncey, *Gay New York*, 358.

60. Echols, *Hot Stuff*, 125.

61. Andrew Holleran's *Dancer from the Dance* quoted in Echols, *Hot Stuff*, 130.

62. Echols, 132.

63. Echols, xxv.

64. For more on how "the Village People became ambassadors of gay macho to the rest of the world," see Echols, *Hot Stuff*, chap. 4, especially 122.

65. John Badham, dir., *Saturday Night Fever* (1977).

66. For more on *Saturday Night Fever*, see Echols, *Hot Stuff*, chap. 5.

67. Randy McBee, conversation with the author, May 1, 2016.

68. Hughes, "In the Empire,"147.

69. "Are You Macho?," Question Man, *San Francisco Chronicle*, May 4, 1974.

70. On machismo as a world of men, see also "In Search of Masculinity: Symposium," *Harper's*, July 1975, 3–10.

71. Charles McCabe, "In Praise of Macho," *San Francisco Chronicle*, August 13, 1975.

72. McCabe.

73. McCabe.

Chapter Three

1. Novella O'Hara, "Are You a Male Chauvinist Pig?," Question Man, *San Francisco Chronicle*, April 8, 1971.

2. Steve Rubenstein, "Novella-O' Hara—'Question Man,'" *SFGate*, March 12, 1997, http://www.sfgate.com/news/article/Novella-O-Hara-Question-Man-2849531.php.

3. O'Hara, "Are You a Male Chauvinist Pig?"

4. For example, men's attempts to enter women's work could pull the rug out from normative gender scripts even as they reasserted rigid notions of male expertise or engendered radical change. Phil Tiemeyer argues that after the sex clause was added to Title VII in 1964, "queer-baiting became a significant preoccupation of the bureau-

crats and lawyers left to interpret the new law after it passed. These considerations took the form of hypothesizing about supposedly absurd gender anomalies who might seek to enter the workplace because of Title VII, including male nurses, female dog catchers, and male Playboy bunnies." Tiemeyer, *Plane Queer*, 82.

5. Dow, *Watching Women's Liberation*, 160.

6. Emphasis in the original. Dow, 166.

7. Meyerowitz, *How Sex Changed*.

8. Cowie, *Stayin' Alive*, 9–10, 48; Cowie and Boehm, "Dead Man's Town."

9. Cowie, *Stayin' Alive*, 2–3.

10. Harrington and Scott-Heron both quoted in Cowie, *Stayin' Alive*, 3; See also Cowie and Boehm, "Dead Man's Town."

11. O'Hara, "Are You a Male Chauvinist Pig?"

12. For a more complex understanding of cultural feminism, see Taylor and Rupp, "Women's Culture."

13. O'Hara, "Are You a Male Chauvinist Pig?"

14. O'Hara.

15. O'Hara.

16. Collins, *When Everything Changed*, 158.

17. O'Hara, "Are You a Male Chauvinist Pig?"

18. Novella O'Hara, "What Is a Male Chauvinist?," Question Man, *San Francisco Chronicle*, November 24, 1971.

19. O'Hara.

20. Novella O'Hara, "Is Your Husband a Male Chauvinist?," Question Man, *San Francisco Chronicle*, December 5, 1971.

21. O'Hara.

22. Collins, *When Everything Changed*, 206–7.

23. O'Hara, "Is Your Husband a Male Chauvinist?"

24. Collins, *When Everything Changed*, 216.

25. Collins, 215.

26. Hewlett quoted in Critchlow, *Phyllis Schlafly*, 214.

27. Critchlow, 222–23.

28. Quoted in Collins, *When Everything Changed*, 225.

29. Collins, 226.

30. For example, even those who supported the ERA were often troubled by the thought of women serving in the military. In the 1970s and against the backdrop of the waning Vietnam War, only 20 percent of Americans supported the concept of women being drafted. Collins, *When Everything Changed*, 224–25. For nuanced discussions of the complicated ways in which equality in the workplace has been understood, see, for example, Tiemeyer, *Plane Queer*; and Turk, *Equality on Trial*.

31. O'Hara, "Is Your Husband a Male Chauvinist?"

32. Schlafly quoted in Collins, *When Everything Changed*, 223.

33. Novella O'Hara, "Is a Man a Chauvinist If He Offers a Woman a Seat on the Bus?," Question Man, *San Francisco Chronicle*, March 14, 1972.

34. O'Hara.

35. Dow, *Watching Women's Liberation*, 200.

36. Joyce Brothers, "Quiz: Are You a Male Chauvinist?," *San Francisco Examiner and Chronicle*, June 9, 1974, 9; Kathleen Neuer, "Happy St. Valentine's Day! The Male Chauvinist Pig Test," *NYT*, February 13, 1972, Sunday Magazine, 21.

37. Brothers, "Quiz."

38. Brothers.

39. Farrell, *Liberated Man*, xi–xxi.

40. Farrell quoted in Faludi, *Backlash*, 302–3.

41. Faludi, 303.

42. Fraterrigo, *Playboy*, 183.

43. Farrell, *Liberated Man*, xi–xxi.

44. Farrell, xi–xxi.

45. Farrell, 368.

46. Alan Alda, "Men: What Every Woman Should Know about Men," *Ms.*, October 1975, 15–16.

47. Emphasis original. Alda, 15–16.

48. Mildred Hamilton, "Male Chauvinism: He Sees Its End," *San Francisco Examiner*, May 30, 1973, 23; Korda, *Male Chauvinism!*

49. Korda, *Male Chauvinism!*, 162.

50. Korda, 163–64.

51. Reilly, *Male Chauvinist Pig!*, 62.

52. James, *Assholes*, 5, 93.

53. James, 4.

54. One of the reasons the chauvinist pig is so easy to dismiss as a static figure is that his actions and attitudes often make it impossible to distinguish political consciousness from the typical condescension associated with any asshole. Indeed, the male chauvinist pig had many of these same characteristics, and thus it seems the asshole in the 1970s became a political figure staunchly opposed to feminism. For James, the asshole, however, is a fixed identity, not a fleeting moment of misconduct. James, 106–7.

55. James, 10. The asshole, he argues, is "a stable trait of character, or type of person—a vice rather than a particular act, mere lapse in conduct, or brief phase of life." According to James, a "single courageous or magnanimous act does not make for a courageous or magnanimous person." Which is why the male chauvinist pig, perhaps, so often seemed unredeemable.

56. James, 11, 10, 16.

57. For James the asshole is not "the bottom of the moral barrel." James, 11. For example, he turns to Jean Jacques Rousseau, who provided the moral theory that informed James's philosophical stance but, according to James, "was unfortunately quite an asshole himself, or maybe something worse." Rousseau, James notes, continued to engage in illicit affairs, but what made him perhaps worse than a typical asshole was "his repeatedly fathering children with Thérèse Lavasseur then summarily sending them away to an orphanage." James, 4n5.

58. James, 10–11.

59. Hamilton, "Male Chauvinism."

60. Michael Korda, "Male Chauvinism in the Office: An Hour-by-Hour Report," *New York Magazine,* January 22, 1973, 29–31, 34–35 (quotes from 35).

61. See "Female Chauvinist," Google Books Ngram Viewer, accessed August 11, 2020, https://books.google.com/ngrams/graph?content=Female+Chauvinist&year _start=1800&year_end=2000&corpus=15&smoothing=3&share=&direct_url =t1%3B%2CFemale%20Chauvinist%3B%2Cco.

62. Levy's study was not focused on the genealogy of the figure featured in her book's title, but rather on a younger generation of women who she argues embrace old-school male chauvinist pig antics and "treat women like a piece of meat." She sees a generation of feminists who have taken their cues from *Penthouse Forum* instead of *Ms.* magazine and a contemporary female chauvinist pig who mistook sexual hedonism for feminist progress and suffers from the old, familiar trope of false consciousness that she is determined to root out. By calling out a younger generation of women who she feels have gone astray as female chauvinist pigs, Levy reveals how a heterosexual prowess has defined so much of the male pig's swagger since the 1970s. Levy, *Female Chauvinist Pigs.*

63. Irene Pines, "Test Fails to Uncover 'True Chauvinist Pig,'" letter to the editor, *Miami News,* August 9, 1972, 14A.

64. Anne Roiphe, "Confessions of a Female Chauvinist Sow," *New York,* October 30, 1972.

65. Dow, *Watching Women's Liberation,* 7.

66. Ehrenreich, *Hearts of Men,* 115.

67. Betty Friedan, "Beyond Women's Liberation," *McCalls,* August, 1972, 82-83,134, 136. Deirdre Carmody, "Feminists Scored By Betty Friedan," *NYT,* July 19, 1972, 43.

68. Dunbar quoted in Bradley, *Mass Media,* 85.

69. By 1971 Steinem had cofounded the National Women's Political Caucus and begun to appear on national news. Dow, *Watching Women's Liberation,* 184, 188.

70. Friedan, "Beyond Women's Liberation;" See also Dee Wedemeyer, "Betty Friedan: Bitter Female Backlash Hits Woman's Lib Champ," *Robesonian* (Lumberton, NC), July 26, 1972, 16, http://news.google.com/newspapers?id=butVAAAAIBAJ&sjid =ooANAAAAIBAJ&pg=7276,2315626&hl=en; and "Betty Friedan Slams 'Female Chauvinists,'" *Daytona Beach Morning Journal,* July 19, 1972, 24, http://news.google.com /newspapers?nid=1879&dat=19720719&id=Pk8fAAAAIBAJ&sjid=r9EEAAAAIBAJ&pg =858,1226761.

71. Bradley, *Mass Media,* 85.

72. See Wedemeyer, "Betty Friedan," 16. For more on Friedan, see Horowitz, *Betty Friedan*; and Coontz, *Strange Stirring.*

73. Douglas, *Where the Girls Are,* 226, 221, 223.

74. Novella O'Hara, "Are You a Female Chauvinist?," Question Man, *San Francisco Chronicle,* November 21, 1973.

75. O'Hara.

76. O'Hara.

77. Dow, *Watching Women's Liberation,* 189.

78. O'Hara, "Are You a Female Chauvinist?"

79. O'Hara.

80. O'Hara.

81. Halley, *Split Decisions*, 9.

Chapter Four

1. Archy L, "Lenny Bruce Hugh Hefner Playboy's Penthouse 1959," YouTube video, 22:57, posted December 21, 2016, https://www.youtube.com/watch?v=3G1F8m363Uw.

2. Archy L.

3. For more on the *Playboy* philosophy, see Ehrenreich, *Hearts of Men*; Pitzulo, *Bachelors and Bunnies*; and Fraterrigo, *Playboy*.

4. On the Sunbelt South, see Schulman, *Seventies*; Dochuk, *From Bible Belt to Sunbelt*; Durr, *Behind the Backlash*; and Lassiter, *Silent Majority*.

5. Fraterrigo, *Playboy*, 175.

6. Dow, *Watching Women's Liberation*, 30.

7. vagabondways2, "Susan Brownmiller Facing Hugh Hefner at the Dick Cavett Show, 1970," YouTube video, 10:25, posted May 3, 2015, https://www.youtube.com/watch?v=KBiFR7rgY2k. Susan Brownmiller published *Against Our Will* in 1975 and brought the discussion of rape to the forefront of the women's liberation movement and hence the nation.

8. *Playboy*, December 1953, 3.

9. "What Hugh Hefner Did for Comedy," Chortle, September 28, 2017, https://www.chortle.co.uk/features/2017/09/28/38011/what_hugh_hefner_did_for_comedy. See also Farmer, *Playboy Laughs*.

10. Nesteroff, *The Comedians*, 213.

11. Farmer, *Playboy Laughs*, 26. Hefner's friend and "second-in-charge" Victor Lownes was inspired by Burton Brown's Gaslight Club in Chicago.

12. "What Hugh Hefner Did."

13. Farmer, *Playboy Laughs*, 27.

14. Farmer, 27–28.

15. Corey Kilgannon, "A Distinguished Professor with a Ph.D. in Nonsense," *NYT*, April 14, 2008, https://www.nytimes.com/2008/04/14/nyregion/14comedian.html.

16. Farmer, *Playboy Laughs*, 29.

17. Kilgannon, "Distinguished Professor."

18. Huber, "Short History of Redneck."

19. Huber, 145, 146, 148–49.

20. Hubbs, *Rednecks*, 25–27.

21. *The Smothers Brothers Comedy Hour* was preceded by *The Smothers Brothers Show* (1965–66). Eskridge, *Rube Tube*, 146.

22. Eskridge, 152, 156, 159, 158.

23. Schulman, *Seventies*, 106–14.

24. On "redneck chic," see Schulman, 114–17.

25. Hall Needham, dir., *Smokey and the Bandit* (1977).

26. Daisy is the "sexy, tomboyish, girl-next-door." She was such an icon in her cut-offs that the short shorts she wears are still referred to as "Daisy Dukes." Eskridge, *Rube Tube*, 197.

27. For more on the television series, see Hofstede, *Dukes of Hazzard*.

28. James Bridges, dir., *Urban Cowboy* (1980).

29. Cheryl Lavin, "Star Power," *Chicago Tribune*, January 4, 2000, https://www .chicagotribune.com/news/ct-xpm-2000-01-04-0001040279-story.html; Nesteroff, *Comedians*, 256–57.

30. *Playboy after Dark* was a CBS variety show Hugh Hefner hosted in 1969–70 and was similar to an early show he hosted, *Playboy's Penthouse* (1959–60). Randal Roberts, "Hugh Hefner's 'Playboy after Dark' was in Tune with Pop Music's Eccentricities," *Los Angeles Times*, September 28, 2017, https://www.latimes.com/entertainment /music/la-et-ms-hefner-playboy-after-dark-20170928-story.html.

31. Hubbs, *Rednecks*, 14.

32. Schulman, *Seventies*, 114–16.

33. "Watch for Artie Kaplan's Sensational Album 'Confessions of a Male Chauvinist Pig' Coming Soon—and Unbelievable!," *Billboard*, November 11, 1972.

34. Nancy Elrich, "A 'Pig' Confesses," *NYT*, February 4, 1973, 132.

35. Kinky Friedman, "Get Your Biscuits in the Oven and Your Buns in the Bed," BluegrassNet, accessed August 9, 2020, https://www.bluegrassnet.com/lyrics/get-your -biscuits-in-the-oven-and-your-buns-in-the-bed#.XpypjVNKhmA.

36. Matt Powell, "The Case for Kinky Friedman," Humor in America, June 22, 2012, https://humorinamerica.wordpress.com/2012/06/22/the-case-for-kinky-fried man/; Enid Nemy, "AT HOME WITH/Kinky Friedman; Married to the Wind," *NYT*, August 31, 1995, http://www.nytimes.com/1995/08/31/garden/at-home-with-kinky -friedman-married-to-the-wind.html?scp=2&sq=%22pig%20of%20the%20year%22&st =cse. Also see Friedman's short biography as contributor for *Texas Monthly*, http:// www.texasmonthly.com/author/kinky-friedman.

37. Strub, *Perversion for Profit*, 167.

38. "Playboy Interview: Billie Jean King," *Playboy*, March 1975, 194.

39. Fraterrigo, *Playboy*, 170.

40. "What Hugh Hefner Did"; Farmer, *Playboy Laughs*, 155–57.

41. Eric Bogosian, introduction to Bruce, *How to Talk Dirty*, vii, viii.

42. Ehrenreich, *Hearts of Men*, chap. 5.

43. "50 Best Stand-Up Comics of All Time," *Rolling Stone*, February 14, 2017, https:// www.rollingstone.com/culture/culture-lists/50-best-stand-up-comics-of-all-time -126359.

44. "What Hugh Hefner Did."

45. Nesteroff, *Comedians*, 214–15.

46. "50 Best Stand Up Comics."

47. *Playboy* quickly found itself the subject of feminist protests but also presented a mixed stance on a range of feminist issues. See Fraterrigo, *Playboy*, 175–83.

48. Morton Hunt, "Up against the Wall, Male Chauvinist Pig!" *Playboy*, May 1970, 95-96; 104, 206-209. For a more in-depth discussion of Cell 16, see Echols, *Daring to Be Bad*, 158–66.

49. Hunt, "Up against the Wall, 95."

50. Hunt, 96, 102.

51. "Dear Playboy," *Playboy*, August 1970, 7–8.

52. "Dear Playboy," 7–8.

53. Reilly, *Male Chauvinist Pig!*, 90. The work of historian Gail Collins and a wealth of feminist literature, including Sara Evans's now classic *Personal Politics*, capture the same double standard women faced in the New Left and are in perfect harmony with some self-deprecating gestures from *Playboy* cartoons and editorials. Collins, *When Everything Changed*; Evans, *Personal Politics*.

54. Krefting, *All Joking Aside*, 144, 145, 146.

55. John Wasserman, "Female Comics at War with the Past," *San Francisco Chronicle*, September 11, 1972.

56. In a recent *New York Times* article, Carrie Pitzulo describes the controversy surrounding *Playboy* and feminism by noting, "'At Playboy's height of influence in the 1960s and early 1970s it was what we might consider the 1960s version of 'woke.'" She adds "'the criticism that it objectifies women, that it privileges white heterosexual men is all true. But there is this other side of *Playboy* that hasn't really been acknowledged.'" In that same article, Gloria Steinem is quoted saying, "*Playboy* wouldn't exist if women and men were equal in our society. . . . It's the gendered version of a minstrel show." Jessica Bennett, "Can Millennials Save Playboy?," *NYT*, August 3, 2019, 1, https://www.nytimes.com/2019/08/02/business/woke-playboy-mille nnials.html.

57. Betty Beale, "Kennedys Prominent on List of Male Chauvinists," *San Francisco Sunday Examiner and Chronicle*, September 10, 1972, 2.

58. Brenda Feigen Fasteau and Bonnie Lobel, "Rating the Candidates: Feminists Vote the Rascals In or Out," *Ms.*, Spring 1972, 82.

59. MacFarquhar, "Gilder Effect," 118, 112.

60. "Power and the Pen: Meet George Gilder, Author of 'Wealth and Poverty,'" *Oscala Star-Banner*, May 25, 1981, 2B, http://news.google.com/newspapers?id=CG8x AAAAIBAJ&sjid=IgYEAAAAIBAJ&pg=7037,4789057&dq=male-chauvinist-pig-of -the-year&hl=en. Also see Kimmel, *Manhood in America*, 274–75.

61. MacFarquhar, "Gilder Effect," 119.

62. MacFarquhar, 119.

63. "The Sexes: The Dangers of Being a Single Male," *Time*, December 9, 1974.

64. MacFarquhar, "Gilder Effect," 119; "Sexes."

65. Faludi, *Backlash*, 297–99.

66. MacFarquhar, "Gilder Effect," 119.

67. Gilder quoted in Moody Watten, "Overhauling the Male Role" call for men's liberation in *California Living* from the *San Francisco Sunday Examiner and Chronicle*, November 16, 1975, 8.

68. "Power and the Pen"; Kimmel, *Manhood in America*, 274–75.

69. Gilder, *Visible Man*; Roger Starr, "A Guide to Capitalism," *NYT*, February 1, 1981, http://www.nytimes.com/1981/02/01/books/a-guide-to-capitalism.html.

70. Review of *Visible Man: A True Story of Post-racist America*, by George Gilder, *Kirkus Reviews*, June 1, 1978, https://www.kirkusreviews.com/book-reviews/a/george -glider/visible-man-a-true-story-of-postracist-america.

71. Zaretsky, *No Direction Home*, 14.

72. Douglas and Michaels, *Mommy Myth*, 185–87.

73. Cowie, *Stayin' Alive*, 171.

74. Cowie, 170, 169.

75. Merle Haggard, "Merle Haggard—Okie from Muskogee (Live)," YouTube video, 2:38, posted October 20, 2014, https://www.youtube.com/watch?v=68cbjlLFl4U.

76. Cowie, *Stayin' Alive*, 169–70.

77. Schulman, *Seventies*, 115.

78. Cowie, "From Hard Hats to the Nascar Dads," 10, 13, 15–16; McBee, *Born to Be Wild*, 185–88.

79. "Presidential Christmas: Ford Is Given Humorous Present by Daughter Susan," *Toledo Blade*, December 26, 1976.

80. Liberals also attempted to tap into the *Playboy* mystique. One of the most infamous examples is Democratic presidential hopeful Jimmy Carter's interview with *Playboy*. Strub, *Perversion for Profit*, 185.

81. Beale, "Kennedys Prominent," 2.

Chapter Five

1. Stephen Talbot, "Wizard of Ooze," *Mother Jones*, May/June 1995, 41–43, https://www.motherjones.com/politics/1995/05/wizard-ooze/. In 1995 Stephen Talbot was inspired to find out "who are these people, and why are they listening to Rush?" and began producing the documentary *Rush Limbaugh's America* for the PBS series *Frontline*.

2. Talbot. For more on Limbaugh, see Chafets, *Rush Limbaugh*; Kornacki, *Red and the Blue*; and David Greene, "Rush Limbaugh's Conservative Charge," Morning Edition, NPR, May 25, 2010, https://www.npr.org/transcripts/127096506.

3. For more on the rise of modern conservatism, see Kruse, *White Flight*; Lassiter, *Silent Majority*; Carter, *Politics of Rage*; McGirr, *Suburban Warriors*; Formisano, *Boston against Bussing*; and Dochuk, *From Bible Belt to Sunbelt*.

4. Wilson, *Most Dangerous Man in America*, 5–6.

5. James Bowman, "Rush: The Leader of the Opposition," *National Review*, August 1, 2003; Clair Suddath, "Conservative Radio Host Rush Limbaugh," *Time*, March 4, 2009.

6. Talbot, "Wizard of Ooze."

7. Jason Schwartz, "Rush Limbaugh Roars Back," Politico, December 21, 2018, https://www.politico.com/story/2018/12/21/rush-limbaugh-trump-comeback-1073726.

8. In 2010, conservative radio hosts Sean Hannity had fourteen million listeners per week and Glenn Beck had nine million. See Berry and Sobieraj, "Understanding the Rise."

9. Phyllis Schlafly, "Rush: On Top Because of Courage," *Eagle Forum*, August 1, 2008, http://www.eagleforum.org/column/2008/aug08/08-08-01.html.

10. Schlafly.

11. Wilson, *Most Dangerous Man in America*, 247.

12. Talbot, "Wizard of Ooze."

13. Talbot.

14. Talbot.

15. Robert D. McFadden, "Paul Harvey, Homespun Radio Voice of Middle America, Is Dead at 90," *NYT*, March 2, 2009; Carlos Watson, "The Rest of the Story: Paul Harvey, Conservative Talk Radio Pioneer," NPR, October 9, 2014, https://www.npr.org/2014/10/09/354718833/the-rest-of-the-story-paul-harvey-conservative-talk-radio-pioneer.

16. Schlafly, "Rush."

17. McLeod, *Pranksters*, 194.

18. Self, *All in the Family*, 346–47.

19. Lewis Grossberger, "The Rush Hours," *NYT*, December 16, 1990, 58.

20. Chafets, *Rush Limbaugh*, 2.

21. Faludi, *Backlash*, 13.

22. James Reston, "The Reagan Joke Book: A Sampler," *NYT*, March 31, 1984, 8.

23. Wickberg, *Senses of Humor*, 197.

24. Kyle Longley, "Why Donald Trump Is Just Following in Ronald Reagan's Footsteps on Race," *Washington Post*, August 4, 2019, http://historynewsnetwork.org/article/172752. See Longley's article for more on the racism embedded in Reagan's rhetoric.

25. Tygiel, "Ronald Reagan," 49–52.

26. "Flashback: Ronald Reagan and the Berkeley People's Park Riots," *Rolling Stone*, May 15, 2017, https://www.rollingstone.com/culture/culture-news/flashback-ronald-reagan-and-the-berkeley-peoples-park-riots-114873/.

27. "Until the mid-1980s, syndicated radio shows required phone lines and were expensive, especially in rural areas. Satellite technology helped make Rush Limbaugh's success possible by reducing the price of distributing syndicated radio at a time when AM stations were desperate to reduce costs due to declining ratings." Wilson, *Most Dangerous Man in America*, 6.

28. Berry and Sobieraj, "Understanding the Rise."

29. Roediger, *Colored White*, 53.

30. Roediger, *Colored White*, 50.

31. Roediger, *Colored White*, 52.

32. (No Author)"Rush Limbaugh: The Master of Racial Poison," *The Journal of Blacks in Higher Education*, 15; Perlman, "Rush Limbaugh," 198.

33. Greene, "Rush Limbaugh's Conservative Charge."

34. Allan Bloom, *Closing of the American Mind*; Jim Sleeper, "Allan Bloom and the Conservative Mind," *NYT*, September 4, 2005, https://www.nytimes.com/2005/09/04/books/review/allan-bloom-and-the-conservative-mind.html.

35. Kruse, *White Flight*; Lassiter, *Silent Majority*; Carter, *Politics of Rage*; McGirr, *Suburban Warriors*; Formisano, *Boston against Bussing*; Dochuk, *From Bible Belt to Sunbelt*.

36. See "Political Correctness," Google Books Ngram Viewer, accessed August 10, 2020, https://books.google.com/ngrams/graph?content=political+correctness&year_start=1800&year_end=2000&corpus=15&smoothing=3&share=&direct_url=t1%3B%2Cpolitical%20correctness%3B%2Cco#t1%3B%2Cpolitical%20correctness%3B%2Cco.

37. Schlafly, "Rush."

38. Linda Lowen, "What Is a Feminazi?," ThoughtCo, November 13, 2019, https://www.thoughtco.com/definition-of-feminazi-3533833.

39. Limbaugh, *Way Things Ought to Be*, 194.

40. Lundberg and Farnham, *Modern Woman*.

41. In *Sexual Politics*, Kate Millett notes that Lundberg and Farnham's study had tremendous influence. They concluded that the "sexual revolution had made women a 'lost sex' around whom 'much of the unhappiness our day revolves, like a captive planet.'" Millett, *Sexual Politics*, 206–7.

42. Lowen, "What Is a Feminazi?"

43. Limbaugh, *Way Things Ought to Be*, 194. In 1996, Gloria Steinem described the term as "cruel and ahistorical" to argue that Limbaugh's desire to undermine women's reproductive freedom was reminiscent of Hitler's regime. Steinem, *Outrageous Acts*, xv.

44. Limbaugh, *Way Things Ought to Be*, 194; Lowen, "What Is a Feminazi?"

45. Limbaugh argues that he used the term *feminazi* to demonize feminists who advocated abortion. The debate over reproductive rights remained part of Limbaugh's critique of feminism, but his use of the trope, as well as its use by others, quickly expanded and caused the term to become synonymous with feminism and a range of murky definitions and anxieties. Limbaugh, *Way Things Ought to Be*, 194. For a discussion of earlier organizations and newspapers that equated feminism with Hitler, see Steinem, *Outrageous Acts*, 332–54.

46. Talbot, "Wizard of Ooze."

47. Evans, *Tidal Wave*, 229.

48. Russell Frank, *Newslore*, 32–34.

49. Suzi Parker, "Rush Limbaugh's Obsession with Hillary Clinton," *Washington Post*, December 17, 2012, https://www.washingtonpost.com/blogs/she-the-people/wp/2012/12/17/rush-limbaughs-obsession-with-hillary-clinton/.

50. Molly Ivins, "Lyin' Bully," *Mother Jones*, May/June 1995, 37–38. http://www.motherjones.com/politics/1995/05/lyin-bully. Ivins, the queen of political satire, found Limbaugh's humor unacceptable.

51. Ivins, 37–38.

52. Ivins's concerns were also articulated in Thomas Frank's 2004 examination of his home state of Kansas and its political shift to the right that all but erased a progressive history of agrarian uprisings. Despite the fact that their state was home to the poorest county in the country, Frank laments, Kansans ignored their radical heritage and, even more surprisingly, their economic self-interest. Frank, *How Conservatives Won*. Nadine Hubbs notes as well that "the book was also marketed internationally under the title *What's the Matter with America?*" She offers an important critique of this work and notions of false consciousness. Hubbs, *Rednecks*, 32–35.

53. Talbot, "Wizard of Ooze."

54. See, for example, Franken, *Rush Limbaugh*.

55. Reid, *Let the People In*, 184.

56. Reid, 182–83.

57. Rick Lyman, "Ann Richards, Plain-Spoken Governor Who Aided Minorities, Dies at 73," *NYT*, September 14, 2006, http://www.nytimes.com/2006/09/14/us

/14richards.html. For more on Williams's infamous sexist jokes, see Reid, *Let the People In*, 240–41.

58. "How Ann Richards Trumped Her Rival Clayton Williams," *Texas Standard*, October 10, 2016, https://soundcloud.com/texas-standard/ann-richards-clayton-williams -10102016.

59. Reid, *Let the People In*, 273.

60. Reid, 271.

61. "100 Greatest Country Songs of All Time," *Rolling Stone*, June 1, 2014, https://www .rollingstone.com/music/music-lists/100-greatest-country-songs-of-all-time-11200/.

62. Reid, *Let the People In*, 331.

63. Reid, 338–39.

64. Reid, 405.

65. Kevin Merida, "Rush Limbaugh Saluted as a 'Majority Maker,'" *Washington Post*, December 11, 1994, https://www.washingtonpost.com/archive/politics/1994/12 /11/rush-limbaugh-saluted-as-a-majority-maker/e4f879c5-a0d2-43b8-ae56-9e24ee b82b62/.

66. Michael Barbaro and Megan Twohey, "Crossing the Line: How Donald Trump Behaved with Women in Private," *NYT*, May 14, 2016, https://www.nytimes.com /2016/05/15/us/politics/donald-trump-women.html.

67. Paul Solotaroff, "Trump Seriously: On the Trail with the GOP's Tough Guy," *Rolling Stone*, September 9, 2015, http://www.rollingstone.com/politics/news/trump -seriously-20150909.

68. Cleeve R. Wootson, "Donald Trump Was Proud of His 1990 Playboy Cover. Hugh Hefner, Not So Much," *Washington Post*, September, 28, 2017, https://www .washingtonpost.com/news/arts-and-entertainment/wp/2017/09/28/donald-trump -was-proud-of-his-1990-playboy-cover-hugh-hefner-not-so-much/.

69. Mark Abadi, "Trump Had an Unusual Reaction to 9/11 Just Hours after the Attacks," Business Insider, September 11, 2019, https://www.businessinsider.com /trump-september-11-interview-tallest-building-manhattan-2017-9.

70. Tom Porter, "The Playboy President: Trump and Hugh Hefner Bonded for Decades over Their Love of Licentiousness, but the Relationship Soured," *Newsweek*, September 28, 2017, https://www.newsweek.com/trump-hugh-hefner-friends-decades -relationship-soured-673205.

71. Solotaroff, "Trump Seriously."

72. Jasmine C. Lee and Kevin Quealy, "The 239 People, Places, and Things Donald Trump Has Insulted on Twitter: A Complete List," *NYT*, June 30, 2016, http://www .nytimes.com/interactive/2016/01/28/upshot/donald-trump-twitter-insults.html?_r=1.

73. Frank Pallotta, "John Oliver Now Regrets Urging Donald Trump to Run," CNN, November 7, 2016, http://money.cnn.com/2016/11/07/media/john-oliver-donald-trump -election/; Indicrat, "Best Compilation—People Who Laughed at TRUMP . . . and Said He Would Never Be President—FUNNY!," YouTube video, 5:32, posted November 15, 2016, https://www.youtube.com/watch?v=ahkMA6JPOHU.

74. Connor Friedersdorf, "Donald Trump Is No Conservative," *Atlantic*, July 13, 2015, http://www.theatlantic.com/politics/archive/2015/07/donald-trump-running-for -president/398345/.

75. Nancy Gibbs, "Sex and Power: Why Powerful Men Abuse Women—and Get Away with It," *Time*, May 30, 2011, 24–30.

76. Stephanie Zacharek, Eliana Dockterman, and Haley Sweetland Edwards, "Time Person of the Year 2017: The Silence Breakers," *Time*, accessed August 9, 2020, https://time.com/time-person-of-the-year-2017-silence-breakers/.

77. Of the nineteen men featured in the who's-who list of lecherous pigs, four men—golfer Tiger Woods, Supreme Court justice Clarence Thomas, boxer Mike Tyson, and rapper R. Kelly—were African American; the rest enjoyed similar privileges of fame, fortune, and whiteness and included everyone from John F. Kennedy to presidential hopeful John Edwards. Gibbs, "Sex and Power."

78. Gibbs, 26–28.

79. Talbot, "Wizard of Ooze."

80. Eliot Nelson, "Does Rush Limbaugh Matter Anymore?," HuffPost, June 3, 2018, https://www.huffpost.com/entry/does-rush-limbaugh-matter-anymore_n_5b0d8f64e4b0568a880f23cd.

81. Peter Beinart, "The New McCarthyism of Donald Trump," *Atlantic*, July 21, 2015, https://www.theatlantic.com/politics/archive/2015/07/donald-trump-joseph-mccarthy/399056/; Brenden Gallagher, "A Timeline of Donald Trump's Most Insane Insults on the Campaign Trail," VH1, February 22, 2016, http://www.vh1.com/news/245354/trump-insult-campaign/; Eric Lichtblau, "Hate Crimes against Muslims Most since Post-9/11 Era," NYT, September, 17, 2016, https://www.nytimes.com/2016/09/18/us/politics/hate-crimes-american-muslims-rise.html.

82. Laura Bates, "Donald Trump's 'Spat' with Megyn Kelly Is Sexism, and It's Abusive," *Time*, January 28, 2016, http://time.com/4198737/donald-trump-megyn-kelly-sexism/.

83. David A. Fahrenthold, "Trump Recorded Having Extremely Lewd Conversation about Women in 2005," *Washington Post*, October 8, 2016, https://www.washingtonpost.com/politics/trump-recorded-having-extremely-lewd-conversation-about-women-in-2005/2016/10/07/3b9ce776-8cb4-11e6-bf8a-3d26847eeed4_story.html?utm_term=.cf21d3eb9e8c.

84. Prachi Gupta, "Donald Trump Gives the Worst Excuse for His Disgusting Comments about Women," *Cosmopolitan*, March 29, 2016, http://www.cosmopolitan.com/politics/news/a55946/donald-trumps-sexist-comments-jokes/.

85. Cecile Richards, "How Ann Richards' Run for Texas Governor Mirrors Clinton vs. Trump," *Rolling Stone*, November 7, 2016, http://www.rollingstone.com/politics/features/how-ann-richards-run-for-governor-mirrors-clinton-vs-trump-w448850.

86. Bre Payton, "Hillary Just Made the Most Excruciating 'Pokemon Go' Joke Ever," *Federalist*, July 14, 2016, http://thefederalist.com/2016/07/14/hillary-clinton-just-made-the-most-excruciating-pokemon-go-joke-ever/.

87. Yoni Hesler, "Watch SNL's Hilarious Spoof of the Trump vs. Clinton Debate," BGR Media, October 3, 2016, https://bgr.com/2016/10/03/snl-donald-trump-vs-hillary-clinton-debate-video/.

88. "READ: Michelle Obama's Speech at 2016 Democratic National Convention," NPR, July 26, 2016, http://www.npr.org/2016/07/26/487431756/michelle-obamas-prepared-remarks-for-democratic-national-convention.

89. Glenn Kessler, "A Guide to the Allegations of Bill Clinton's Womanizing," *Washington Post*, December 30, 2015, https://www.washingtonpost.com/news/fact-checker/wp/2015/12/30/a-guide-to-the-allegations-of-bill-clintons-womanizing/?utm_term=.b3eb75880de9.

90. Patrick Healy, "The Clinton Conundrum: What's behind the Laugh," *NYT*, September 30, 2007, https://www.nytimes.com/2007/09/30/us/politics/30clinton.html.

91. *Real Time with Bill Maher*, season 14, episode 24, aired July 20, 2016, on HBO, http://play.hbogo.com/episode/urn:hbo:episode:GV4UF5A2kwQLDQgEAAAAf.

92. Maureen Dowd, "Judd Apatow Freaking Out over Donald Trump," *NYT*, January 14, 2017, *NYT*, https://www.nytimes.com/2017/01/14/opinion/sunday/judd-apatow-freaking-out-over-donald-trump.html?_r=0.

Epilogue

1. Elspeth Reeve, "The Ghost of Sandra Fluke Is Haunting Rush Limbaugh's Mega-Deal," *Atlantic*, May 6, 2013, https://www.theatlantic.com/politics/archive/2013/05/rush-limbaugh-contract-sandra-fluke/315587/. A few days later, after losing sponsors and facing heavy criticism, Limbaugh apologized for his remarks, suggesting that he was merely trying to be funny. See Todd Cunningham, "Rush Limbaugh Loses Another Sponsor over Sandra Fluke Remarks," Reuters, March 4, 2012, https://www.reuters.com/article/us-rushlimbaugh-sponsors/rush-limbaugh-loses-another-sponsor-over-sandra-fluke-remarks-idUSTRE8230VY20120304. Also see Manne, *Down Girl*.

2. "Full Transcript: Trump's 2020 State of the Union Address," *NYT*, February 5, 2020, https://www.nytimes.com/2020/02/05/us/politics/state-of-union-transcript.html.

3. Gerald M. Boyd, "President Honors Sinatra and Mother Theresa," *NYT*, May 24, 1985, https://www.nytimes.com/1985/05/24/us/president-honors-sinatra-and-mother-theresa.html; Kerri Lawrence, "Celebrating Mr. Rogers at the National Archives," National Archives News, March 20, 2019, https://www.archives.gov/news/articles/celebrating-mr-rogers-at-the-national-archives; Nardine Saad, "Read Barack Obama's Tribute to 'National Treasure' Toni Morrison," *Los Angeles Times*, August 6, 2019, https://www.latimes.com/entertainment-arts/story/2019-08-06/barack-obama-toni-morrison-tribute.

4. David Sims, "The Feedback Loop of *Saturday Night Live* and Donald Trump," *Atlantic*, December 5, 2016, https://www.theatlantic.com/entertainment/archive/2016/12/the-feedback-loop-of-saturday-night-live-and-donald-trump/509618/.

5. Sims.

6. Steve Hendrix, "'SNL' Has Skewered Every President since Ford, and All of Them Reacted the Same Way—Until Now," *Chicago Tribune*, October 14, 2018, https://www.chicagotribune.com/entertainment/tv/ct-ent-snl-presidents-20181014-story.html.

7. Dean Obeidallah, "Can SNL Topple the Trump Administration?," CNN, March 15, 2017, https://www.cnn.com/2017/02/12/opinions/can-snl-bring-down-trump-administration-obeidallah-opinion/index.html.

8. S. E. Cupp, "Sean Spicer Has a Problem: Melissa McCarthy," CNN, February 7, 2017, https://www.cnn.com/2017/02/06/opinions/sean-spicer-cupp/index.html.

9. James Doubek and Maquita Peters, "Melissa McCarthy's 'Spicey' and Alec Baldwin's Trump Return to 'SNL,'" NPR, February 12, 2007, http://www.npr.org/sections/thetwo-way/2017/02/12/514800509/melissa-mccarthys-spicey-and-alec-baldwins-trump-return-to-snl.

10. Scott Powers, "Sean Spicer: No Regrets, Except Maybe That Melissa McCarthy Thing," Florida Politics, April 8, 2019, https://floridapolitics.com/archives/293014-sean-spicer-no-regrets-except-maybe-that-melissa-mccarthy-thing.

11. Saturday Night Live, "Jeff Sessions Gump Cold Open—SNL," YouTube video, 5:37, posted March 5, 2017, https://www.youtube.com/watch?v=8ZM3jvlvgVw.

12. Chas Danner, "Trump Will Not Attend White House Correspondents' Dinner," New York Magazine, February 25, 2017, http://nymag.com/daily/intelligencer/2017/02/trump-will-not-attend-white-house-correspondents-dinner.html; David Itzkoff, "Samantha Bee to Roast Trump on Same Night as Correspondents' Dinner," NYT, January 30, 2017, https://www.nytimes.com/2017/01/30/arts/television/donald-trump-correspondents-dinner-samantha-bee.html?_r=1; Emily Heil, "Samantha Bee Plans an Anti-White House Correspondents' Dinner: Will Journalists Go?," Washington Post, January 30, 2017, https://www.washingtonpost.com/news/reliable-source/wp/2017/01/30/samantha-bee-plans-an-anti-white-house-correspondents-dinner-will-journalists-go/?tid=a_inl&utm_term=.4164786bb0d2.

13. Beth Shilliday, "George W. Bush Dissing Donald Trump? 'The Best Humor Is Making Fun of Yourself,'" Hollywood Life, March 3, 2017, http://hollywoodlife.com/2017/03/03/george-w-bush-disses-donald-trump-best-humor-laughing-at-self/.

14. Howard Stern Show, "Hillary Clinton on the Howard Stern Show Pt. 1," YouTube video, 25:57, posted December 6, 2019, https://www.youtube.com/watch?v=2kHUA-Zma1U.

15. Howard Stern Show. Also see Clinton, What Happened, esp. 111–45.

16. Maggie Astor, "'A Woman, Just Not That Woman': How Sexism Plays Out on the Trail," NYT, February 11, 2019, https://www.nytimes.com/2019/02/11/us/politics/sexism-double-standard-2020.html.

17. Clinton, What Happened, 119.

18. Clinton, 121.

19. Howard Stern Show, "Hillary Clinton."

20. Howard Stern Show.

21. Lorna Bracewell and Nancy D. Wadsworth, "The 'Pussyhats' (and Other Things) Make Protests Fun—Which Keeps People Coming Back," Washington Post, February 22, 2017, https://www.washingtonpost.com/news/monkey-cage/wp/2017/02/22/the-pussyhats-and-other-things-make-protests-fun-which-keeps-people-coming-back/?utm_term=.28058a242b9d.

22. Willett and Willett, Uproarious.

23. Leng, "When Politics Were Fun, 5."

24. Amber Jamieson, Nicola Slawson, and Nadia Khomami, "Women's March Events Take Place in Washington and around the World—as It Happened," Guardian, January 21, 2017, https://www.theguardian.com/lifeandstyle/live/2017/jan/21/womens-march-on-washington-and-other-anti-trump-protests-around-the-world-live-coverage; Scott Malone and Ginger Gibson, "Women Lead Unprecedented Worldwide

Mass Protests against Trump," Reuters, January 22, 2017, http://www.reuters.com/article/us-usa-trump-women-idUSKBN15608K.

25. "Muslim Comedian Uses Humor to Cope with Trump," CBC News, February 17, 2017, https://www.cbc.ca/radio/tapestry/lighten-up-1.3972222/muslim-comedian-uses-humour-to-cope-with-trump-1.3972223.

26. Mukhopadhyay and Harding, *Nasty Women*; Regina R. Robertson, "Meet the Comedian behind the 'How to Medical' TikTok Everyone Is Sharing," *Essence*, April 27, 2020, https://www.essence.com/entertainment/sarah-cooper-comedian-donald-trump-how-to-medical/.

27. Monica Hesse, "Women on TikTok Have Cracked the Code on How to Satirize Trump," *Washington Post*, May 22, 2020, https://www.stamfordadvocate.com/opinion/article/Women-on-TikTok-have-cracked-the-code-on-how-to-15288586.php.

28. Hesse.

29. Elle Hunt, "'People Still Need to Laugh': How Lipsyncing Spoofs Saved Lockdown," *Guardian*, May 16, 2020, https://www.theguardian.com/technology/2020/may/16/people-still-need-to-laugh-how-lipsyncing-spoofs-saved-lockdown#maincontent.

30. Hunt.

31. James Poniewozik, "Trump Said, 'I Have the Best Words.' Now They're Hers," *NYT*, May 29, 2020, https://www.nytimes.com/2020/05/27/arts/television/trump-sarah-cooper.html.

32. Howard Stern Show, "Hillary Clinton."

33. Jim Rieger, "When a Rallygoer Suggested Shooting Immigrants in May, Trump Made a Joke," *Washington Post*, August 5, 2019, https://www.washingtonpost.com/politics/2019/08/05/when-rally-goer-suggested-shooting-immigrants-may-trump-made-joke/.

34. Rover Costa, Seung Min Kim, and Josh Dawsey, "Trump Calls Governors 'Weak,' Urges Them to Use Force against Unruly Protests," *Washington Post*, June 1, 2020, https://www.washingtonpost.com/politics/trump-governors-george-floyd-protests/2020/06/01/430a6226-a421-11ea-b619-3f9133bbb482_story.html.

35. ABC News, "All 4 Officers Charged in George Floyd's Death," YouTube video, 14:41, posted June 3, 2020, https://www.youtube.com/watch?v=oe4Y36UZ6Qs.

Bibliography

Archives and Special Collections

Billy Ireland Cartoon Library and Museum, Ohio State University, Columbus, Ohio
Peter Tamony Collection, 1890–1985, State Historical Society of Missouri, University
of Missouri–Columbia
Raising Our Voices: The History of San Diego State and San Diego in Sound, Special
Collections and University Archives, San Diego State University

Periodicals

Atlantic
Business Insider
Chicago Defender
Chicago Tribune
Chortle
Cosmopolitan
Crimson (Harvard)
Daily Beast
Daytona Beach Morning Journal
Democrat and Chronicle
Eagle Forum
Ebony
Ellensburg (WA) Daily Record
Essence
Guardian
Harper's Magazine
Jezebel
Kirkus Reviews
Life
Los Angeles Times
Mademoiselle
McCalls
Mother Jones

Ms.
Nation
National Archives News
National Review
New Republic
Newsweek
New York
New Yorker
New York Magazine
New York Times
Playboy
Politico
Rolling Stone
San Francisco Chronicle
San Francisco Examiner
San Francisco Examiner and Chronicle
SFGATE (San Francisco)
Swaddle
Texas Standard
Time
Toledo Blade
Vanity Fair
Washington Post

Secondary Sources

Abramson, Kate. "Turning Up the Lights on Gaslighting." *Philosophical Perspectives*
28, no. 1 (December 2014): 1–30.

Adler, Richard P., ed. *All in the Family: A Critical Appraisal*. New York: Praeger, 1979.

Ahmed, Sarah. *Living a Feminist Life*. Durham, NC: Duke University Press, 2017.

Auslander, Philip. "'Brought to You by Fem-Rage': Stand-Up Comedy and the Politics of Gender." In *Acting Out: Feminist Performances*, edited by Lynda Hart and Peggy Phelan, 315–36 Ann Arbor: University of Michigan Press, 1993.

Bailey, Beth, and David Farber, eds. *America in the Seventies*. Lawrence: University of Kansas Press, 2004.

Barreca, Regina. *They Used to Call Me Snow White. . . . but I Drifted: Women's Strategic Use of Humor*. New York: Penguin Books, 1991.

Benson, Susan Porter. *Household Accounts: Working-Class Family Economies in the Interwar United States*. Ithaca, NY: Cornell University Press, 2015.

Berry, Jeffrey, and Sarah Sobieraj. "Understanding the Rise of Talk Radio." *Political Science and Politics* 44, no. 4 (October 20, 2011): 762–67.

Biskind, Peter, and Barbara Ehrenreich. "Machismo and Hollywood's Working Class." *Socialist Review* 10, nos. 2/3, 50/51 (May–June 1980): 109–30.

Blee, Kathleen. *Women in the Klan: Racism and Gender in the 1920s*. Berkeley: University of California Press, 2008.

Bloom, Allan. *The Closing of the American Mind: How Higher Education Has Failed Democracy and Impoverished the Souls of Today's Students*. New York: Simon and Schuster, 1987.

Bloom, Joshua, and Waldo E. Martin Jr. *Black against Empire: The History and Politics of the Black Panther Party*. Berkeley: University of California Press, 2013.

Bodnar, John. *Blue-Collar Hollywood: Liberalism, Democracy, and Working People in American Film*. Baltimore: Johns Hopkins University Press, 2003.

Bornstein, Kate. *A Queer and Pleasant Danger: A Memoir*. Boston: Beacon, 2012.

Bow, Leslie. *Asian American Femininisms*. New York: Routledge, 2012.

Bradley, Patricia. *Mass Media and Shaping of American Feminism, 1963–1975*. Jackson: University Press of Mississippi, 2003.

Brownmiller, Susan. *Against Our Will*. New York: Simon and Schuster, 1975.

Bruce, Lenny. *How to Talk Dirty and Influence People: An Autobiography*. New York: Simon and Schuster, 1992.

Burchfield, R. W., ed. *A Supplement to the Oxford English Dictionary*. Vol. 2. Oxford: Oxford University Press, 1976.

Cahones, Carolyn. *Women's Lip: Male Chauvinist Reading Matter*. Tucson: Apocrypha Books, 1974.

Carter, Dan. *The Politics of Rage: George Wallace, the Origins of the New Conservatism, and the Transformation of American Politics*. 2nd ed. Baton Rouge: Louisiana State University Press, 2000.

Chafets, Zev. *Rush Limbaugh: An Army of One*. New York: Sentinel, 2010.

Chauncey, George. *Gay New York: Gender, Urban Culture, and the Making of the Gay Male World, 1890-1940*. New York: Basic Books, 1995.

Chisholm, Shirley. *Unbought and Unbossed*. Boston: Houghton Mifflin, 1970.

Chudakoff, Howard P. *The Age of the Bachelor*. Princeton, NJ: Princeton University Press, 2000.

Clinton, Hillary Rodham. *What Happened*. New York: Simon and Schuster, 2017.

Cobble, Dorothy Sue. *The Other Women's Movement: Workplace Justice and Social Rights in Modern America*. Princeton: Princeton University Press, 2005.

Cobble, Dorothy Sue, Linda Gordon, and Astrid Henry. *Feminism Unfinished: A Short, Surprising History of American Women's Movements*. New York: Liveright, 2014.

Cohen, Lizabeth. *A Consumers' Republic: The Politics of Mass Consumption in Postwar America*. New York: Vintage Books, 2003.

Cohen, Yael. *We Killed: The Rise of Women in American Comedy*. London: Picador, 2013.

Collins, Gail. *When Everything Changed. The Amazing Journey of American Women from 1960 to the Present*. New York: Little, Brown, 2009.

Coontz, Stephanie. *A Strange Stirring: "The Feminine Mystique" and American Women at the Dawn of the 1960s*. New York: Basic Books, 2012.

Cowie, Jefferson. "From Hard Hats to the Nascar Dads." *New Labor Forum* 13, no. 3 (Fall 2004): 9–17.

———. *Stayin' Alive: The 1970s and the Last Days of the Working Class*. New York: New Press, 2012.

Cowie, Jefferson, and Lauren Boehm. "Dead Man's Town: 'Born in the U.S.A.,' Social History and Working-Class Identity." *American Quarterly* 58, no. 2 (June 2006): 353–78.

Crenshaw, Kimberlé. "Mapping the Margins: Intersectionality, Identity Politics, and Violence against Women of Color." *Stanford Law Review* 43, no. 6 (July 1991): 1241–99.

Critchlow, Donald. *Phyllis Schlafly and Grassroots Conservatism: A Woman's Crusade*. Princeton, NJ: Princeton University Press, 2005.

Dagnes, Alison. *A Conservative Walks into a Bar: The Politics of Political Humor*. New York: Palgrave Macmillan, 2012.

Davis, Angela. *Blues Legacies and Black Feminism: Gertrude "Ma" Rainey, Bessie Smith, and Billie Holiday*. New York: Vintage, 1999.

De León, Arnoldo. *They Called Them Greasers: Anglo Attitudes towards Mexicans in Texas, 1821–1900*. Austin: University of Texas Press, 1983.

De Puymège, Gérard. "The Good Soldier Chauvin." In *Realms of Memory: The Construction of the French Past*, vol. 2, *Traditions*, edited by Pierre Nora, 332–60. New York: Columbia University Press, 1997.

Dochuk, Darren. *From Bible Belt to Sunbelt: Plain-Folk Religion, Grassroots Politics, and the Rise of Evangelical Conservatism*. New York: W. W. Norton, 2010.

Domínguez-Ruvalcaba, Héctor. *Modernity and the Nation in Mexican Representations of Masculinity: From Sensuality to Bloodshed*. New York: Palgrave Macmillan, 2007.

Douglas, Mary. *Purity and Danger: An Analysis of the Concepts of Pollution and Taboo*. New York: Praeger, 1966.

Douglas, Susan J. *Enlightened Sexism: The Seductive Message That Feminism's Work Is Done*. New York: Times Books, 2010.

———. *Where the Girls Are: Growing Up Female with the Mass Media*. New York: Times Books, 1995.

Douglas, Susan J., and Meredith W. Michaels. *The Mommy Myth: The Idealization of Motherhood and How It Has Undermined All Women*. New York: Free Press, 2005.

Dow, Bonnie J. *Prime-Time Feminism: Television, Media Culture, and the Women's Movement since 1970s*. Philadelphia: University of Pennsylvania Press, 1996.

———. *Watching Women's Liberation, 1970: Feminisms Pivotal Year on Network News*, Urbana: University of Illinois Press, 2014.

Durr, Kenneth D. *Behind the Backlash: White Working-Class Politics in Baltimore, 1940–1980*. Chapel Hill: University of North Carolina Press, 2003.

Echols, Alice. *Daring to Be Bad: Radical Feminism in America, 1967–1975*. Minneapolis: University of Minnesota Press, 1989.

———. *Hot Stuff: Disco and the Remaking of American Culture*. New York: W. W. Norton, 2011.

Ehrenreich, Barbara. *The Hearts of Men: American Dreams and the Flight from Commitment*. New York: Anchor, 1987.

Enstad, Nan. *Ladies of Labor, Girls of Adventure: Working Women, Popular Culture, and Labor Politics at the Turn of the Century*. New York: Columbia University Press, 1999.

Eskridge, Sara K. *Rube Tube: CBS and Rural Comedy in the Sixties*. Columbia: University of Missouri Press, 2018.

Essig, Mark. *Lesser Beasts: A Snout-to-Tail History of the Humble Pig*. New York: Basic Books, 2015.

Estes, Steve. *I Am a Man! Race, Manhood, and the Civil Rights Movement*. Chapel Hill: University of North Carolina Press, 2005.

Evans, Sara. *Personal Politics: The Roots of Women's Liberation in the Civil Rights Movement and the New Left*. New York: Knopf, 1979.

———. *Tidal Wave: How Women Changed America at Century's End*. New York: Free Press, 2003.

Faludi, Susan. *Backlash: The Undeclared War against Women*. New York: Broadway Books, 2006.

Farber, David. *The Age of Great Dreams in the 1960s*. New York: Hill and Wang, 1994.

Farmer, Patty. *Playboy Laughs: The Comedy, Comedians, and Cartoons of Playboy*. New York: Beaufort Books, 2017.

Farrell, Warren. *The Liberated Man: Beyond Masculinity: Freeing Men and Their Relationships with Women*. New York: Random House, 1974.

Finley, Jessyka. "Black Women's Satire as (Black) Postmodern Performance." *Studies in American Humor* 2, no. 2 (2016): 236–65.

———. "Raunch and Redress: Interrogating Pleasure in Black Women's Stand-Up Comedy." *Journal of Popular Culture* 49, no. 4 (August 2016): 780–98.

Finney, Gail, ed. *Look Who's Laughing: Gender and Comedy*. Langhorne, PA: Gordon and Breach, 1994.

Formisano, Ronald. *Boston against Bussing: Race, Class, and Ethnicity in the 1960s and 1970s*. Chapel Hill: University of North Carolina Press, 1991.

Frank, Gillian. "'The Civil Rights of Parents': Race and Conservative Politics in Anita Bryant's Campaign against Gay Rights in 1970s Florida." *Journal of the History of Sexuality* 22, no. 1 (January 2013): 126–60.

Frank, Russell. *Newslore: Contemporary Folklore on the Internet*. Oxford: University Press of Mississippi, 2013.

Frank, Thomas. *How Conservatives Won the Heart of America*. New York: Metropolitan Books, 2004.

Franken, Al. *Rush Limbaugh Is a Big Fat Idiot and Other Observations*. New York: Dell, 1999.

Fraterrigo, Elizabeth. *Playboy and the Making of the Good Life in Modern America*.

Freedman, Estelle. *No Turning Back: The History of Feminism and the Future of Women*. New York: Ballantine, 2002.

Freeman, Joshua B. "Hardhats: Construction Workers, Manliness, and the 1970 Pro-war Demonstrations." *Journal of Social History* 26, no. 4 (Summer 1993): 725–44.

Friedan, Betty. *The Feminine Mystique*. New York: W. W. Norton, 1963.

Gabin, Nancy. *Feminism in the Labor Movement: Women and the United Auto Workers, 1935-1975*. Ithaca, NY: Cornell University Press.

García, Alma M., ed. *Chicana Feminist Thought: The Basic Historical Writings*. New York: Routledge, 1997.

Gilder, George. *Visible Man: A True Story of Post-Racist America*. New York: Basic Books, 1978.

Gilmore, Stephanie. *Groundswell: Grassroots Feminist Activism in Postwar America*. New York: Routledge, 2014.

Ginzberg, Lori. *Women and the Work of Benevolence: Morality, Politics, and Class in the Nineteenth-Century United States*. New Haven, CT: Yale University Press, 1990.

González, Ray. *Muy Macho: Latin Men Confront Their Manhood*. New York: Doubleday, 1996.

Gordon, Linda. *The Great Arizona Orphan Abduction*. Cambridge, MA: Harvard University Press, 2001.

Gornick, Vivian. *Woman in Sexist Society: Studies in Power and Powerlessness*. New York: Basic Books, 1971.

Green, Viveca S., and Amber Day. "Asking for It: Rape Myths, Satire, and Feminist Lacunae." *Signs* 45, no. 2 (Winter 2020): 449–72.

Guy-Sheftall, Beverly, ed. *Words of Fire: An Anthology of African-American Feminist Thought*. New York: New Press, 1995.

Haggins, Bambi. *Laughing Mad: The Black Comic Persona in Post-soul America*. New Brunswick, NJ: Rutgers, 2007.

Halley, Janet. *Split Decisions: How and Why to Take a Break from Feminism*. Princeton, NJ: Princeton University Press, 2006.

Harris, Marvin. *Good to Eat: Riddles of Food and Culture*. Long Grove, IL: Waveland, 1998.

Hennefeld, Maggie. *Specters of Slapstick and Silent Film Comedians*. New York: Columbia University Press, 2018.

Hernández-Avila, Inés. "In Praise of Insubordination, or, What Makes a Good Woman Go Bad?" In *The Chicana/o Cultural Studies Reader*, edited by Angie Chabram-Demersesian, 191–202. New York: Routledge, 2006.

Hewitt, Nancy A., ed. *No Permanent Waves: Recasting Histories of U.S. Feminism*. New Brunswick, NJ: Rutgers University Press, 2010.

Hill Collins, Patricia. *Black Feminist Thought*. Minneapolis: University of Minnesota Press, 1998.

Hill Collins, Patricia, and Sirma Bilge. *Intersectionality*. Cambridge, UK: Polity, 2016.

Hilliard, David, Keith Zimmerman, and Kent Zimmerman. *Huey: Spirit of the Panther*. New York: Basic Books, 2006.

Hofstede, David. *The Dukes of Hazzard: The Unofficial Companion*. London: St. Martin's Griffin, 2005.

Horowitz, Daniel. *Betty Friedan and the Making of the Feminine Mystique: The American Left, the Cold War, and Modern Feminism*. Amherst: University of Massachusetts Press, 1998.

Hubbs, Nadine. *Rednecks, Queers, and Country Music*. Berkeley: University of California Press, 2014.

Huber, Patrick. "A Short History of Redneck: The Fashioning of a Southern White Masculine Identity." *Southern Cultures* 1, no. 2 (Winter 1995): 145–66.

Hughes, Walter. "In the Empire of the Beat: Discipline and Disco." In *Microphone Fiends: Youth Music and Youth Culture*, edited by Andrew Ross and Tricia Rose, 147–57. New York: Routledge, 1994.

Hull, Gloria T., Patricia Bell-Scott, and Barbara Smith, eds. *All the Women Are White, All the Blacks Are Men, but Some of Us Are Brave: Black Women's Studies*. New York: Feminist Press, 1982.

Hunt, Lynn. "The Many Bodies of Marie-Antoinette: Political Pornography and the Problem of the Feminine in the French Revolution." In *Marie-Antoinette: Writings on the Body of a Queen*, edited by Dena Goodman, 117–38. New York: Routledge, 2003.

Hurewitz, Daniel. *Bohemian Los Angeles and the Making of Modern Politics*. Berkeley: University of California Press, 2007.

James, Aaron. *Assholes: A Theory*. New York: Anchor Books, 2014.

Jones, Charles E., ed. *The Black Panther Party (Reconsidered)*. Baltimore: Black Classic, 1998.

Kelley, Robin D. G. *Race Rebels: Culture, Politics, and the Black Working Class*. New York: Free Press, 1996.

Kennedy, Flo. *Color Me Flo: My Hard Life and Good Times*. New York: Simon and Schuster, 2017.

Kerber, Linda. *Women of the Republic: Intellect and Ideology in Revolutionary America*. New York: W. W. Norton, 1986.

Kimmel, Michael. *Manhood in America: A Cultural History*. New York: Free Press, 1996.

Kiple, Kenneth F., and Kriemhild Coneè Ornelas, eds. *The Cambridge World History of Food*. Cambridge: Cambridge University Press, 2000.

Kiverst, Cory. *The Male Chauvinist's Cookbook*. New York: Winchester, 1974.

Korda, Michael. *Male Chauvinism! How It Works*. New York: Random House, 1973.

Kornacki, Steve. *The Red and the Blue: The 1990s and the Birth of Political Tribalism*. New York: Ecco, 2018.

Kray, Christine A., Tamar W. Carroll, and Hinda Mandell, eds. *Nasty Women and Bad Hombres: Gender and Race in the 2016 US Presidential Election*. Rochester, NY: University of Rochester Press, 2018.

Krefting, Rebecca. *All Joking Aside: American Humor and Its Discontents*. Baltimore: Johns Hopkins University Press, 2014.

Kruse, Kevin. *White Flight: Atlanta and the Making of Modern Conservatism*. Princeton, NJ: Princeton University Press, 2005.

Lassiter, Matthew. *Silent Majority: Suburban Politics in the Sunbelt South*. Princeton, NJ: Princeton University Press, 2007.

Leng, Kirsten. "When Politics Were Fun: Recovering a History of Humor in U.S. Feminism." *Synoptique* 5, no. 1 (2016): 1–21.

Levy, Ariel. *Female Chauvinist Pigs: Women and the Rise of Raunch Culture*. New York: Free Press, 2006.

Limbaugh, Rush. *The Way Things Ought to Be*. New York: Pocket Star Books, 1993.

Lott, Eric. *Love and Theft: Blackface Minstrelsy and the American Working Class*. Oxford: Oxford University Press, 1993.

Lundberg, Ferdinand, and Marynia F. Farnham. *Modern Woman, the Lost Sex*. New York: Universal Library, 1947.

MacFarquhar, Larissa. "The Gilder Effect." In *The New Gilded Age: The New Yorker Looks at the Culture of Affluence*, edited by David Remnick, 111–24. New York: Random House, 2000.

Major, Reginald. *A Panther Is a Black Cat*. Baltimore: Black Classic, 1971.

Manne, Kate. *Down Girl: The Logic of Misogyny*. Oxford: Oxford University Press, 2017.

Mansbridge, Jane, and Katherine Flaster. "The Cultural Politics of Everyday Discourse: The Case of 'Male Chauvinist.'" *Critical Sociology* 33, no. 4 (July 2007) 627–60.

———. "Male Chauvinist, Feminist, Sexist, and Sexual Harassment: Different Trajectories in Feminist Linguistic Innovation." *American Speech* 80, no. 3 (Fall 2005): 256–79.

Marable, Manning. *Race, Reform, and Rebellion: The Second Reconstruction and Beyond in Black America, 1945-2006*. Oxford: University of Mississippi Press, 2007.

Martin, Del, and Phyllis Lyon. *Lesbian/Woman*. San Francisco: Glide, 1972.

Marx, Nick, Matt Sienkiewicz, and Ron Becker, eds. *Saturday Night Live and American TV*. Bloomington: Indiana University Press, 2013.

McBee, Randy. *Born to Be Wild: The Rise of the American Motorcyclist*. Chapel Hill: University of North Carolina Press, 2015.

McCrohan, Donna. *Archie and Edith, Mike and Gloria: The Tumultuous History of "All in the Family."* New York: Workman, 1988.

McGirr, Lisa. *Suburban Warriors: The Origins of the New American Right*. Princeton, NJ: Princeton University Press, 2002.

McLeod, Kembrew. *Pranksters: Making Mischief in the Modern World*. New York: New York University Press, 2014.

Meyerowitz, Joanne. *How Sex Changed: A History of Transsexuality in the United States*. Cambridge, MA: Harvard University Press, 2004.

Millett, Kate. *Sexual Politics*. New York: Simon and Schuster, 1969.

Mirandé, Alfredo. *Hombres y Machos: Masculinity and Latino Culture*. Boulder, CO: Westview, 1997.

Mizejewski, Linda. *Pretty/Funny: Women Comedians and Body Politics*. Austin: University of Texas Press, 2014.

Mizejewski, Linda, and Victoria Sturtevant, eds. *Hysterical! Women in American Comedy*. Austin: University of Texas Press, 2017.

Mukhopadhyay, Samhita, and Kate Harding, eds. *Nasty Women: Feminism, Resistance, and Revolution in Trump's America*. London: Picador, 2017.

Murch, Donna Jean. *The Living for the City: Migration, Education, and the Rise of the Black Panther Party in Oakland, California*. Chapel Hill: University of North Carolina Press, 2010.

Nesteroff, Kliph. *The Comedians: Drunks, Thieves, Scoundrels and the History of American Comedy*. New York: Grove, 2015.

Nevins, Joseph. *Operation Gatekeeper: The Rise of the "Illegal Alien" and the Remaking of the U.S.-Mexico Boundary*. London: Routledge, 2001.

Newton, Huey P. *Revolutionary Suicide*. New York: Penguin, 2009.

Norton, Mary Beth. *Liberty's Daughters: The Revolutionary Experience of American Women, 1750-1800*. Ithaca, NY: Cornell University Press, 1980.

Nystrom, Dereck. *Hard Hats, Rednecks, and Macho Men: Class in 1970s American Cinema*. Oxford: Oxford University Press, 2009.

Orwell, George. *Animal Farm: A Fairy Story*. New York: Signet Classics, 1996.

Paredes, Américo. "The United States, Mexico, and *Machismo*." *Journal of the Folklore Institute* 8, no. 1 (1971): 17-37.

Partridge, Eric. *A Dictionary of Slang and Unconventional English*. 8th ed. New York: Routledge, 2002.

Peiss, Kathy. *Zoot Suit: The Enigmatic Career of an Extreme Style*. Pittsburgh: University of Pennsylvania Press, 2014.

Perea, Juan F., ed. *Immigrants Out! The New Nativism and the Anti-immigrant Impulse in the United States*. New York: New York University Press, 1996.

Pérez, Raúl, and Viveca S. Greene. "Debating Rape Jokes vs. Rape Culture: Framing and Counter-framing Misogynist Comedy." *Social Semiotics* 26, no. 3 (January 2016): 265-82.

Perlman, Allison. "Rush Limbaugh and the Problem of the Color Line." *Cinema Journal* 51, no. 4 (Summer 2012): 198-204.

Pitzulo, Carrie. *Bachelors and Bunnies: The Sexual Politics of Playboy*. Chicago: University of Chicago Press, 2011.

Primm, Eric Stephen. "The American Bad-Ass: A Social History of the Biker." PhD diss., University of Colorado, Boulder, 2004.

Reed, Jennifer. *The Queer Cultural Work of Lily Tomlin and Jane Wagner*. London: Palgrave Macmillan, 2013.

Reid, Jan. *Let the People In: The Life and Times of Ann Richard*. Austin: University of Texas Press, 2012.

Reilly, Donald. *Male Chauvinist Pig! Cartoons from Playboy*. Chicago: Playboy, 1972.

Remnick, David, ed. *The New Gilded Age: The New Yorker Looks at the Culture of Affluence*. Random House, 2000.

Riggs, Thomas, ed. *St. James Encyclopedia of Pop Culture*. 2nd ed. Farmington Hills, MI: St. James, 2013.

Roberts, Selena. *A Necessary Spectacle: Billie Jean King, Bobby Riggs, and the Tennis Match That Leveled the Game*. New York: Crown, 2005.

Roediger, David. *Colored White: Transcending the Racial Past*. Berkeley: University of California Press, 2003.

———. "White Looks: Hairy Apes, True Stories and Limbaugh's Laughs." *Minnesota Review* 47, no. 1 (Fall 1996): 37–47.

Rosen, Ruth. *The World Split Open: How the Modern Women's Movement Changed America*. New York: Viking, 2000.

Rowe, Kathleen. *The Unruly Woman: Gender and Genres of Laughter*. Austin: University of Texas Press, 1995.

Rubin, Gayle. "The Valley of the Kings: Leathermen in San Francisco, 1960–1990." PhD diss., University of Michigan, 1994.

Schulman, Bruce. *The Seventies: The Great Shift in American Culture, Politics, and Society*. New York: Free Press, 2001.

Scott, James C. *Domination and the Arts of Resistance: Hidden Transcripts*. New Haven, CT: Yale University Press, 1990.

Self, Robert. *All in the Family: The Realignment of American Democracy since the 1960s*. New York: Hill and Wang, 2012.

Shakur, Assata. *Assata: An Autobiography*. Chicago: Lawrence Hill Books, 2001.

Shapiro, Fred R. "Historical Notes on the Vocabulary of the Women's Movement." *American Speech* 60, no. 1 (Spring 1985): 3–16.

Spears, Richard A. *Slang and Euphemism: A Dictionary of Oaths, Curses, Insults, Sexual Slang and Metaphor, Racial Slurs, Drug Talk, Homosexual Lingo, and Related Matters*. 2nd ed. New York: Jonathan David, 1981.

Stansell, Christine. *City of Women: Sex and Class in New York, 1789–1860*. Urbana: University of Illinois Press, 1987.

Steinem, Gloria. *Outrageous Acts and Everyday Rebellions*. 2nd ed. New York: Holt, 1995.

Strub, Whitney. *Perversion for Profit: The Politics of Pornography and the Rise of the New Right*. New York: Columbia University Press, 2011.

Tackett, Timothy. *When the King Took Flight*. Cambridge, MA: Harvard University Press, 2003.

Tarrow, Sidney. *The Language of Contention: Revolutions in Words, 1688–2012*. Cambridge: Cambridge University Press, 2013.

———. *Strangers at the Gate: Movements and States in Contentious Politics*. Cambridge: Cambridge University Press, 2012.

Taylor, Verta, and Leila J. Rupp. "Women's Culture and Lesbian Feminist Activism: A Reconsideration of Cultural Feminism." *Signs* 19, no. 1 (Autumn 1993): 32–61.

Tickner, Lisa. *The Spectacle of Women: Imagery of the Suffrage Campaign, 1907–14*. Chicago: University of Chicago Press, 1988.

Tiemeyer, Phil. *Plane Queer: Labor, Sexuality, and AIDs in the History of Male Flight Attendants*. Berkeley: University of California Press, 2013.

Turk, Katherine. *Equality on Trial: Gender and Rights in the Modern American Workplace*. Philadelphia: University of Pennsylvania Press, 2016.

Tygiel, Jules. "Ronald Reagan and the Triumph of Conservatism." In *What's Going On? California and the Vietnam Era*, edited by Marcia A. Eymann and Charles Wollenberg. Berkeley: University of California Press, 2004.

Wallace, Michele. *Black Macho and the Myth of the Superwoman*. London: Verso, 2015.

Ware, Susan. *Game, Set, Match: Billie Jean King and the Revolution in Women's Sports*. Chapel Hill: University of North Carolina Press, 2011.

Warner, Sara. *Acts of Gaiety: LGBT Performances and the Politics of Pleasure*. Ann Arbor: University of Michigan Press, 2012.

Webber, Julie. *The Joke Is on Us: Political Comedy in (Late) Neoliberal Times*. Lanham, MD: Lexington Books, 2018.

Wickberg, Daniel. *The Senses of Humor: Self and Laughter in Modern America*. Ithaca, NY: Cornell University Press, 1998.

Willett, Cynthia. *Irony in the Age of Empire: Comic Perspectives on Democracy and Freedom*. Bloomington: Indiana University Press, 2008.

Willett, Cynthia, and Julie Willett. *Uproarious: How Feminists and Other Comics Speak Truth*. Minneapolis: University of Minnesota Press, 2019.

Wilson, John K. *The Most Dangerous Man in America: Rush Limbaugh's Assault on Reason*. New York: Thomas Dunne Books, 2011.

Zaretsky, Natasha. *No Direction Home: The American Family and the Fear of National Decline, 1968–1980*. Chapel Hill: University of North Carolina Press, 2007.

Zoglin, Richard. *Comedy at the Edge: How Stand-Up in the 1970s Changed America*. New York: Bloomsbury, 2008.

Index

Note: page numbers in italics refer to illustrations

laughter. *See* humor; jokes; Clinton, Hillary

Lavasseur, Thérèse, 146n57

lecherous men, 23–24, 122, 155n77

Lemieux, Jamilah, 46

Leng, Kirsten, 7, 126

Lennon, John, 87

Levy, Ariel, 69, 147n62

liberals, 2, 9, 10, 12, 14, 43, 76, 85, 89–90, 98, 102, 104–5, 108–10, 113; chauvinistic qualities, 98; mainstream and, 89; *Playboy* and, 79, 151n80; pluralism and, 33. *See also* New Left

Liberated Man, The (Farrell), 65–66

Limbaugh, Millie, 101, 102

Limbaugh, Rush, 9–10, 69, 98, 99–110, 113, 115, 117, 153nn43,45, 156n1; as antiwoman, 121; background of, 101–2; cancer diagnosis, 121; characterization of, 99; dittoheads, (fans), 100, 101, 109, 110; feminazi epithet and, 107; political influence of, 113; Presidential Medal of Freedom and, 121; significance of, 101; style of, 99, 100, 102–4, 106–8, 110, 115, 199

Loftus, Joseph A., 135n11

Longley, Kyle, 103–4

Lopez, Sonia, 48–49

Lord, Jack, 50

Lott, Eric, 42

Louis XVI, king of France, 37–38

Lundberg, Ferdinand, *Modern Woman, the Lost Sex*, 107, 153n41

Lurie, Diana, 77

Lynn, Loretta, 85

Lysistrata (Aristophanes), 34

Mabley, Moms, 6, 126

MacFarquhar, Larissa, 92–93

macho/machismo, 45–54; Black Panthers, 45–46; chauvinism vs., 48–50, 52; definitions of, 47–48, 51–52, 143n43; gay men, 144n64; legacy of, 46; male chauvinist pig vs., 8, 54; misogyny and, 36, 45, 54

"Macho Man" (song), 50–52

Maher, Bill, 120

Mailer, Norman, 93

male chauvinism, 52–54, 65, 97; as bullying, 4; fluid conceptions of, 63; Gilder award, 92–93; history of term, 14–15; popular conception of, 7; strains of, 36; women's definitions of, 59–60

Male Chauvinism, How It Works (Korda), 67–68

"Male Chauvinist Pig Calendar," 23–24

male chauvinist pig of the year, 86, 92, 102

Male Chauvinist's Cookbook, The (Kiverst), 20

male gaze, 79

male supremacists, 20

Man, the (term), 38–39

Marie Antoinette, 37–38

marital gender roles, 60–61, 64

Martin, Dick, 34

Martin, Judith, 48

Martin, Ron, 63

masculinity, 8, 9, 35–36, 38, 47–48, 50–61, 83, 84, 94, 97. *See also* male chauvinism

Maude (TV program), 19

McBee, Randy, 51–52

McCabe, Charles, "In Praise of Macho," 53–54

McCarthy, Melissa, 122–23

McGirr, Lisa, 3

McGovern, George, 61

McKinnon, Kate, 123

McLaurin, Melton, 85

McLeod, Kembrew, 33, 102

Meadows, R. L., 89

men. *See* male chauvinism; male chauvinist pig of the year; masculinity; misogyny

men's liberation, 65–66

merchandising, 17, 20–25; male chauvinist products, 9, 11, 20, 21, 22, 23, 77, 97; "redneck chic," 82

→ Hashtags at the intersection of
gender and religion.